Starve The Beast

JOIN THE GLOBAL
TAX REVOLT

J. WILLIAM PFEIFFER Ph.D., J.D.

CONTEXT: **Trying to understand our world from the media is like trying to tell time by looking at the second hand of a watch – The information is virtually meaningless without the context of the other hands.**

To stay current on the context of issues about the future of work and the global tax revolt of the underground economy, check our website.

drjobs.org

b-zine Format

This book is printed in an innovative, and hopefully useful, new format. In the wired world, an electronic magazine is called an e-zine – a magazine in an electronic format. This book, like its predecessor, *RoadKill on the Information Highway*, is a b-zine, a book in a magazine format. And, of course, there is a companion website for my updates, your comments, and our mutual observations.

Design and graphics: **John Robertson**

Senior editor: **Marian Prokop**

Permissions editor: **Kimeiko Hotta-Dover**

Editorial assistant: **Katherine Arcus**

Pfeiffer & Company **2 St. Clair Ave East**
Suite 903
Toronto, Ontario, Canada
M4T 2R1

Toll Free Tel.: 1-888-734-6058
Toronto Orders: 416-924-2628

drjobs@sympatico.ca

Canadian Cataloguing in Publications Data

Pfeiffer, J. William
Starve The Beast!
Join The Global Tax Revolt

1. Economics   2. Geopolitics   3. Business

ISBN: 1-894334-19-1

Printed in Canada

Printing   1 2 3 4 5 6 7 8 9 10

MARKETED IN COOPERATION WITH

McClelland & Stewart Inc.
THE CANADIAN PUBLISHERS

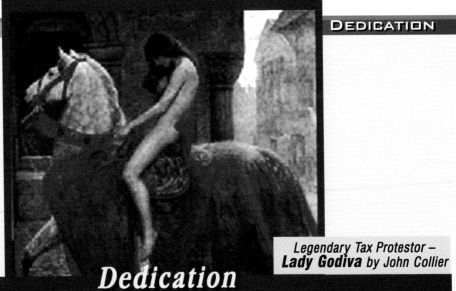

Legendary Tax Protestor –
Lady Godiva *by John Collier*

Dedication

To all those incredibly open people who freely shared with me detailed stories about their experiences in participating in the Underground Economy – and to their countless and diverse creative justifications for their actions.

Perhaps the most insightful data for this book came from surprisingly vivid anecdotes from people in all walks of life who took the time to discuss both their attitudes toward and their participation in some very creative aspects of the Underground Economy (UgEcon). In dozens of radio and TV call-in shows from Canada to South Africa, I heard the same refrain: *"Screw all the governments, they waste my money anyhow! Why should I give them anything? I need, and I deserve the money."*

At social events, people frequently came up to me and said, "Are you going to talk about the 'xyz' scam? Let me tell you how it works!" Almost no one ever asked me to keep the data anonymous, and many of the people on the call-in shows were not very circumspect about their identities. They would often start with information like, "I run the boat repair shop on Highway X, 6 miles north of the junction with Highway Y, and I always . . . or I never . . ."

What struck me was the range of people: taxi drivers, plumbers, doctors, lawyers, and dentists, who found no moral issue involved in outright tax evasion. The most pervasive practice was among the self-employed who "forget" to record some income, but had a fairly strong habit of classifying most expenses as business-related. Two people even told me that they had buried personal "Love Connection" ads and responses as "help wanted" business expense ads.

The major premises that I had about the Underground Economy (UgEcon) when I started this book was that tax evasion in developed countries is not a victimless crime. It punishes the captive and compliant taxpayers, and it is a very sobering indicator of the "me-first" degradation of our social morality.

After spending a year researching all the issues, I have come to the conclusion that **the tax revolt is justified by the outlandish nincompoopery of the bureaucrats and politicians who squander our hard-earned money.**

What started as a search to find solutions for curbing the UgEcon has turned me into an ardent advocate of the global tax revolt – Given the passive national character of most adults in developed countries, we are not going to have flagrant tax revolts, like the Boston Tea Party or the Whiskey Rebellion favored by the early Americans.

STARVE THE BEAST **— The most viable way that taxpayers have to curb the arrogance of profligate bureaucrats and politicians is to withhold all the taxes we possibly can until somebody in government gets the message.**

Post Script: I grew up in a different age. My father prided himself on his honesty; he was a law-abiding citizen and proudly a voluntarily compliant taxpayer. One of the earliest moral lessons that I can remember from him, just after *"Always share your toys,"* was *"Being honest is just like being pregnant – either you are or you aren't."*

JWP, *Toronto, February, 2000*

Acknowledgments

Creating a book like this is a bit like playing the part of famous film director Cecil B. DeMille, whose name became synonymous with opulent spectacle films, such as *Cleopatra, The Crusades,* and *Samson and Delilah.* His trademark was "a cast of thousands."

The Broadcast Media

In many ways, this book, like a DeMille film, has a cast of thousands. It was conceived somewhere on the media trail promoting my last book, *RoadKill on the Information Highway: The Future of Work in Canada.* Many people influenced the development of this book; broadcast personalities, such as Charles Adler (CJOB in Winnipeg), Duane Lowe (Global in Halifax), Leanne Cusack (CTV in Ottawa), and David Ingram (Rogers in Vancouver) stand out clearly in my mind. Dozens of people have called, faxed, or e-mailed after hearing me with Raif Mair and Peter Warren (CKNW and the WIC network in Vancouver); the Motts (CFRB in Toronto); and Jim Duff (CIQC in Montreal). All in all, I appeared on about a hundred different radio and TV shows. These appearances were not only in the major cities of each of the provinces, but just as importantly from the perspective of this book, also in many places that most Canadians rarely visit, cities like Antigonish, Belleville, Hamilton, Kitchener, London, Moncton, New Glasgow, Sarnia, Sherbrooke, Summerside, Sydney, and Waterloo.

The broadcast media were very gracious, and their counterparts on the print side were equally congenial. Early in my tour, someone labelled me **"Dr. Jobs,"** and the title stuck and was picked up by subsequent hosts and interviewers.

The Print Media

With the longer newspaper interviews, I had the chance to exchange ideas with some seasoned veterans: Kevin O'Connor (*Regina Leader-Post*), Rob Matthews (*Halifax Herald*), John Campbell (*Cape Breton Post*), and my equally "seasoned" friend, Judi McLeod (formerly with the *Toronto Sun* and now the owner/publisher of *Toronto Free Press*). My website, drjobs.org, has copies of the reviews from these papers as well as *The Calgary Herald, The Charlottetown Guardian, The Edmonton Journal, The New Glasgow Evening News, The Hamilton Spectator, The Montreal Gazette, The Newfoundland Herald,*

The Ottawa Citizen, The Vancouver Sun, and *The Winnipeg Free Press.* One of my favorite reviews came from *The Alberta (and BC) Report,* where, to my absolute delight, the reviewer could not peg me as right or left and concluded, *correctly,* that my objectivity sets me outside either of those labels.

By my nature, I love to chat with people, and I chatted on planes, trains, buses, and especially taxis as I crisscrossed the country. I chatted in the waiting rooms of newspaper offices and the greenrooms of radio and TV stations, in good restaurants and coffee shops. I also spent considerable time "researching" in the favorite watering holes of dozens of cities and towns. Mostly I listened to what people had to say, and they had a lot to say about feeling overtaxed, about feeling detached from government. I heard lots of complaints about wasting money, cronyism, and patronage. I experienced people particularly frustrated by the sense that the government was out of control and there was nothing that they could do about it.

The late summer and fall of 1999 brought confirmation of what I had been hearing, in the form of clear messages from the voters in Manitoba, New Brunswick, Nova Scotia, and Saskatchewan: Incumbents, regardless of their stripes, were turned out or pressed into a minority government, as the clean broom swept out the old ways. Is someone in Ottawa listening?

Key Staff

All but one of the key contributors from *RoadKill* have returned to play key roles in *The Global Tax Revolt;* they are named on the copyright page. My most sincere appreciation goes to Marian, John, Kimeiko, and Katherine.

Marketing and Distribution

Ken Thomson, VP, Sales and Marketing at McClelland & Stewart, has been helpful far beyond my expectations. Joe, Mark, Andrew, Doug, and especially Elga and Parisa of M&S were fantastic in their support. I owe Brad Chambers, General Manager of Canbook, a very special acknowledgment for sponsoring me to speak at Canbook's inaugural publishers conference. Several of the wonderful folks that I met there have made me feel welcome in the Canadian publishing industry.

JWP, Toronto, February, 2000

Table of Contents

JOIN THE GLOBAL TAX REVOLT

Global Perspective Series

Preface

> *"Our new Constitution is now established, and has an appearance that promises permanency; but in this world, nothing can be said to be certain, except death and taxes."*

Benjamin Franklin had no way of knowing that his statement of absolute certainty, written more than 200 years ago, would be found to be so false in this latter half of the 20th century. For now, in addition to death and taxes, we also can be certain of *tax evasion*.

Globally, we are experiencing a massive tax revolt that is driving the world's economy underground. This boom in the Underground Economy (UgEcon) is a mixed blessing: it represents an opportunity to control the runaway spending by our governments, but it also will cause many casualties, because tax evasion is *not* a victimless crime.

By examining something under a microscope, you can see many details that are invisible to the naked eye. This book should reinforce that point; your awareness of both the size and complexity of the UgEcon will be significantly enhanced.

Owning the Problem

The UgEcon is not just a problem of governments. Rather, it is a very real problem for law-abiding, compliant, and captive (taxed-at-the-source) taxpayers who are saddled with the burden of paying more than their fair share to support both legitimate and wasteful government functions.

The problems associated with defining and measuring the size and impact of the UgEcon are more complex and convoluted than most taxpayers really want to know. Much of the information about the UgEcon is written *by* economists *for* economists and can be too obscure for the average taxpayer (or politician) to understand. The purpose of this book is to cut through this esoteric complexity and to confront the moral and social implications of the exploding growth of a vast array of activities that make up the UgEcon.

We are sure that this book will give you a clear understanding of what the UgEcon comprises. You will quickly grasp the size, velocity, and far-reaching social impact of the many facets of the UgEcon. We are equally confident that your ultimate question will be, "Is there anything that can be done, particularly to stop the most detrimental activities?"

We hope you will reject the notion that stricter enforcement and harsher penalties will ever be the best answers. Instead, we hope you come to see that the answer lies in a combination of factors such as redesigning various aspects of our tax systems and recognizing that social marketing (*selling* people on the idea of voluntary compliance) will not work if they are tired of government waste and suffering from tax fatigue. This book will explore many factors that lead to the conclusion that the time is right for a tax revolt and may, ultimately, draw you into the cause of forcing our governments to be more responsible and less arrogant.

Focus of the Book

Although this book is intended for a global audience, the vast majority of the quantified data is gleaned from OECD sources – the world's 29 most economically advanced countries. This biasing of source data unfortunately is necessary because many less-developed nations do not have reliable economic databases. Where we have tried to address the problems that are unique to the less-developed countries, we have often had to rely more on anecdotal sources than on hard data.

Many of the examples come from our Canadian experience, not only because of the author's first-hand familiarity with that information, but also because of the "laboratory quality" of the country. For the last 6 consecutive years, Canada has been named by the UN as the "Best Country in the World" in terms of "quality of life." It also is a country that has the highest proportion of immigrant and refugee residents, one of the highest tax rates in the world, and an UgEcon that is growing at triple the rate of its already robust formal economy.

There are even more examples from the US – both because it is the world's largest economy and because it is probably most experienced with tax revolts. Even though this book is somewhat Canada/US-centric, we have taken great care to ensure that the comparisons and contrasts to other countries at various stages of economic development are crisp and that there is a liberal use of examples from all corners of the world.

This book is quite unique in its design. It is focused on what is conclusively a robust global issue – the dynamics of the UgEcon – and it attempts to address very complex topics from both the global panorama and from the distinctive perspectives of particular countries. For example, a **"Global Perspectives"** feature at the end of each chapter highlights some of the unique characteristics of other countries at different stages of economic development. It offers an opportunity to view many of these riddles from a transnational point of view. The reason for this is that some aspects of the UgEcon (such as illicit drugs, money laundering, people smuggling, and tax havens) cannot be properly addressed by any single nation. These issues have evolved to a level where they are the purview of transnational organizations such as the United Nations, World Bank, International Monetary Fund, OECD, and the various trade groups (APEC, EU, NAFTA, MERCOSUR, MUWAS, and WTO).

Key Causes of the UgEcon

Although it may be a little bit like telling you "The butler did it!" on the 1st page of a murder mystery, let us alert you to what we believe are the key causes of the rapidly escalating growth of the UgEcon in all parts of the world:

1. A perception of unfairness of taxes.
2. An aggregate tax rate in excess of 25% of GDP.
3. A perception of high levels of government waste.
4. A cultural bias against voluntary compliance.
5. An above-average risk orientation on the part of the individual taxpayer.
6. Using punishments for non-compliance, which studies show are not effective deterrents.
7. A feeble economy with a high unemployment rate.
8. A proliferation of jobs, such as self-employment, that invite entry into the UgEcon.
9. Taxes designed so that collection and monitoring of compliance are both difficult and expensive.

We have no strong *political* perspectives. *However, we do have a strong economic commitment to promoting a tax revolution.* We have, at all times, tried to keep our economic objectivity and to remember that we are writing for the average taxpayer and not for other economists. It is our fervent hope that you will finish this book with a more enlightened perspective on one of the great economic challenges of our time – how to control pompous politicians and self-serving bureaucrats.

In our opinion, the UgEcon is a moral issue as well as an economic one. When taxpayers perceive that gains from tax evasion outweigh its risks, it creates incentives for dynamic UgEcon activity.

Internationally, we find a trend toward non-compliance. It has become a lot more acceptable not to report all your income and to inflate your deductions. Some moralists argue that we are experiencing a downgrading of civic commitment and that people have less respect for the law in general, and tax law specifically, than they did 20 years ago.[1] Our view is that the tax laws deserved more respect 20 years ago than they do now – which is why the global tax revolt is happening.

Clear Answers Exist

Our experience in having assorted friends and colleagues read pieces of this book at various stages of development is that most people are unacquainted with many of the basic facts about the evolution of taxes. Government workers, union workers, individuals over the age of 50, those on the extreme political left, and the less educated and less financially successful tend to have high expectations that governments will take care of them.

Younger workers, particularly those who have taken the self-employment option, are better educated and are integrated into the world of knowledge workers. They tend to expect less from government and are resentful about getting the bill for the profligate ways of the last 2 generations.

Relatively simple actions can vanquish the forces that create the climate for our flourishing UgEcon. As you wend your way through this book, you will see that the answers are not rocket science, but thoughtful common sense.

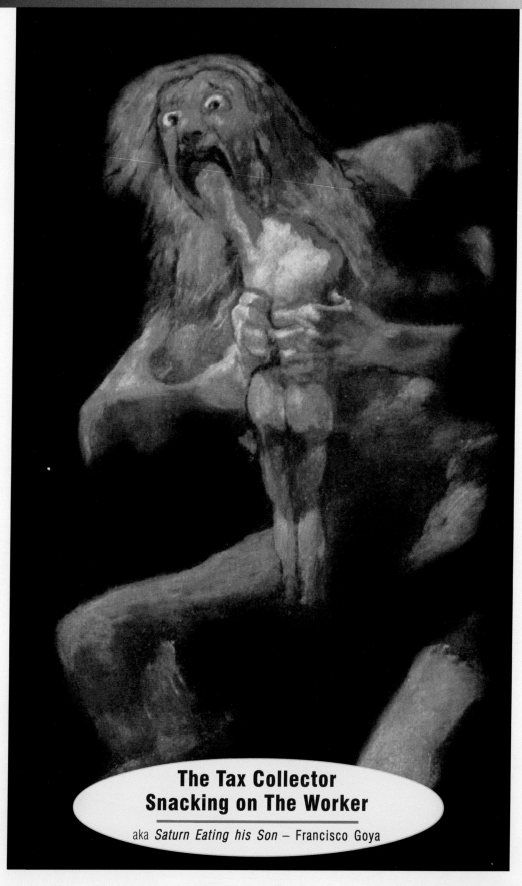

**The Tax Collector
Snacking on The Worker**

aka *Saturn Eating his Son* – Francisco Goya

STARVE THE BEAST!

What Is the UgEcon?

Tax avoidance is the **legal** reduction of taxes; tax evasion is any **illegal** reduction of taxes.

Tax Evasion Is an Epidemic

Taxes are unpopular and breed resentment today – as they undoubtedly always have – and to some degree probably always will. Accordingly, some people will evade taxes no matter what tax system is used; but perhaps some tax systems will provoke less tax evasion than others.

Under today's income tax systems, tax evasion is a critical epidemic. Notwithstanding the sky-rocketing growth in tax agency scrutiny, burgeoning sophistication in computerized record keeping, more burdensome information reporting requirements, increasingly stiff and numerous penalties, and a host of legislative initiatives, the problem is increasingly pernicious. Based on US data, tax evasion increased by 67% during the past decade. Despite relatively moderate tax rates, strong enforcement procedures, and a generally tax-compliant population, US tax evasion on legal activities continues to amount to approximately 20-25% of all income taxes collected. These government figures do not even attempt to measure taxes lost on *illegal* sources of income.

Defining the UgEcon

One of the many complexities of examining and measuring the UgEcon is the wide range of definitions applied. Governments tend to be very restrictive in their definitions while journalists tend to be very broad, which helps to sensationalize copy. We have opted for a similarly broad perspective, not so much to sensationalize, but to educate readers about the true breadth of the issues involved.

The operations of the UgEcon sectors in various contemporary economies are also referred to as "parallel" or "shadow" economies; in developing countries as the "informal" economy; and as the "second" economy in former socialist countries. One of the more benign labels, frequently used by those who fail to grasp the adverse impact of the UgEcon, is "operating under the table."

Our formal definition for this book is that the UgEcon is: **All economic activities, legal and illegal, that escape inclusion in national income accounts because the sellers' practices are such that the accounting procedures do not detect the transaction.**[2]

This comprehensive definition leads to many different types of activities that we include as part of the UgEcon. When the average person thinks of the

Sitcoms: A Reflection of Public Tax Morality

Cultural values are often reflected in TV programs and movies. A 1953 episode of Jackie Gleason's classic American sitcom, *The Honeymooners*, dramatizes the American commitment to taxes during that period. Ralph Kramden, the down-at-the-heels bus driver, is at first angry at discovering he owes the government $15 in extra taxes – he had saved that money toward a new bowling ball. But when he considers the matter, he decides he is glad to pay the tax. "We're living in a great country," he tells his wife, Alice, in a display of remorse that one is hard put to imagine finding in *Seinfeld-era* sitcoms. "I didn't mean that before what I said about the income tax. Boy, we should give everything to the government. Especially this government."

> **The only moral difference between small and large businesses is that the latter can afford expensive tax advice and offshore tax havens to reduce taxes.**

UgEcon, his or her thoughts tend to be limited to paying cash for repairs or services or buying goods from small shops that offer:

Price A – the "regular" on-the-books price that includes a traceable payment (check, credit, or debit card) plus sales, VAT, or excise taxes; or

Price B – the cash price, lower than Price A, which does not include taxes. Although Price B transactions are commonplace examples of the UgEcon, they represent only a fraction of the value of this economic sector.

The next line of thinking about the UgEcon leads to thoughts of illegal activities, such as illicit drug trade, prostitution, theft, and unsanctioned gambling. Although such illegal activities do represent a significant part of the UgEcon, the real definition must also include an equally far-reaching variety of legal activities that are not reported for income tax purposes.

A few economists also include goods and services produced in the home as part of the UgEcon, reasoning that if someone else did this work, it would be taxed. We have excluded consideration of the work done for yourself or immediate family, represented by the kinds of activities that are typically described as homemaking or "sweat equity" in property improvements.

A reasonable, and less formal, working definition of the UgEcon is *any economic activity that would generally be taxable if reported to the tax authorities*. Thus, the UgEcon would include unreported rental incomes, skimming by business owners, barter activities, off-the-books employment, and unreported income from the sale of home-produced goods. A good example of sectors that have a high percentage of unreported income include domestic service and child care. For these services, it is relatively easy to be paid in cash and never have any record of the transaction.

There are, of course, many positive aspects to the UgEcon, particularly in less economically developed countries, where significant evidence indicates that a more vital economy exists than we are led to believe by the official statistics. (See Russia on pages 102-103.)

Measuring the UgEcon

Many measures attempt to estimate the UgEcon. Obviously, the answer cannot be as simple as getting figures from people who did not report all of their income. More complex methods include measuring different types of payment systems, such as currency and demand deposits; polling people to see how much they have bought from the "informal vendors;" surveys of consumer purchases; and the currency ratio method.

These different estimations do have one thing in common: They all show the UgEcon to be a major part of all economies.

Recently the world has become captivated with this informal sector of the economy. First, the public is fascinated with the illegal nature of the UgEcon. Second, policymakers would like an accurate measurement to help determine how to create "better" tax laws. They also would like to have adjusted figures for poverty levels, because many people who are classified as living *below* the poverty level according to reported figures are actually *above* the poverty level because of the UgEcon income.

Confronting the Big Myth

Four major factors stimulate the UgEcon:
• higher tax rates,
• the perception of government waste,
• recessions (periods of high unemployment) and
• changes in public attitudes toward tax evasion.

However, those who do business in the UgEcon must be aware of the social inequities and casualties arising from the unpaid taxes.

It puts honest businesses at a competitive disadvantage, and in some cases, out of business. It also causes compliant taxpayers to bear the tax load of those who choose this form of protest. Enforcing tax laws is not easy, and it should not be seen as a war between taxing authorities and the rest of us.

If taxes are fair, equitable, and used properly, the taxing authority works for all of us and deserves the support of all taxpayers. *If the tax revenues are excessive and wasted on bureaucracy, we have the right, and maybe even the obligation, to withhold taxes by every means possible.*

Born in 1755, the youngest daughter of the Holy Roman Emperor Francis I and Maria Theresa, Maria Antonia, spent her childhood in the Schönbrunn Palace in Vienna. From her earliest youth it was planned that she would marry the French king's heir, to strengthen the alliance between France and Austria. Thus, in 1770, the young archduchess

"Qu'ils mangent de la brioche."

"Only little people pay taxes."

The Bookend Queens

In 1989, in a much publicized case, the US tax authorities prosecuted Leona Helmsley, known from media ads as "The Queen of Harry Helmsley's Hotels." Her crime was that she treated personal renovations to her home (mansion) as business expenses.

The New Yorker, frequently referred to as "the Queen of Mean," eventually served 18 months in

moved to France. She lived her life at the royal court of Versailles as any spoiled 15-year-old would, throwing herself into a life of amusements and distractions. Her marriage to Louis XVI, who became king in 1774, was unpopular and was unconsummated for 7 years. The new queen's notorious reputation led to several scandals; but it was with the outbreak of the French Revolution that the queen was able to demonstrate once and for all that there was nothing beneath her veneer of frivolity and superficiality.

In case you missed all your history lessons: On being told her people were rioting because they had no bread, Marie-Antoinette reputedly replied, "Qu'ils mangent de la brioche." (This normally is translated as "Let them eat cake," although brioche is more a kind of sweet bread than cake.) Although historians now believe the remark to be apocryphal, it nonetheless served to further discredit the queen with her subjects.

Both Louis XVI, the last King of France, and Marie Antoinette, its last Queen, were tried for treason and condemned to death under the guillotine in 1793.

prison, paid over $7 million in restitution, and performed 900 hours of community service. Her prison sentence had been shortened to allow her to care for her ailing husband. An extra 150 hours of community service, however, were added on after it was revealed that Mrs. Helmsley had ordered her domestic workers to do some of the community service chores assigned to her.

Her husband, billionaire real estate magnate Harry B. Helmsley, died January 4, 1997, leaving an estate estimated at over $1.7 billion, which included the Empire State Building and some of New York City's most upscale hotels.

By far the best-remembered line from the case was one reported by her maid:

Mrs. Helmsley, the maid testified, had told her that "people like the Helmsleys didn't pay taxes; only the little people pay taxes."

The public was infuriated. It was not so much what or how she said what she did; rather, it was the stark realization that "Queen Leona" had spoken the unspeakable truth. But, as the new promotional ads for Helmsley Hotels testify: "Say what you will, she runs a hell of a hotel."

Your conduct was the product of naked greed, the arrogant belief that you were above the law.
– Judge John M. Walker, Jr., who sentenced Leona Helmsley to 4 years in prison, 750 hours of community service, and millions in fines for mail fraud and tax evasion.

Lack of Perceived Fairness: The Engine of the UgEcon

When a taxpayer perceives that gains from tax evasion outweig[h] any associated risks and cos[ts] this creates an incentive f[or] underground activity.

Federal governments must take the tax revolt warnings seriously. In a decentralized economy, taxes rely substantially on voluntary compliance. If taxpayers find a particular tax very unfair, they will refuse to pay it. *Perceived unfairness is the single most self-justificatory reason that people have for participating in the UgEcon.*

Taxpayer Fatigue

Psychological studies of taxpayer behavior have found that evasion increases when people can convince themselves that a tax is unfair. For their own self-esteem, most people like to think of themselves as honest. However, significant numbers of taxpayers around the world believe that they do not receive enough benefits for the taxes they are required to pay.

In his 1994 pre-budget consultation document, Ontario's Minister of Finance articulated:

"Government understands... the fatigue taxpayers are feeling, and that there are limits to how much revenue the tax system can deliver. The Government is also aware of the problem of the underground economy and how it means honest taxpayers have to pick up more than their fair share of the cost of services."

Clearly, this statement could be made today by any government official in any nation, and it reflects a change in taxpayers' attitudes. Contrast this with the you-get-what-you-pay-for views of a local newspaper editor in the US 40 years earlier:

"Taxes are the prorated costs of things we can only buy from the government. We get about what we pay for. We should get more and better fire and police protection, education, sanitation, recreation, food inspection, control over fraudulent transactions and reduction in the risk of our investments if we paid more taxes. Yet by listening to the low-tax people all these years

we have cheated ourselves out of the essentials only government can give us. It is time we examined the economy-in-government interests and determined whether we should listen to them or decide for ourselves how much government service we need and want and can afford." [3]

The Growth of Public-Debt Interest

One cause of increasing levels of taxation is the growth of public-debt interest. The reality of the situation is that a large proportion of the taxes people are paying today goes to pay for services consumed in the past by people who may no longer even be alive. *Current taxpayers find it hard to derive pleasure from past deficits.* Tax rates that increase without any offsetting benefits to taxpayers are deeply resented, as psychological studies of tax evasion suggest.

For example, with debt-servicing in Canada eating up 25% of the expenditure budget, a federal move to balance the national budget through spending cuts would leave Canadians with only 75¢ worth of services for every dollar of taxes that they pay.

The Rich As Role Models

In some cases, big corporations and family trusts in many countries have been able to evade substantial taxes. These high-profile cases send an appalling message to the average taxpayer, reinforcing what we all think we know: People with means find ways to avoid taxes. This reality justifies the average citizen who does not feel it is immoral if he is trying to save on his tax bill by participating in the UgEcon. The difference between tax avoidance and tax evasion gets very blurry at this point.

The UgEcon in Developed Countries

This self-serving rationalization is premised on the notion that 2 wrongs make a right. It forces the captive and compliant taxpayers to pay much higher taxes, although almost everyone sees governments as taking too much in taxes.

A passive tax revolt does not directly address the problem of eliminating waste and the abuse of the right to tax.

Many people who earn near the poverty level justify involvement in the UgEcon as necessary to supplement their incomes because no one should have to live in poverty. However, this thinking is also flawed, in that individuals do not have the right to cheat the government just because they think that they "deserve" extra money. A viable counter argument is that this unreported income often raises these people's standards of living above people who are trying to earn an honest living – the so-called "working poor." A 3rd argument is that some of these people still accept transfer payments;

some taxpayers end up supporting people whose standard of living is higher than their own.[4]

Despite obvious incentives to sell in the UgEcon, the reasons to buy are more varied. In the illegal UgEcon, for example, people buy things because they cannot get those goods or services anywhere else, e.g., illicit drugs and prostitution. However, for the legal economy, various reasons exist. Sometimes they are goods or services that cannot be found in other markets, but, more typically, it is simply because the goods or services are less expensive, and, for some, it is just an ingrained part of their general tax revolt against government. Increased participation in the UgEcon is an act of protest against profligate government spending. [2]

COUNTERPOINT

Fair Corporate Taxes

To the average taxpayer, a key ingredient of a fair tax system is that corporations should pay their fair share of tax. We, and many other economists, contend that corporations do not pay taxes at all since most corporate taxes are simply built into the price of goods and services and are passed along to the consumer. Therefore, sooner or later, all corporate income ends up in the hands of individuals, where it is taxed as personal income.[5]

Regarding the 3 key arguments that frequently are made for taxing corporations – we rebut them:
• *Businesses benefit from public services much the same as individuals do.* Although valid for municipal taxes (fire and police protection, school taxes, snow removal, street repairs, etc.), this argument does not justify corporate income tax.
• *In the absence of income tax on corporations, it would be possible for individuals to postpone tax on income or capital gains indefinitely by placing income-producing assets in a corporation and thereby having the income or gains accrue within the corporation.* Many countries have a concept of "excess accumulations," which is a way of forcing corporations to pay taxable dividends when they accumulate more money than they

need to operate their businesses. Investment companies can be taxed a flat rate on the basis of their accumulated capital, perhaps 1%.
• *Corporate taxes allow the taxation of income accruing to foreigners and ensure that foreign-based corporations operating in Canada pay tax on income earned in Canada.* This could be addressed with a low, flat-rate tax on companies with foreign ownership, perhaps 5% of profits. Every country wants to encourage foreign investment – which is universally viewed as a measure of economic stability. However, just as automobiles are made from components manufactured in a dozen or more countries, it is difficult to define who is a foreign owner and which corporations are foreign-based. Multi-national companies defy citizenship labels. If Sony, for example, operates in more than 100 countries, often with local partners, always with international *and* local shareholders, are its operations in Singapore "foreign"?

Corporations also pay a variety of other taxes and contributions, such as payroll taxes (contributions to unemployment insurance, pensions, and workers' compensation programs), property taxes, and sales and excise taxes. This does not include indirect taxes paid, such as fuel taxes.

The UgEcon – Good, Bad, or "It Depends"

Most academics, when asked a tough question, rely on a classic qualifier: "It depends." The tough question that this book forces on us has become: **"Is society better off or worse off as a consequence of a robustly growing UgEcon?"** Not surprisingly, the answer is, "It depends." In this case, it depends ultimately on the level of economic development of the particular tax jurisdiction and on the level of fiscal responsibility of the taxing authorities.

1. **In economically developed economies,** taxes lost as a result of participation in the UgEcon are virtually always pernicious, both economically and socially, unless they are *consciously* used as weapons of tax revolt. One might argue convincingly on behalf of those who struggle at the poverty level, but ultimately benefit fraud creates adverse social repercussions, because abused wealth redistribution plans are one of the favourite targets of the far right.

2. **In transitional economies,** the UgEcon is an important crutch until appropriate alternative support systems are established. The danger lies in developing a dependency on the crutch and not giving it up as stronger formal systems develop.

A continued reliance on the crutch of the UgEcon thwarts the development of new formal systems because it denies them the support

> *A culture of evasion has come into being.*
>
> *It's a problem with social and ideological, as well as economic, implications.*
>
> *There have always been people who've tried to cheat, but it's only recently become something they openly boast about.*

(nutrition) that they need to grow. Transitional economies need to plan in terms of at least 2 generations to make the kinds of changes required to reorient people.

3. **In developing economies,** the UgEcon is an essential element because it does what the governments cannot do: It provides sustenance to those on the edge of survival. When formal systems are corrupt or inadequate, people have no alternative but to go outside those systems. However, as necessary as it may be for survival, rampant reliance on an informal economy creates a power vacuum that promotes anarchy, bringing with it extreme social unrest, crushing personal hardships, as well as fanning the fires of ethnic resentments.

4. **In justifying the positive side of the tax revolt:** The next chapter on the history of taxation will explore some of the best-known tax revolts.

What is most distinctive about the current tax revolt is that it is so pervasive, yet it remains passive. Governments know it is happening, but they pretend that it is business as usual.

Soooo... I HEAR YOU ARE A PAINTER...

Conclusion

Pillars of the UgEcon: Arbitrary and Direct Taxes

> **There is no such thing as a good tax.**
> – Sir Winston Churchill

Adam Smith on Bad Taxes

Adam Smith, in *The Wealth of Nations*, sets forth 4 signs of a bad tax system:

1. A large bureaucracy for administration.
2. A system that puts taxpayers through "odious examinations...and exposes them to much unnecessary trouble, vexation, and oppression."
3. A system that encourages evasion.
4. A system that obstructs the industry of the people and discourages enterprise which might otherwise give "employment to great multitudes," [jobs], that obligates people to excessive payments and thereby takes away the funds that would promote commerce, industry, and employment.[6]

Arbitrariness

"The most pernicious of all taxes are the arbitrary," said David Hume, the great Scottish philosopher. "They are commonly converted into punishments on industry... It is surprising, therefore, to see them have place among any civilized people." (See page 14.) Alexander Hamilton, a leading proponent of broad taxing powers, had no use for arbitrary taxes. "Whatever liberty we may boast of in theory, it cannot exist in fact while [arbitrary] assessments continue."

No tax laws have been more arbitrary than US income tax rates in the last half of the 20th century. In the 1950's, Congress decided that the top bracket should be 91%; President Kennedy brought it down to 70%; President Reagan slashed it to 28%, and President Clinton has tried on several occasions to raise it back to around 40%. Exemptions, tax credits, and other tax loopholes have varied from legislature to legislature – making a field day for tax lobbyists. This is arbitrariness and inconsistency to the utmost extreme, the kind of behaviour that adds fuel to the UgEcon.

Is Tax Evasion a Real Crime?

Many people today are amazed to learn that the great thinkers of the Enlightenment, William Blackstone (law), Adam Smith (political economy), and Montesquieu (political philosophy), all opposed making tax evasion a crime. Montesquieu said it was contrary to the spirit of moderate government. Severe punishment for tax offenses, said Blackstone, "destroys all proportion of punishment and puts murderers upon equal footing with such as are really guilty of no natural, but merely a positive offense [not a real crime]."

Adam Smith reasoned this way: A tax evader was usually a person not capable of committing a true crime, and in every respect an excellent citizen, had not the laws of his country made a crime something that nature never meant to be so.

Canada has about as many tax evasion convictions per capita as the US (about 2,500 per year). However, a recent study disclosed that only 6 taxpayers ever saw jail and then only on a short-term basis. In the US everybody goes to jail, and not for short terms. America has a kind of gulag for disloyalty to the tax system, not unlike the gulag in the former Soviet Union for disloyalty to the political system.

Direct Taxes Damage Liberty

Besides the disastrous consequences of arbitrary and excessive taxation, Montesquieu described direct taxation as being "natural to slavery," saying that "a duty on merchandise is more natural to liberty, because it is not so direct a relation to the person."

More than 2,000 years earlier, the Greeks observed that many empires of the world were despotic tyrannies. All had direct forms of taxation, such as wealth taxes, income or production taxes, poll taxes, and the like.

They therefore concluded that tyranny was the inevitable consequence of direct taxation.

UK Taxes
Ancient & Modern

Stamp Taxes

William III imported the idea of stamp duty, which had been invented in The Netherlands in 1624. Duties between 1p and £2 were levied mostly on legal documents, including policies of insurance. The duties were later extended to playing cards, dice, and newspapers. Although stamp forgery was punishable by death, in 1710, one of the Commissioners of Stamps was found guilty of selling counterfeit stamps.

The End of the King's Prerogative

English customs taxes were the King's prerogative before Parliament existed. In 1606, James I levied a tax on the importation of currants; the House of Commons petitioned the King, saying that such impositions were unlawful without its consent. In 1637, James's son, Charles I, imposed "ship money," again without Parliament's consent. A wealthy landowner's refusal to pay his share helped to lead to the civil war and the execution of the King. Although the monarchy was restored in 1660 with Charles II, control of taxation moved to the House of Commons by 1688.

Excise Taxes

In 1643, during the civil war, excise duties (used successfully elsewhere in Europe) were imposed on home-produced goods. The hearth tax of 1662 was particularly disliked because an official had the authority to go inside each house to count hearths. Unusually, William III himself requested its repeal in 1694. However, the next few years saw the excise tax extended to windows, hackney coaches, glass, burials, births and marriages, bachelors and hawkers. The coal tax was revived and the salt duty increased. In 1701, the malt tax was also revived. Between 1710 and 1712, candles, leather, paper, hops, and soap became permanent sources of excise revenue.

Introduction of Income Taxes

In 1784, William Pitt the Younger identified 68 different kinds of customs duties; a pound of nutmegs alone was subject to 9 different duties! He reformed the tariff, and, in 1799, introduced a temporary tax: income tax at 10%. The fact that this temporary income tax still exists after 200 years is largely due to Henry Addington, who reintroduced it in 1803 with key fundamental changes. This remained the case until Lloyd George introduced supertax in 1911.

Income tax lapsed in 1816 after the defeat of Napoleon. In 1842, Robert Peel reduced the number of dutiable articles from 1,200 to 750. To make up the difference, he reintroduced income tax at 3%, again temporarily. (*To this day, income tax has to be reimposed annually.*) By 1874, income tax had fallen to less than 1%.

20ᵗʰ Century Taxes

Lloyd George's Finance Bill of 1909 was so radical that the House of Lords rejected it. The crisis led to 2 general elections in 1910, which produced identical results. In 1911, the Lords' powers were curbed, and to obtain the Lords' agreement, George V threatened to create sufficient peers to pass the necessary act.

To meet the costs of WWII, the US, Canada, and the UK all increased the rates of income tax. To facilitate its collection, they also introduced deduction of tax by employers – the least expensive and most efficient method of tax collection.

Whatever Turns You On

The British Chancellor of the Exchequer, **Sir Kinsley Wood**, was so excited at being able to announce the UK tax increase to fund WWII, that he collapsed and died of a heart attack. The scheme started without him – on schedule.

Formal Name:	**United Kingdom of Great Britain and Northern Ireland**
Local Name:	United Kingdom
Location:	Europe
Status:	UN Country
Capital City:	**London**
Main Cities:	Birmingham, Manchester, Glasgow, Edinburgh, Belfast
Population:	**57,956,000**
Area [sq.km]:	**244,880**
Currency:	**1 pound sterling = 100 pence**
Main Languages:	English, Welsh, Scots Gaelic, Irish Gaelic
Main Religions:	Protestant, Roman Catholic, Muslim, Hindu, Judaism

Capital Gains & Corporate Taxes

James Callaghan caused fiscal indigestion by introducing both capital gains tax and corporation tax in 1965. When Edward Heath took Britain into the EC in 1972, value-added tax replaced the much narrower purchase tax. In 1974, Denis Healey increased the top rate of income tax to 98%, an even higher rate than that imposed during World War II.

The UgEcon Yesterday and Today

In the UK, a cavernous gulf exists between the public perception of the UgEcon and the academic and official evaluations. The true UgEcon ranges from crack cocaine dealers through benefit fraud and moonlighting, and on to the continued growth of the theft industry. Studies in the early 1980's used multiple techniques and came up with a wide variety of estimates of its size, ranging from a low of 3% to a high of 22% of GDP.[7]

A cynic might be forgiven for thinking that the government figure of 7.5% is a particularly comfortable one. It is large enough to cause official concern and warrant further manpower resources to the Inland Revenue. However, it is not so large that it would give the impression that the Board of Inland Revenue is ineffective.

The total size of the UK UgEcon is likely to be considerably larger, because the government guesstimate referred only to "unreported economy."

The full UgEcon – or what some economists call the "shadow economy" – also includes the "illegal economy" (drug trafficking, alien smuggling, theft, fraud, arson, prostitution) and the "self-service economy" involving household work, home repairs, gardening, and child care. Everyone in the UK knows of, and commonly deals with, "cash only" entrepreneurs – window cleaners, builders and painters, and all types of small business proprietors.

Prognosis

If we examine the 5 elements that tend to increase the size of the UgEcon, we can easily see that all of these factors are working *against* curbing its growth in the UK:

Taxation: While significant cuts in the marginal rate of income taxation were made in 1988, the overall burden of taxation rose under Mrs. Thatcher, from 41% to 43% of GDP. This trend continued as sharp tax increases were introduced in 1994.

Regulation: A tidal wave of regulation was imposed on the UK by the EU – from the color of mushy peas to the curvature of cucumbers.

Tax morality: No evidence of any surge in British tax morality has been found over the past 15 years: if anything, we have seen a sharp deterioration of tax morality.

Unemployment: Unemployment continues to hover at around 10% of the workforce. This may be a low figure compared with some other European countries (for example, Spain has averaged 18% over the last decade), but it is high by UK standards of the 1960's and 1970's. Many more people may be being pushed into the UgEcon.

Illegal economy: There is little doubt that the illegal economy components of the UgEcon have grown significantly in the UK over the past 2 decades, notably in such areas as car theft, burglary, and drug trafficking. It is estimated that 65% of illegal drugs enter the UK from other EU countries.

The History of Money and Banking

Putting the UgEcon in Context

Before we can begin to understand the complex web of tax evasion, we need to take a couple of steps backward and look at the origins of money and banking. Both are integral components of tax systems, and the UgEcon is a well-scripted and creative response to taxation.

What Is Money?

At first, the answer to this question seems obvious; average consumers would agree that money is coins and banknotes, but would they accept them from any country? What about cheques? Bank money (i.e., anything for which you can write a cheque) actually accounts for (by value) the greatest proportion of the total supply of money. What about IOU's, credit cards, and gold? The gold standard belongs to history, and in economic retrospect it is recognized as a major contributing cause of the Great Depression. (The US abandoned it in 1933; France did so in 1936).

The global eradication of "real money" took place when gold and the US dollar were "decoupled" on August 15, 1971. However, even today, when many central banks are selling their gold stores, many people prefer to keep some of their wealth in the form of gold rather than in official, inflation-prone currencies.

The attractiveness of gold, from an aesthetic point of view, and its resistance to corrosion are 2 of the properties that led to its use for monetary transactions for thousands of years. In complete contrast, a form of money with virtually no tangible properties whatsoever – electronic money – seems set to gain rapidly in popularity.

The Invention of Banking

Banking originated in Ancient Mesopotamia where the royal palaces and temples provided safe-keeping for grain and other commodities. Receipts came to be used for transfers to the original depositors and to third parties. Eventually private houses in Mesopotamia also got involved, and laws regulating them were included in the code of Hammurabi.

In Egypt, the centralization of harvests in state warehouses also led to the development of a system of banking. Even after the introduction of coinage, these grain banks reduced the need for precious metals, reserving them for foreign purchases, particularly in connection with military activities.

Precious metals, in weighed quantities, were a common form of money in ancient times. The transition to quantities that could be counted rather than weighed came gradually. However, many primitive forms of money were counted just like coins. Among the earliest countable metallic money or "coins" were "cowries" made of bronze or copper, in China.

What Is Money?

It is almost impossible to define money in terms of its physical form or properties. Therefore, any meaningful definition must be based on its functions.

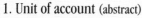

Specific functions (mostly micro-economic)
1. Unit of account (abstract)
2. Common measure of value (abstract)
3. Medium of exchange (concrete)
4. Means of payment (concrete)
5. Standard for deferred payments (abstract)
6. Store of value (concrete)

General functions (mostly macro-economic, abstract)
7. Liquid asset
8. Framework of the market allocative system (prices)
9. A causative factor in the economy
10. Controller of the economy.

Professor Glyn Davies, a noted scholar on this subject, concludes that the best definition is as follows: "Money is anything that is widely used for making payments and accounting for debts and credits." [9]

These quasi-coins were easy to counterfeit and, being made of base metals, of low intrinsic worth and thus not convenient for expensive purchases. True coinage developed in Asia Minor with the Lydians, who stamped small round pieces of precious metals as a guarantee of purity. Later, when their metallurgical skills improved and these pieces became more regular in form and weight, the seals served as symbols for both purity and weight.

Money Exchange and Credit Transfer

The great variety of coinages in use in the Hellenic world meant that money changing was the earliest and most common form of Greek banking. Usually money changers would do business in or around temples and other public buildings, setting up trapezium-shaped tables (which usually carried a series of lines and squares for assisting calculations), from which the Greek bankers, the trapezitai, derived their names (much as the English name for bank comes from the Italian *banca* for bench or counter).

Credit transfer was a characteristic feature of the services provided in Delos, which rose to prominence in banking during the late 2nd and 3rd centuries BCE. Whereas in Athens banking had been carried on exclusively in cash, cash transactions in Delos were replaced by real credit receipts and payments were made on simple instructions with accounts kept for each client. After the fall of the Roman Empire, banking was forgotten and had to be re-invented much later.

Thus, banking re-emerged in Europe at about the time of the Crusades. In Italian city-states such as Rome, Venice and Genoa, and in the fairs of medieval France, the need to transfer sums of money for trading purposes led to the development of financial services including bills of exchange. The Crusades gave a great stimulus to banking because payments for supplies, equipment, allies, and ransoms required safe and speedy means of transferring cash. Consequently the Knights of the Temple and the Hospitallers began to provide banking services such as those in some of the Italian city-states.

The Royal Monopoly of Minting

When coins were first introduced their use spread rapidly because of their great convenience. In situations where coins were generally acceptable at their nominal value, there was no need to weigh them. In everyday transactions involving relatively small numbers, counting was quicker and far more convenient than weighing.

By the Middle Ages, monarchs were able to use this convenience as a source of profit. Wholesale recalls of coinage were far more frequent than was justified by wear and tear on the coins. The profits from minting, known as seigniorage, provided a supplement to other revenues.

Despite the challenges of counterfeiters, governments controlled coin production and hence the money supply. Not until the rise of commercial banking and the widespread adoption of paper money was this monopoly broken, with profound consequences for the growth of democracy.

Relevance of History

Economists, especially monetarists, tend to overestimate the narrow and technical functions of money and have placed insufficient emphasis on its wider social, institutional, and psychological aspects. These issues are not simply of academic interest. Economists still argue about how to measure and control the money supply, and these disputes have implications for the material well-being of everyone. Hence the importance of learning from history.[9]

Zappozats

All sorts of things have been used as money at different times in different places: Amber, beads, cowries, drums, eggs, feathers, gongs, hoes, ivory, jade, kettles, leather, mats, nails, oxen, pigs, quartz, rice, salt, thimbles, vodka, wampum, yarns, and zappozats (decorated axes).[9]

A Short History of Taxation

tax (taks), n.
1. A sum of money demanded by a government for its support or for specific facilities or services, levied upon incomes, property, sales, etc. 2. A burdensome charge, obligation, duty, or demand.[10]

It's no wonder that, since the beginning of recorded history, taxes have been considered a plague. Even the dictionary definition focuses on "demands" and "burdens." History is littered with myriad schemes for collecting taxes in a variety of creative ways, but taxpayers have traditionally been even more creative than the tax collectors.

Ancient Egypt

During the reigns of the Pharaohs, the scribes were the tax collectors. During one period, a tax was imposed on cooking oil. To ensure that citizens were not avoiding the tax, scribes began to audit households. Their job was to check that appropriate amounts of cooking oil were consumed and that citizens were not using substitutes for the taxed oil.

Ancient Greece

In times of war, the Athenians imposed a head tax referred to as eisphora. No one was exempt from this tax, which was used to pay for special wartime expenditures. However, the Greeks were one of the few societies that actually rescinded the tax once the emergencies were over. When additional resources were gained by the war effort, those resources were used to refund the tax.

Athenians also imposed a monthly poll tax on foreigners, those who did not have *both* an Athenian mother and father. This tax, a metoikion, amounted to one drachma for men and a half drachma for women.

The Roman Empire

Empire founder, Caesar Augustus, is considered to have been a brilliant tax strategist and might well be crowned the "father of modern taxation." He ordered a tax census throughout the Roman world at the time attributed to the birth of Jesus. Prior to his rule, each conquered province paid a fixed sum; Augustus' innovation was to add a tax that fluctuated with the value of each piece of land.

Inheritance taxes of 5% on all gifts (except to children and spouses) were imposed to provide retirement funds for the military. Import and export duties (portoria) varied from 2-5%, and a 5% tax was placed on the value of freed slaves. Other lasting changes included a 1% sales tax on public auctions and a 4% tax on sales of slaves.

During Caesar Augustus' reign as "First Citizen," the "old" publicani were virtually eliminated as tax collectors for the central government. In their place, he introduced a civil service and transferred the responsibilities for tax collection to the cities.

England

The Roman Empire's occupation of England was marked early on by a tax revolt. Boadicea, Queen of the Iceni, an ancient Celtic tribe of eastern England, headed an insurrection against corrupt Roman tax collectors in the year 61. With an army of 230,000 soldiers behind her, the Queen's revolt allegedly killed all Roman soldiers within 100 miles, seized London, and killed more than 80,000 people. When the revolt was crushed by Emperor Nero, new administrators were appointed for the British Isles.

After the disintegration of the Roman Empire in the early 5th century, England was invaded and settled by Anglo-Saxons; Viking raids in the late 8th century turned into full-scale invasions in 865. The conquest of Norman William I in 1066 marked the start of feudalism. With this rich history of occupation, the rulers could select from a variety of tax traditions. For example, in addition to customs duties, people were subject to additional taxes on land, known as Danegeld.

Lady Godiva, another famous tax resister, was the wife of Leofric, Earl of Mercia. According to legend, she rode naked through the streets of Coventry to persuade her husband to lower heavy taxes. By the 12th century, the symbolic head of tax resistance was a character known as Robin Hood.

In 1369, during the 100 Years War between England and France, one key factor that renewed fighting was the rebellion of the nobles of Aquitaine over the oppressive tax policies of Edward, The Black Prince. It's worth noting that the taxes of that time were very progressive; the 1377 Poll Tax noted that the tax on the Duke of Lancaster was 520 times the tax on a common peasant.

Under the earliest English taxing schemes, an income tax was imposed on the wealthy, office holders, and the clergy; a tax on movable property was imposed on merchants. The poor paid little or no taxes. *The King's Writ stated that individuals should be taxed according to status and means. Hence the idea of a progressive tax on those with the ability to pay was developed very early.*

Disputes over the taxation rights of the King and those of Parliament plagued the reign of King Charles I. To pay for the army commanded by Oliver Cromwell, Parliament imposed excise taxes on essential commodities (grain, meat, etc.) in 1643. The taxes imposed by Parliament extracted even more funds than taxes imposed by Charles I, especially from the poor. The excise tax was very regressive, lowering the rural laborers' abilities to buy wheat to the point that families were starving. This, in addition to the fact that the common lands used for hunting were enclosed and the peasants forbidden to hunt, led to the Smithfield riots in 1647. As for Charles, he was ultimately charged with treason and beheaded.

A precursor to the modern income tax we know today was invented by the British in 1800 to finance the war with Napoleon. When the tax was repealed in 1816, opponents of the tax, who thought it should only be used to finance wars, wanted all records of the tax destroyed. Records were publicly burned by the Chancellor of the Exchequer but copies were retained in the basement of the tax court.

North America

The US was essentially the by-product of a tax revolt against the British. In contrast, Canadians did not object to paying the taxes that caused the American Revolution and that passive capacity to shoulder excessive taxation is an ingrained part of Canadian culture today. *Most governments have long since forgotten that the intent of taxes is defense and not wealth redistribution.*

Unfair Taxes Push People Into the UgEcon

Creating Tax Dissatisfaction

Although a variety of causes push people into the UgEcon, no single cause has more potency than the belief that the taxes are unfair.

In December of 1998, more than 1,000 Canadians were polled by Gallup on behalf of *Reader's Digest*. Respondents were instructed to think about **all the taxes** they paid to federal, provincial, and local governments, including income, sales, and local property taxes.

The poll found that Canadians at every income level think they are overtaxed. An astounding 83% of respondents feel their own total tax payments are "too high." Overall, just 15% of respondents say the taxes they pay are fair.

This represents a dramatic increase in the level of dissatisfaction; 1962 Gallup data found Canadians almost equally divided between those who thought their taxes were "too high" (47%) and those who thought they were "about right" (43%).

Fair Equals 25-29% of Income

Interestingly, the poll showed a strong consensus on the issue of tax fairness. When asked to name the highest total tax a family of 4 should pay, respondents across economic, ethnic, ideological, and age lines answered with surprising uniformity: 29%. (See page 91 for more detail on this poll.)

This number is corroborated by a 1995 poll by the well-regarded Roper Center for Public Opinion Research at the University of Connecticut. The Roper poll, also published by *Reader's Digest*, showed that a broad majority of people felt that 25% was about the share of their money Americans should pay in all their taxes.

David Hume's classic, *Of Taxes*

Modernized and condensed here, it is as sage today as it was more than 200 years ago.

Governments hold a prevailing assumption that every new tax creates a new ability in taxpayers to bear it, and that each increase of the public burdens increases proportionately the productivity of the people. This maxim is hazardous, because it is almost certain that it will be abused. It is particularly dangerous too, because its truth cannot be altogether denied; it has some foundation in reason and experience. However, it is true only when kept within bounds. When a tax is laid on commodities that are consumed by the common people, the necessary consequence is either that the poor must reduce something from their way of living or be able to increase their wages.

But there is a third consequence, which often follows taxes: Namely, that workers increase their productivity and live as well as before, without demanding more for their labor. Where taxes are moderate, are laid on gradually, and do not threaten the necessities of life, this often happens.

We may observe that the most commercial nations have not always possessed a great amount of fertile land; on the contrary, they have labored under many natural disadvantages.

Singapore, Switzerland, and Hong Kong are strong 20th century examples.

In all history, we find only 3 instances of large and/or fertile countries with much trade: The Netherlands, England, and France. The Netherlands and England have the advantages of their maritime resources and access to foreign ports to procure what their own

Robin Hood's Nemesis:
The Tax Collecting Sheriff of Nottingham

climates refused them. In France, trade came late and seems to have been the effect of reflection and observation by an ingenious and enterprising people who noticed the riches acquired by The Netherlands and England.

Sir William Temple's Theory of Laziness

Some deficits of natural resources that might be perceived as disadvantages may, if fact, actually encourage enhanced productivity. The Dutch productivity, based entirely on their natural disadvantages, demonstrates a striking contrast with Ireland, where because of the abundance of good soil and scarcity of people, all things necessary to life are cheap. An industrious Irishman can eat for a week with 2 days' work.

An easy life, therefore, is the basis of the laziness in people. People naturally prefer ease over labor and will not take pains if they can live idle. When necessity has inured them to it, they cannot leave it. The places where trade has most flourished, both in ancient and modern times, are commonly observed to be such confined territories that they have created a necessity for higher individual productivity.

1. The best taxes are levied on **consumption**, particularly on luxury items, because such taxes are least felt by the ordinary people. They seem in some measure voluntary, because a man may choose how much he wants to use a taxed commodity. Such taxes are paid gradually and sensibly. They naturally produce sobriety and frugality, if judiciously imposed. Being confounded with the natural

STARVE THE BEAST!

price of the commodity, they are scarcely perceived by the consumers. Their only disadvantage is that they are expensive to collect.

2. *Property taxes* are inexpensive to collect, but have every other disadvantage. Most states, however, are obliged to use them, in order to supplement other taxes.

3. In general, all *poll or head taxes* are dangerous, because it is so easy for the government to add a little more, and then a little more, to the sum demanded, so that these taxes eventually become altogether oppressive and intolerable.

4. *Duties on imports* are self-regulating. The government will soon find that an increase of the customs tax does not increase revenue. It is not easy, therefore, for a people to be harmed by such taxes.

5. *The most pernicious of all taxes are the **arbitrary** ones.* They are commonly converted into punishments on productivity; also, by their unavoidable inequality, they are more grievous. It is surprising, therefore, to see them have a place among any civilized people.

Historians tell us that one of the most fundamental causes of the collapse of ancient Rome was Constantine's introduction of a universal poll-tax, which replaced the tithes, customs, and excises that formerly composed the revenue of the empire. The people in all the provinces were so oppressed by these taxes that they took refuge in the conquering arms of the barbarians, whose tax needs were lower and therefore preferable to the more refined tyranny of the Romans.

Tax the Land!

Placing all taxes on land is an opinion zealously promoted by many political writers. These restricted thinkers assert that inasmuch as all taxes ultimately fall on land, it is better to lay them there initially, thereby abolishing every tax on consumption. But it is not true that all taxes fall ultimately on land. If a duty is laid on a commodity consumed by an artisan, he has 2 obvious expedients for paying it: he may cut back on his expenses, or he may increase his labor. Both these resources are easier than raising his wages. In years of scarcity, the weaver either consumes less or labors more, or both, by which he is able to reach the end of the year.

The manufacturer who employs him cannot give him more, because the merchant, who exports the cloth, cannot raise his prices; the merchant himself is limited by the price the product can demand in foreign markets. Everyone, to be sure, desires to push the tax burden from himself and lay it on others. Everyone has the same inclination; therefore, no set of men can prevail completely in this contest. Why the landed gentleman should be the victim and should not be able to defend himself, I cannot readily imagine.

This 200-year-old perspective on taxes is interesting to read in the context of the very current Basic World Tax Code (see page 109). The key issue is that income taxes (unless they are flat) are by their very nature both direct and arbitrary.

A Footnote from David Hume's Treatise, *Of Taxes*

I will conclude my observations on taxes with an example of what frequently happens in political institutions: Namely, that the consequences of some taxes are diametrically opposed to expectations. It is regarded as a fundamental maxim of the Ottoman (Turkish) government that although the Sultan is the absolute master of the lives and fortunes of each individual, he has no authority to impose new taxes.

One might imagine that this limitation would be the firmest barrier in the world against tax oppression. Yet, the reality is quite the contrary. Because the Sultan has no regular method of increasing revenue from his subjects, he squeezes his lieutenants and governors to the point that *they* oppress and abuse the subjects. However, if the Sultan could impose new taxes directly, as is done in European governments, his interests would be more in concert with those of his people, and he would more quickly understand the sinister effects of increased tax levies. Ultimately he would find that: *A pound, raised by fair taxes, would have a less pernicious effect than a shilling raised in an unfair and arbitrary manner.*

The Progressive Tax Rate Trap – Taxes on Being Successful

> Let me tell you how it will be. There's one for you, nineteen for me.
> 'Cos I'm the taxman.
>
> – George Harrison, "The Taxman" from the album *Revolver* (1966)

Not unlike the words in the Beatles' Taxman song, successful people are paying "progressive tax rates" in the 30, 40, and even 50% range. The taxes that come with this new prosperity are, in reality, "success taxes."

Taxes can be categorized as proportionate or progressive. In a proportionate system, when the tax rate is 25%, a person who earns $100 pays $25 in taxes. Logically, a person who earns $200 pays more: $50. Most countries, however, do not have proportionate tax systems.

A system that taxes people at higher rates when they increase their income is a progressive system. The 1st dollars earned are taxed at lower rates, ranging from nothing at all to 10-20% at most. But the last dollars earned are taxed at higher rates, often exceeding 50%, after taking into consideration the taxes of all levels of government with taxing authority. Taxpayers encounter the progressivity problem at many points; for example, it is at the heart of the marriage penalty that exists in many countries' tax systems.

What those working in the trenches of everyday life have come to realize is that progressivity does not, in fact, tax the rich. The progressivity trap sets a very high tax rate on "ordinary income." So the super rich, and even people who are merely very prosperous, arrange deferred-compensation plans that pay them in years when their taxes are lower. Those who are truly successful, the super rich, get to stay that way and even build their wealth.

In plain and simple terms, a progressive tax system taxes the process of becoming successful or significantly improving one's lot. Progressivity is the mother of all taxes, the tax that dominates taxpayers' lives like no other. And it institutionalizes the class warfare that politicians tell us they are waging on our behalf.

Public Policy and the UgEcon

Many important public policy decisions at both national and meta-national levels now call for analytical and empirical knowledge of the size, growth, causes, and consequences of the UgEcon.

For example, allowing for US business holdings of currency, the whereabouts of more than 80% of the US currency supply is presently unknown. These anomalous findings give rise to what has been labeled the "currency enigma," which consists of a stock and a flow component.[11] The inability to identify the holders and locations of a large portion of the US currency stock further complicates attempts to measure the size of the UgEcon in any country. Although direct measures of overseas holdings indicate that no more than 25% of US currency is presently held abroad, indirect methods yield estimates that between 30% and 70% of US currency is held abroad, with the "composite" estimate being roughly 40%. It would not be a surprise if the actual foreign holdings were equal to or exceeded 50% of the US currency stocks.

The Role of the Euro

The euro will soon become the single currency of Europe, replacing the French franc, German mark, Italian lira, and 12 other national currencies. The EU has recently decided to fight the encroachment of dollars into its nations' UgEcon by printing 500 euro notes (about $500),* which will be much more attractive to drug dealers and the like because of the volume of cash necessary for their large transactions. We share the view of at least one noted economist who says that the European decision to print 500 euro notes is an explicit effort to compete for the business of the UgEcon.[12] (See more on the euro on page 25.)

* All amounts of money in this edition of the book are in US dollars unless otherwise specified.

Conclusion
Taxes: Past, Present and Future

The Case for Consumption Taxes

Tax evasion will undoubtedly be a problem under any tax system. It is a major and growing problem under the current tax systems, despite very substantial efforts and increasingly harsh treatment of the tax-paying public. In the US, a generally tax-compliant country, almost 40% of the taxpayers are out of compliance with the tax system, mostly unintentionally, because of the enormous complexity of the system itself.[13] This complexity breeds disrespect for the tax system as well as the law, and makes a system based on taxpayer self-assessment less and less viable.

"This will be a truly great tax, because another tax is sure to drive them to drink more."

Punch,
the very British humor magazine, understood how tax policy was made. This illustration is from an 1877 edition.

A consumption (sales) tax is likely to reduce rather than exacerbate the problem of tax evasion. The increased fairness, transparency, and legitimacy of the system will induce more compliance. The 90% reduction in the number of filers will enable tax administrators to more narrowly and effectively address non-compliance and will increase the likelihood that tax evasion will be uncovered.

The relative simplicity of a sales tax also will promote compliance. Businesses will need to answer only 1 question to determine the tax due: How much was sold to consumers? Finally, the dramatic reduction in marginal tax rates will reduce gains from evasion. If the cost of non-compliance remains comparable (or even increases, based on the increased likelihood of being caught among the much smaller number of filers), then the expected profit from tax evasion will decline and the magnitude of tax evasion will decline.

> **Unreported economic activity leads to unfairness in the distribution of the tax burden.**

Remembering Who Pays the Taxes

There is a persistent misunderstanding among those modern-day "Robin Hoods" who see taxes as a wealth redistribution scheme. The belief that taxes are paid by the rich and corporations persists despite overwhelming evidence to the contrary.

For example, in Canada, the country with the highest personal income tax in the G-7 and the highest corporate tax in the OECD, only 6% of all taxes collected come from the "rich," which the taxing authority defines as anyone making more than $55,000 a year. Only 9% of all taxes collected come from corporations; and, as we have said elsewhere, we believe these costs are ultimately passed along to the consumers anyway.

This means that the tax burden falls squarely on the shoulders of taxed-at-the-source, captive taxpayers and law-respecting, compliant taxpayers. Sadly, both of these groups are members of shrinking sectors of the workforce.

The World's Best Tax Cheaters

The word itself is derived from the Latin *fasces*, a symbol of authority in ancient Rome.

The fasces was a bundle of rods that were strapped around an axe, and it represented the unbreakable power of the state.

Italy truly is a land of ironies. Despite the 2000-year-old grand tradition of the Roman Empire, Italy is an infant state; it did not become a democratic republic until 1946, when the last Italian monarch, King Umberto II, was deposed by popular referendum. Italy boasts 2 non-reigning royal families as well as 3 non-reigning grand ducal houses. In addition, 3 sovereign governments exist entirely within Italian borders (San Marino, Vatican City, and The Order of Malta). It so happens that the only reigning Italian dynasty, a branch of an old Genoese family, rules a sovereign Italian principality, Campione, an area within *Switzerland.*

Given this context, it understandably could be difficult to figure out to whom one rightfully owed taxes. The prevailing practice became *"when in doubt about tax obligations – don't pay anyone."* A little historical review will be helpful in understanding the unique attitude of Italians toward paying taxes.

Mussolini and Fascism

Benito Mussolini came to power after the infamous 1922 "March on Rome" and was appointed Prime Minister by King Victor Emmanuel; he ruled until 1945, when he was hanged by an angry mob. From his beginnings as the editor of a small socialist newspaper, Mussolini went on to almost a quarter-century of leadership in a new political movement called "fascism."

The Fasces

Fascism dictates that expansion of the nation is an essential manifestation of its vitality. As such, it is the kind of doctrine best adapted to the aspirations of a citizenry, like the Italians, who were rising again after many centuries of subservience. But expansion of a nation demands discipline and a deeply felt sense of duty and sacrifice.

Even though Italy's economy was devastated by WWI, Mussolini's fascism dictated colonial-type expansionism in Libya and Ethiopia, as well as expensive involvement in the Spanish Civil War. Therefore, the combination of the debt incurred in WWI, the manoeuvers in Africa, and the war games in Spain required excessively high taxes.

One of our major hypotheses on the UgEcon is that *when taxes reach a certain level, taxpayers rebel.*

In a famous speech, IL DUCE said:

The Government has been compelled to levy taxes which unavoidably hit large sections of the population. The Italian people are disciplined, silent and calm; they work and know that there is a Government which governs, and know, above all, that if this Government hits cruelly certain sections of the Italian people, it does not come out of caprice, but from the supreme necessity of the national order.

– Benito Mussolini, Italian Prime Minister, 1923

Formal Name:	**Italian Republic**
Local Name:	*Italia*
Local Formal Name:	*Republica Italiana*
Location:	*Europe*
Status:	**UN Country**
Capital City:	**Rome (Roma)**
Main Cities:	Milan, Naples, Turin, Florence, Venice
Population:	**57,867,000**
Area [sq.km]:	**301,270**
Currency:	*1 lira = 100 centesimi*
Main Languages:	*Italian*
Main Religions:	*Roman Catholic*

The US, with its intense valuing of personal rights over those of the state, has a long history of aggressive tax revolts. In contrast, countries that are more passive or less unified have more covert tax revolts. This is particularly true for countries with authoritarian governments, like Italy. As a result, tax evasion is practiced on a scale unequalled in any other developed country.

Economic Development

Italy has few natural resources. No substantial deposits of iron, coal, or oil exist. Proven natural gas reserves have grown in recent years, however, and they constitute the country's most important mineral resource. With much of the land unsuited for farming, Italy is a net food importer. In addition, most raw materials needed for manufacturing and more than 80% of the country's energy sources are imported. Italy's economic strength lies in the design, processing and manufacturing of goods, primarily in small- and medium-sized family-owned firms. Its major industries are precision machinery, motor vehicles, chemicals, pharmaceuticals, electric goods, fashion and clothing.

Italy's economy, however, has deceptive strength because it is supported by a substantial UgEcon that functions outside of government controls. The Mafia continues to exert a strong influence in Southern Italy, often hindering or opposing governmental programs aimed at economically and politically integrating the region more fully into the national economy. A major problem in Southern Italy is the widespread use of illicit drugs.

This area has the highest incidence of drug use in the country. The spread of drugs has become a major social problem in Europe. Corruption probes, begun in 1992, led to the arrest of hundreds of business and political figures and the investigation of many others, including several party leaders and former premiers.

After the Italian government raised its official GDP statistics (see page 62) to reflect off-the-books economic activity, Italy became the world's 5th largest economy. But whatever the truth statistically, tax evasion in Italy is rampant.

What is distinctive in the Italian model is that tax evasion is not just the choice of mom-and-pop businesses and the self-employed; rather, it also is practiced at a high level of sophistication by large companies. Even large public companies, compliant taxpayers in almost every other country, are infamous for hiding income and inflating expenses. Celebrities such as fashion designer Giorgio Armani have admitted bribing tax officials for favorable audits, evidence of the bribery and corruption that abound at the highest levels of government.

Official Numbers vs. Reality

A study of the manufacture of coral jewelry in the Bay of Naples area:

According to official figures, about 1,000 people are employed in this industry, in approximately 100 small enterprises which chalk up aggregate export earnings of some $13 million annually.

But the researchers, who studied the matter on site, found 400 small companies employing a total of 4,500 people and achieving annual export earnings of about $163 million.

Defining and Measuring Underground Economies

Until recently, studies of the UgEcon lacked an accepted taxonomy for classifying underground activities. These activities were diversely labeled as subterranean, hidden, irregular, informal, gray, shadow, clandestine, parallel, and black, but these descriptors lacked explicit definitions to support empirical investigation.

Underground activities can be differentiated by the rules they violate; therefore, 4 specific types of UgEcon activity exist, often overlapping: illegal, unreported, unrecorded, and informal.

The *illegal* economy consists of economic activities that violate the laws that govern legitimate commerce. Most commonly this includes illicit drugs, bribes, prostitution, theft, graft, and unauthorized gambling. Recently, it has expanded to include money laundering and people smuggling. Because of the fact that the activities are illegal, no real measures exist to estimate the size of this sector.

The *unreported* economy consists of economic activities that evade the fiscal reporting requirements of our tax codes. Such activities include failing to declare income on tax returns, benefit fraud, false claims to benefits or subsidies to which the claimants are not legally entitled, and skimming (failing to report sales).

The unreported economy is measured by the "gross tax gap," the difference between the amount of tax revenues legally due and the amount of tax revenues voluntarily paid. The "net tax gap," in contrast, represents the difference between the amount of revenue due and the amount actually collected. Therefore, the difference between the gross and net equals the revenues collected as a result of enforcement activities.

The *unrecorded* economy includes those activities that circumvent the reporting requirements of government statistical agencies. A summary measure of unrecorded economy is the amount of income that should be recorded in the national accounts that measure economic activity such as GDP. Because national accounting conventions differ regarding the inclusion of illegal incomes, unrecorded income may or may not include components from the illegal sector.

The *informal* economy encompasses activities that circumvent the costs, benefits, and rights of property, licensing, labor contracts, torts, financial credit, and social security systems. A summary measure of the informal economy is the income generated by economic agents operating informally on a global basis – the most common example is street vendors.

He was the leader of the highly regarded Chicago school of monetary economics, which stresses the importance of controlling the amount of money in circulation as an instrument of government policy and as a determinant of business cycles and inflation.

This is a key concept in the most effective measurements of the UgEcon.

He received the 1976 Nobel Prize for Economics and has been a senior research fellow at the Hoover Institution (Stanford University) since 1977.

Dr. Milton Friedman

Formulas to Measure the Invisible

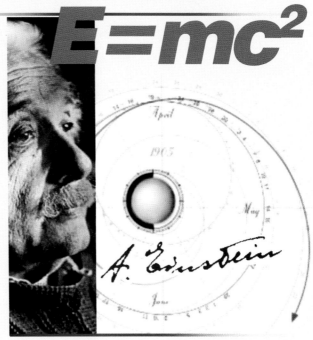

Econometric estimates abound for most types of behavior, but empirical studies of tax evasion are particularly difficult. By its very nature, the UgEcon defies measurement. One basic method simply subtracts total reported income from total expenditure, but more complex measures also exist.[4] Some of these more complex methods include measuring different types of payment methods such as currency and demand deposits, polling people to see how much they have bought from the "informal vendors," and other estimates. Obviously, UgEcon participants are trying to escape detection, making measurement of the phenomenon extremely difficult.

One very prominent UgEcon measurement relies on the assumption that the ratio of currency to demand deposits would have remained constant were it not for growth in the UgEcon.[16] To the author and to many other economists, this assumption seems to be an unreasonable *ad hoc* supposition. A multitude of other factors influenced the choice between currency and demand deposits over time – changing regulations, growth of nearby banks, credit and debit cards, automatic teller machines, coins of larger denominations, and many other bank innovations.

Our preferred method for estimating the UgEcon is a variation on the currency ratio method. This method, in its purest form, assumes that virtually all UgEcon transactions use currency. The 3 major exceptions to this are barter, pages 26-27; multiple business bank accounts, page 108; and blatantly excessive business deductions, page 22.

In its purest form, this method looks at the amount of currency that exists in the economy compared to the amount of demand deposits that are used in the non-UgEcon. If the amount of currency demanded increases, then the UgEcon estimate increases proportionately. However, several modifications of this method include:

1. Observing the ratio of large denomination bills to smaller denominations, determining the demand for currency using interest rates, and then comparing this amount to the actual demand for currency. This assumes that UgEcon transactions predominantly use large denomination bills. Although this is clearly true of transactions for illicit drugs and organized car theft, much of the "legal" UgEcon comprises small, unreported transactions, requiring modification of this method.

2. Another variation determines the demand for currency measured in the market funds available for loans and compares this amount to the actual demand for currency: The demand for money should be less than the actual demand for currency, so the difference is assumed to be a part of the UgEcon. However, because the funds market for loans is not always in a state of equilibrium, this method also has a flaw that requires some kind of compensation in its application.[17]

3. The 1st and 2nd assumptions are based on the foundation that only the country's national currency is involved in UgEcon transactions. From an examination of the amount of US currency in use outside the US – especially $100 bills – we can be sure that much of the world's UgEcon is conducted in US dollars. (See page 29.)

Blatantly Excessive Business Deductions (BEBD)

One of the advantages of being "in business" rather than being an employee is that you have the option of writing off certain expenses, that is, off-setting business expenses against income that you generate. This legitimate option *invites abuse*, particularly among small business owners and the self-employed. Specific rules list the records that need to be kept, but they typically are minimal – names of guests, companies they represent, and topics of business discussed – the kinds of things that you can jot on the back of the credit card slip.

This has always been a "perk" of owning your own business. The practice of "bending the rules" for meals and entertainment is universally practiced. What has changed over the years, based on anecdotal data and observation, is the frequency and the flagrancy of categorizing personal activities as business activities. The proliferation of small business and self-employment has dramatically increased the number of people eligible to exploit the BEBD options.

However, this practice is by no means merely the purview of small businesses; large corporations pay for memberships at country clubs and health clubs, and they lease skyboxes at sports venues. Senior executives are virtually never questioned about their expenses. The practice of inflated and falsified costs among road warriors was common among caravan operators of Marco Polo's day, and a lucrative variation was practiced by ship captains since the 1st ship was hired.

Alternative Methods of Measuring the UgEcon

Another way to measure the UgEcon is by looking at unemployment. This method says that the economy is smaller than what is actually thought: Because the unemployment rate has remained relatively constant in recent years, the UgEcon must also have remained approximately constant.

Another way to use unemployment to estimate the UgEcon is by comparing employment with payroll estimates; the difference is the UgEcon.

However, because most other methods have determined that the UgEcon is growing rapidly, these methods clearly are not totally accurate. [18]

Yet another major method used to determine the size of the UgEcon is to take a survey of consumer purchases. Every transaction has 2 components, a buyer and a seller. The sellers will not tell how much they are not reporting, either because they do not want to get caught doing something illegal, or because they just want to avoid paying taxes. So the only other way to determine that a transaction is a part of the UgEcon is to ask the buyer.[18] However, a variety of small flaws arise when this approach is taken. First, a buyer may not know that the seller does not want to report the income for tax purposes. Second, consumers are not willing to admit that they did something illegal, so the illegal components of the UgEcon cannot be accurately measured. Third, the sample taken may not be large enough and specific enough to give an accurate representation of the UgEcon. Nevertheless, this approach has been used many times to try to estimate the size of the UgEcon.

Reconciling the Estimates

These different estimates do have something in common: They all show that the UgEcon represents a considerable part of the global economy. In 1981, an estimate of the US UgEcon was over $40 billion, while the reported GDP was $3 trillion – not a major problem.[18] Last year, it was estimated that the size of the US UgEcon was around $1 trillion[20] while the GDP was about $7 trillion.[21] This alarming growth has several implications for the future. First, it points to the fact that Americans are viewing the UgEcon as a more acceptable way to do business. This reflects growing hostility toward the government and also changing moral values in today's society. Second, it shows that governments need to restructure the tax system. People would not need to be in the UgEcon if they were willing to pay taxes, so a better system needs to be developed in order to encourage people to report all of their income.

As we have discussed at several points, agreeing on the definition of what is to be included in the UgEcon has proven to be almost as difficult as agreeing on which methodologies are most accurate. Again, it is our view that all transactions that involve illicit commodities being covertly traded to avoid tax or regulation should be included in the size of the UgEcon. One reason for this is that what is illegal in one country may be legal in other countries – for example, many European countries have decriminalized drugs and prostitution. Therefore, in our opinion, the GDP includes all production without regard for legality.[14]

Contaminated Statistical Data

The inescapable conclusion that the UgEcon is considerably larger than governments are willing to acknowledge and that it is growing at a ferocious rate has some critical implications: The adverse impact of the 1990's recession, particularly the slow recorded recovery in many countries, along with the stubbornly high unemployment rate of the mid-1990's, *may have been only an illusion.* If a large number of workers evaded their fair share of the tax burden, it would have contaminated governments' statistical data collection – producing highly unreliable data.

The same kind of reasoning may help to explain the size of the gap between US and Canadian productivity. If, as we estimate, Canadians are 25% more likely than Americans to bury productivity in the UgEcon, this would explain a significant proportion of the estimated 40% productivity gap between the 2 countries.

Worms:
Real Underground Work

Of all of the businesses that operate in the UgEcon, here is one that you probably had not considered: Ontario's multi-million dollar worm-picking industry. The common dew-worm, one of Canada's most populous wild animals, represents capitalism at its crudest – the harvesting and wholesaling of a perishable, seasonal commodity in a largely unregulated cut-throat industry.

Ontario alone has at least a trillion dew-worms. Night after night, indefatigable immigrants stoop to conquer their own poverty out in the rural darkness where the tax collectors cannot see them. This is the bottom rung of an industry whose annual exports have been estimated at anywhere between $26 and $66 million. On a good, warm, wet night, a skillful picker can gather upwards of 6,000 dew-worms – at $10 to $20 per thousand, depending on the seasonal demand. The reputed record is 22,500 worms in one night, by one man.

To find worms in significant numbers, pickers follow the rain. They monitor weather forecasts as keenly as any farmer or fisher. Southeast Asians – Vietnamese, Laotians, Cambodians – make up the vast (and very silent) majority of the pickers and drivers in this physically gruelling work, replacing the Greek immigrants of earlier generations. Except for the use of rechargeable batteries in their lights, worm harvesting has changed little in the last 50 years.

A scientist with Agriculture and Agri-Food Canada guesses that the total wholesale value of worms exported annually is in the $33-million range.

The pickers themselves take home a third of that amount, in cash. A mid-sized company might export 50 million worms in a single year. If the pickers receive $13 per thousand, and the worms retail for $2 per dozen in the US, that leaves a lot of room for profit. And because the work is low profile, decentralized, and done at night, it has never been a priority for the taxing authorities. [109]

The Effects of Unreported Income

As we have noted previously, by its very nature and complexity of definition, the size of the UgEcon is always difficult to measure accurately. There are, however, some indirect ways to get a tolerably precise indication of its size. One way is to compare income reported to the taxing authorities with other measures of income. Another is to compare the public's use of large-denomination currency. The latter aspect is of some global importance for the strongest currencies: the British pound, the German mark, the Japanese yen, and most importantly, the US dollar – the favorite currency of the large scale UgEcon around the world.

Failure to Report Income

In the US, the IRS collects data on adjusted gross income (AGI) from tax returns – what people say they earn. The Commerce Department calculates a measure of AGI from sources such as total wages paid by corporations and total interest paid by banks. Comparing IRS and Commerce Department data gives a good idea of how much income is going unreported.

In 1995, using the IRS/Commerce Department data, Americans failed to report almost $420 billion in AGI on their tax returns. If that income were taxed at 22% (the average marginal tax rate for all US taxpayers), the revenue loss for that single year is almost $100 billion in individual income taxes alone. It is important to remember that this measure only applies to a very small segment of the UgEcon, cases in which a group of taxpayers, almost always businesses, are claiming tax-deductible expenses paid to individuals who are failing to report that income.

Although this segment of the UgEcon is very limited, it can give us a solid idea of how this form of tax evasion has changed over time. Using this measure, unreported income increased from 10% of AGI in 1988 to 13% in 1995. This represents an increase of 30% over a 7-year period. The increase, although significant, is not as dramatic an increase as in many of the other segments of the UgEcon.

Tax rates increased in 1990 and 1993, but there were significant tax cuts in 1986. We will demonstrate elsewhere that lower tax rates have the potential to reduce evasion because the cost of reporting one's true income is lower, which affects the very important risk/reward ratio associated with tax evasion.

Currency in Circulation

Another intriguing way to gauge the growth rate of the UgEcon is to look at the growth of currency in circulation, especially large bills such as US$100 bills. Because the UgEcon operates almost exclusively in cash, unusual increases of cash in circulation are considered a valid indicator of its growth. "Currency in circulation" refers, in the US context, to the amount of the national currency held outside the Treasury and Federal Reserve. Except for small amounts of currency that may have inadvertently been lost or destroyed by the public, currency in circulation includes the holdings of financial intermediaries and the public. Reliable data on financial intermediary holding of vault cash are readily available; therefore, it is possible to obtain accurate estimates of the total stock of currency outside the banking system.

Currency, as an anonymous medium of exchange, is viewed as the preferred means of payment in transactions that UgEcon workers are trying to conceal. This makes cash stocks and flows a natural starting point in our search for the UgEcon. The total amount of currency in circulation is one of the best-measured macroeconomic indicators, since the production and distribution of currency by governments is strictly monitored and carefully recorded.[15]

The chart that follows shows the growth of $100 bills as a percentage of the value of all outstanding US currency. According to the US Treasury Department, $100 bills, which accounted for less than 20% of the value of currency outstanding in 1967, accounted for about 65% of its value in 1999.

In 1997, total US currency increased by $31 billion – and $30.2 billion of it was in $100 bills.

$100 Bills As a Share of US Currency

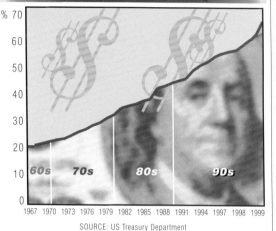

% 70

60

50

40

30

20

10

60s   70s   80s   90s

0

1967 1970 1973 1976 1979 1982 1985 1988 1991 1994 1997 1998 1999

SOURCE: US Treasury Department

We also can estimate the size of the UgEcon from currency data by looking at the real increase in currency per capita. The assumption is that law-abiding citizens will not ordinarily increase their needs for cash day-to-day. Hence, any significant increase in cash per capita must be being used in the UgEcon. In fact, it is reasonable to assume that the increased use of debit and credit cards should have reduced the per capita need for cash. However, despite widespread predictions of the advent of the cashless society and decades of cash-saving financial innovation, per-capita holdings of US currency increased from $110 in 1961 to $1,000 by the end of 1994. Adjusting for inflation, real per capita currency increased by 70% and the proportion of the money supply composed of currency rose from 20% to 30%.

The US Government has not printed notes larger than $100 since 1946 and withdraws from circulation those that come into its possession.

EURO
The UgEcon's Newest Cash of Choice

The euro will soon become the single currency of Europe, replacing the French franc, German mark, and Italian lira, among others. It is destined to edge out the dollar as the currency of choice in the world's huge UgEcon – and, in the process, end a highly profitable American monopoly. As issuer of dollars, the US has benefited by having foreign "customers" hold and use US currency. It is the equivalent of being able to get an interest-free loan. With $400 billion of its currency in circulation, the US Government is saving $28 billion a year, the amount of interest saved if all that currency had to be replaced with 7% T-bills.

The EU has decided to issue the euro in very large denominations, including 100, 200 and 500 euro notes – approximately $100, $200, and $500 at the current rate of exchange. On the surface, these denominations are intended to copy those of the German mark and thus make the new currency seem reassuringly familiar to those with doubts about monetary union.

However, the larger euro bills will help the EU rival the US for UgEcon customers – Colombian narco lords, New York mafia bosses, and Russian gangsters – as well as run-of-the-mill tax dodgers. Cash is anonymous, portable, and easy to hide – the bigger, the better.

Until now, they have had an overwhelming penchant for US dollars because there are so many of them, they are easily convertible anywhere, and they are relatively in-flation-proof. With large-denomination euro notes, all will now have a more compact mechanism for doing business and hoarding their profits. A person will be able to smuggle a million euros in or out of the country in a purse instead of a suitcase.[26]

Thus, faced with the choice of an even better product, the euro, criminals will switch. And the US will see a dramatic increase in interest costs on the national debt because of the loss of the UgEcon "business."

Dodging the Tax of Dividends ... Worldwide interest and dividends reported as paid by corporations will exceed those reported as income received by more than $150 billion.

Bartering

The Origins of Commerce

Worldwide, bartering is prospering again; it is a sector of the UgEcon that is difficult to measure because of the lack of formal records. Knowledgeable analysts estimate that Asia alone has a bartering business worth almost $100 billion a year. Direct bartering of goods and services is a core aspect of many rural economies, especially in lesser developed countries.[24]

The barter system, a significant sector of the legal UgEcon, is an ancient tradition with a modern computerized twist – Electronic Bartering Clubs have turned into a multi-billion-dollar industry, with millions of individuals and businesses participating in formal barter organizations.

It works like this:

- Entrepreneur X and Company A are both members of the same barter company.
- Entrepreneur X sells computers to Company A; his account with the barter company is credited, and Company A's account is debited.
- If Entrepreneur X then decides to print brochures to advertise his computers, he contacts a printing company in his barter system and uses the credit in his account to pay for the printing.
- Entrepreneur X's barter account is debited for that transaction, and the printing company's account is credited.

Business owners say the advantages are 2-fold: They save cash and receive free publicity when their services or goods are traded. Barter is particularly good for businesses with excess capacity or extra time, and those that have a good cash flow. Small businesses with services or goods in demand do especially well in barter.

Taxes on Barter

In its simplest form, bartering consists of trading by exchanging goods or services. The economic foundation of a barter transaction is that each person considers that the value of whatever is received is at least equal to the value of whatever is given up in the exchange.

In all transactions, the amount that must be treated as income is whatever the taxpayer would have normally charged a stranger for the goods or services. When one set of goods or services cannot readily be valued but the other can, the taxing authority will normally accept them as equivalent if the parties were dealing at arm's length.

In general, the official position of tax authorities is that *the taxes on barter are treated on the same basis as if cash were the consideration.*

Services: When a taxpayer barters his or her services, the value of those services must be considered as income when they are related to the taxpayer's business or profession. Examples are a dentist or the *owner* of a plumbing business who agrees to fix someone's teeth or drains (respectively) in return for services or property provided by the other party.

A gray area is introduced by the distinction between an owner and an employee and how the word "occasionally" is interpreted. Where a taxpayer is an *employee, occasional* help given to a friend or neighbor in exchange for something would not be taxable unless the taxpayer made a regular habit of providing such services for cash or barter.

Goods: When a taxpayer barters goods, the value of those goods must similarly be considered as income when they are related to the taxpayer's business. For example, the value of groceries given by a grocer to someone in exchange for something else must be brought into the grocer's income. In addition, some goods that are bartered may give rise to capital gains, such as when capital property (such as a valuable painting, a sailboat, or land) is bartered for goods or service.

I prefer to think of community support through community money as contribution TO the body social/political/economic rather than taxation, which feels more like extraction FROM.

Michael Linton, designer of the LETSystem. He emigrated from Britain to the west coast of Canada in the 1970's. In 1983, the 1st LETSystem in the world was implemented in the Comox Valley on Vancouver Island.

Complementary Community Currency Systems and Local Exchange Networks

One of the more recent innovations in barter is the development of complementary currency models, types of locally issued money that facilitate barter exchanges in much the same way that national currencies facilitate formal commerce. Complementary currencies may be issued as:

• **"Fiat" currency,** such as in Ithaca Hours, (See sidebar.) that is issued, managed, and guaranteed by a central authority;

• **Mutual credit,** such as Local Exchange Trading Schemes (LETS) and Robust Complementary Community Currency Systems (ROCS) that use Green Dollars;

• **Commodity-backed money** or scrip that may be redeemed for a particular product or service. (Airline and hotel points are prominent examples of this kind of scrip.)

In these systems, the amount of money exchanged in any transaction is negotiable. These systems are more popular in diverse communities, where products or services requiring greater variety of skills, experience, training, equipment, or risk are exchanged.

Basically, a Community Currency System is simply an alternative form of exchanging one's work for goods or services provided by others, rather than being dependent on national currencies and the people who control them. Unlike barter trade, which requires a direct exchange, local currencies commit the individual who receives a good or service to supplying goods or services to the community at a future date.

Community currency offers numerous potential benefits to the community:

• Support for locally produced goods and services;
• Boost to small-enterprise development and traditionally undervalued activities;
• Discouraging environmentally destructive activities; and
• Strengthened social relationships.

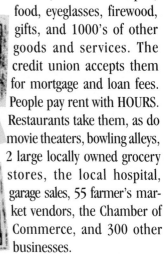

Ecological Economics with Local Currency

Since 1991, residents of Ithaca, New York, have been gaining control of commerce by issuing over $68,000 of local paper money to more than 1,450 participants.

Here's how it works: The Ithaca HOUR is Ithaca's $10.00 bill, because $10/hour is the local average of wages/salaries. HOUR notes, in 5 denominations, buy plumbing, carpentry, electrical work, roofing, nursing, chiropractic, child care, car and bike repair, food, eyeglasses, firewood, gifts, and 1000's of other goods and services. The credit union accepts them for mortgage and loan fees. People pay rent with HOURS. Restaurants take them, as do movie theaters, bowling alleys, 2 large locally owned grocery stores, the local hospital, garage sales, 55 farmer's market vendors, the Chamber of Commerce, and 300 other businesses.

Everyone who agrees to accept HOURS is paid 2 HOURS ($20.00). Every 8 months, they may apply to be paid an additional 2 HOURS, as a reward for continuing participation. This is how the per capita supply of money is gradually and carefully increased.

Ithaca's HOURS are real money, backed by real people, real time, and real skills. Dollars, in contrast, are the true "funny money," no longer backed by gold or silver but by less than nothing – the trillions of dollars of national debt.

Local currency is a lot of fun, and it's legal – HOURS are taxable income when traded for professional goods or services. Local currency is also a lot of work and responsibility.

For more information, Ithaca HOURS provides a Hometown Money Starter Kit and Video.[22] (See Sources page 120.)

Conclusion
Learning to Speak The Same Language

The Tower of Babel by Pieter Brugel (1563)

for per capita GDP which is, in essence, the total GDP of any political entity divided by the number of people in that particular region. The size of the unreported and unmeasured productivity of the UgEcon clouds any implications that we might draw from this information. For example, the amount of money earned in a rural farming economy cannot be accurately compared to the same amount of money in an urban setting because farm income typically is *in addition to food and shelter* and has a significant component of barter. Urban dwellers have to pay for food and shelter and usually have nothing to barter except their labor.

Lies, Damn Lies and Statistics

This book is full of statistical data; this chapter, in particular, has highlighted some of the myriad problems in attempting to gather and present data that give an accurate perception of the causes, size, and impact of the UgEcon. Part of the issue we have discussed from several perspectives – the overwhelmingly inherent complexity of trying to agree on definitions of something as evasive as the size and growth of the UgEcon.

The other significant complexity that makes it difficult to comprehend the tumultuous nature of the UgEcon is that politicians and bureaucrats find it in their best interest to systematically *understate* this aspect of the economy. Accepting the real numbers would mean accepting the reality that the situation is spinning out of control and that government policies of excessive taxation, over-regulation and misguided social engineering are fuelling the global tax revolt.

From a public policy perspective, perhaps the most misleading set of statistics surrounds the frequently cited information on employment levels and average income of a particular region or country. Average income is a popular media term

Systematic Understating of the GDP

The GDP measures consumer purchases, private investment, and government spending. Yet these figures substantially underestimate the GDP because they ignore goods and services produced in the UgEcon. For instance, illicit drugs, unauthorized gambling, and prostitution are not included. Because of their criminal nature, it is understandably hard to estimate the dollar volume of these activities. It is also difficult to estimate the value of legal goods and services provided in an illegal fashion ("off the books") as well as products produced and exchanged through barter systems.

The UgEcon affects economic statistics and policy. Official unemployment and poverty rates may be overestimated because of employment and earnings people do not report. Governments lose billions in tax revenues. On the positive side, the economic activity significantly enhances the official reports of average annual income.

If the proportional size of the UgEcon remains relatively constant, then economic data expressed in rates, such as the growth rate in GDP, will be

The UgEcon that governments are willing to acknowledge is, at most, equivalent to the tip of an iceberg.

accurate despite ignoring the UgEcon. But such consistency is unlikely; as tax rates rise, and the momentum of the tax revolt increases, UgEcon activity rises disproportionately faster than the measured GDP.[21]

Distinguished researchers like Edgar Feige limit the definition of the UgEcon to legal "off-the-books" production. Even so, his estimates suggest that the US UgEcon is about 20% of the formal economy. If we define the UgEcon to include all production not accounted for in the GDP, estimates increase to the range of 15% to 40% of the economy in economically developed countries and in excess of 50% in countries in economic transition.

Stacking other types of UgEcon activity on top of the official measurement further increases its size. The greatest unaccounted-for production is both legal and ethical: "sweat equity." This includes do-it-yourself auto and home repairs, cooking, cleaning, and vegetable gardening – virtually everything that we do ourselves that could be done by someone else. A very credible estimate of the economic value of unpaid work done in the home alone is in excess of 30% of the official GDP. [25]

You Already Know the Real Answer

At some level it is sheer nonsense for us to use highly contaminated data to tell you what you already know. You know which taxes you evade, and you know at least some of the evasion activities of your family, friends, and neighbors.

You also know how you feel about government waste and personally experience the bite of the high taxes. Many of you have already gone offshore with some assets – or you are contemplating such a move when your assets reach a level that justifies the costs.

A Need for Stronger Medicine

Like strains of bacteria that become resistant to formerly effective antibiotics, governments shrug off compelling data and informed opinions and proceed on their self-serving paths.

Dozens of think tanks all over the political spectrum have good ideas, but most of their information is shunned by governments and is often over the head of the average taxpayer. They end up preaching to their own choirs and occasionally to each other.

Taxes are the backbone of any politico-economic regime and limitations on a government's power to tax are constraints on its power to act. Withholding income tax at the source, an invention to finance WWII, is the paramount administrative mechanism enabling the federal government to collect, without significant protest, sufficient private resources to fund a vast welfare state. Governments of virtually all the OECD countries now view withholding as the cornerstone of administering individual income tax.

Yet the history of income tax withholding involves extensive misrepresentation by government office holders. Since withholding itself alters perceptions of private tax burdens, one may legitimately be concerned about political deception. The scam used by politicians and bureaucrats is to create the optics that a situation is a crisis. In a crisis, actions can be taken, usually without direct opposition, that would otherwise be considered gross violations of regime boundaries.

The time has come to actively challenge the publicly accepted scope of government authority.

There also appears to be a quietly deployed rule of thumb in the contemporary economics profession that "if you can't (convincingly) estimate something, it is best to ignore it."

Morditas,
like piranha, mean lots of little bites

A Nation Built on Bribes

The ambitious economic model adopted by the Mexican government in the 1980's is the main cause for the growth of the informal sector. Complex, globally oriented policies were developed and implemented to restructure the manufacturing base to be more competitive and integrated into international markets – particularly NAFTA. Given the gigantic difference between the levels of economic development in Mexico, Canada and the US, this was akin to running before learning how to walk. The result has been a lot of skinned knees, in the form of massive unemployment. The UgEcon in Mexico is very big compared with what is reported for most industrialized nations, but fairly "normal" in terms of standards for developing countries.

The informal economy in developing countries is certainly part of the worldwide UgEcon issue, but the motivation is survival at the most basic level. Unlike most UgEcon activity in developed countries where the motivation is a tax revolt, the motivation to enter the informal sector in developing countries has occurred mainly because of the failure of the formal sector to provide for the population's job needs.[27]

The Size of the Informal Economy

One of the reasons that information on the size of the informal economies varies so dramatically is that old enemy – a lack of common definition. The major variable tends to be whether or not part-time and 2nd (or 3rd) jobs should be counted. It is our view that the picture is inaccurate unless everyone, full- and part-time, is counted. A study by the Mexico City daily newspaper, *El Financiero*, reports that 21.5 million people now work in the informal economy, while only 15.2 million people are formally employed. A generally reliable source, using the more restrictive definition, estimates that about 16 million people will be full-time in the informal sector by 2000.

Governments in almost all countries are fearful of identifying the true size of the UgEcon for fear it will show their incompetence in managing the problem. Additionally, if people really knew the extent of the UgEcon sectors, they might be encouraged to join in. A quasi-governmental agency acknowledges that while the informal economy is extensive, it represents, depending on the method employed, only between 25% and 35% of the GDP. Most recent estimates show that the size of the informal economy as a proportion of GDP has never surpassed 35%, even though there has been a clear increase in these activities in the major cities.[28]

Why People Join the Informal Economy

Informal workers commonly mention low earnings in the formal economy as the reason for turning to unofficial work. The national average for the minimum wage is less than $2.50 a day, and survival is even more difficult now with the significant drop in buying power. As many as 40% of the street vendors earn up to twice the minimum wage.[29]

Bureaucratic obstacles discourage the aspiring entrepreneur. In the late 1980's, the number of bureaucratic procedures required to establish a business was about 20 *official* steps. In 1992, the government committed to reduce red tape, and that number fell to 9; and the process is continuing to be simplified, according to government claims.

Formal Name:	**United Mexican States**
Local Name:	**México**
Local Formal Name:	**Estados Unidos Mexicanos**
Location:	**North America**
Status:	**UN Country**
Capital City:	**Mexico City**
Main Cities:	**Guadalajara, Monterrey, Puebla**
Population:	**91,840,000**
Area [sq.km]:	**1,958,200**
Currency:	**1 Mexican peso = 100 centavos**
Main Languages:	**Spanish**
Main Religion:	**Roman Catholic**

La Mordita

In a country plagued by the tradition of the mordita (literally, the "little bite"), bribes are a part of the way of life. Every step in the process of formalizing a business is an opportunity for another mordita.

Street vendors, on the other hand, are often led by fellow workers who juggle their demands while making sure that the right bribes are paid. Under this informal system of patronage, city streets have become a complex patchwork of loyalties to certain leaders who are expected to manage relationships with city authorities. The National Chambers of Commerce Association reports that vendors pay in excess of 10 times more in bribes than they would have to pay if they actually paid the tax that would be assessed at the current rates.

Merchants charge that corruption stands in the way of a viable solution to the growth of the formal economy. "The government sometimes gives the vendors a piece of paper to legitimize them, but they continue to escape taxes. The government helps the informal economy grow by looking the other way." [30]

In 1993, the smuggling of all kinds of contraband (goods subject to tariffs) was estimated at the equivalent of 30% of the total imports.

Pancho Villa & Emiliano Zapata
Mexican Legends and role models

> *As tariffs have fallen under NAFTA, the economic incentive of contraband has been dramatically reduced.*

Strategies to Combat the Informal Economy

The Mexican government has undertaken a series of measures to diminish the informal economy that include reducing administrative procedures and general taxes for both individuals and companies, plus a very strident effort to punish tax evaders. Law enforcement in this area has recently been very strong – some would say draconian – with dramatic results. The number of active federal taxpayers – as distinct from those considered captive because they work for a company that collects their taxes and remits them to the tax authorities – grew from 1.5 million people in 1988 to almost 5 million in 1993.

Although the number of tax filers continues to grow, it is difficult to expect anything like full compliance in a country where a recent president's brother and his cronies siphoned billions into Swiss bank accounts.

Meanwhile, the debate persists over whether a solution is necessary or whether the informal sector is itself an answer to Mexico's continuing economic woes. [31] For unskilled workers, their destiny is in the informal economy and/or emigration to the US. Certainly NAFTA has created jobs, but not in the numbers needed to absorb the more than 1 million people entering the Mexican labor market annually.

The Mafia

Crime with a Brand Name

When they think about organized crime, Westerners tend to concentrate specifically on the criminal enterprises of the "Mafia" or "Cosa Nostra" ("our affair") in North America and Italy (specifically, Sicily). The Mafia and Cosa Nostra, of course, represent particular branded versions of a more general species of organized criminal enterprise that includes the Yakuza in Japan, the Triads in the Chinese diaspora, yardie gangs in Jamaica and the UK, the cocaine cartels of Colombia, Russia's "New Mafia" and other Italian crime organizations such as the Camorra of Naples. All of these criminal enterprises share certain similarities, but they also exhibit significant differences.

Marlon Brando as the Godfather

The Disorganized Crime Hypothesis

Conventional wisdom in post-war US law enforcement circles was inclined strongly to the "octopus" view of the Cosa Nostra – a centralized organization whose tentacles stretched out into a number of activities. Therefore, when economists started to apply their analytical tools to the study of crime in the late 1960's and early 1970's, the tendency was to accept the octopus view advocated by earlier investigations. These studies, like the governmental inquiries they followed, lacked a solid basis in terms of management and economic research into the realities of organized crime as a business.

Finally, in 1983, a detailed empirical study of certain organized crime activities was conducted. This study of the operations of the numbers, illicit bookmaking, and loan-sharking businesses in New York City marked an important step in casting considerable doubt on the conventional perception of how well the Mafia was organized.

The researchers were unable to find evidence in these 3 "enterprises" that the markets were being centrally controlled. Although incentives exist to create a dominant group in any setting where violence is involved, other economic factors tend to undermine monopolies in the underworld economy and keep them localized, fragmented, and unintegrated, just the opposite of the case in legitimate industries.

This led to the **disorganized crime hypothesis** – the contention that what we thought was supposedly very-organized crime activities are actually typified by fragmentation, as contrasted with their "above-ground" counterparts.[32]

Franchising Criminal Activities

The Mafia is not a centrally controlled industry, but rather a brand name for licensed operators in the private protection industry.
* In the late 1980's, the industry was made up of more than 100 separate "firms." Membership in each protection firm is relatively restricted, typically from 2 to 100 associates.
* Mafia families in Sicily and North America are separate and independent. Linkages do exist, but they are weak.
* The opportunities for effective centralized marketing of protection services are better in the US than in Sicily. The US is home to only 24 "firms" (families), 5 of which are located in New York City. This means that the franchised territories are large.
* As in legitimate business, success breeds competition. Here, the competition is from youth, biker, and prison-based gangs like the Black Guerillas and Nuestra Familia, and others who have the capability to service a demand for protection from illicit businesses.[33]

Benefit Fraud

Pretending to be Robin Hood – taking from the rich to give to the poor – is a major preoccupation of most governments today. It has been a main plank in the political platform of most liberal agendas since the Great Depression. This redistribution of resources from richer to poorer individuals is accomplished in most advanced economies by a system of welfare payments generally referred to as "transfer payments." These transfer payments are typically very complex in design and often involve some sliding level of benefit or "clawback" of payment based on the economic and demographic circumstances of the recipient.

Benefit fraud is the transfer system's counterpart to tax evasion, and, again, we have 2 major public policy alternatives: even more aggressive compliance policies or the reconstruction of the design of the tax and transfer systems. In most cases, more aggressive compliance only drives the activity further underground (a recurring pattern). On the other hand, creative constructive solutions have the potential to eliminate or at least dramatically reduce the undesired behavior.

Public transfer programs – including cash transfers, tax-linked benefits, and in-kind benefits – have grown substantially over the past 30 years. For obvious reasons, at the lower income levels, the size of the UgEcon is influenced almost as much by benefit fraud as by tax evasion.

Some liberal analysts apply the term "benefit fraud" solely to multiple welfare claims and similar manoeuvers. They argue that concealing earnings from welfare authorities is understandable and non-culpable in view of the low level of benefits and the high "clawback" penalties on earnings. This view naively echoes the argument that inasmuch as tax evasion is so commonplace, it is not really a criminal activity.

Mimicking the distinction between the UgEcon and pure tax evasion (see page 23), benefit fraud can involve either participation in the underground economy or simple non-reporting of income from the "above-ground" economy. Most candidates for public transfers have little capital other than

FDR Signs US Social Security Act, 1935

Welfare is a narcotic, a subtle destroyer of the spirit.
– *Franklin D. Roosevelt, 32nd US President, 1933-45*

FDR, US President during The Great Depression and WWII was the Father of the world's welfare systems.

consumer durables and possibly home equity, so their income tends to be derived almost exclusively from labor earnings. In addition, most of the work in the above-ground economy is highly visible; this fact tends to drive public transfer recipients into the UgEcon, where they hope to conceal their earnings from the transfer authorities.

The 2nd type of benefit fraud occurs when a beneficiary conceals assets that would be counted against benefits or fails to report capital or investment income. Such "pure benefit fraud" commonly happens when 2-parent households present themselves as single-parent families to conceal 1 partner's earnings. Then the 2nd parent can work in the above-ground economy with less risk that visible earnings will be traced back to the partner who is claiming the transfers.

Breaking Point
The problem is that people get to a breaking point at which they will find ways of saving money. When a taxpayer perceives that gains from tax evasion outweigh any associated risks and costs, this creates an incentive for underground activity.

Illicit Drugs

The most contentious contraband traffic in the world today is in illicit drugs and psychotropic substances. Because the US is the world's largest consumer of illicit drugs and because of its superpower status, it is able to dictate world drug policy through its massive, yet totally ineffective, anti-drug spending. Increasingly, the EU is seriously debating legalization of certain drugs, while the Inter-American Drug Abuse Control Commission, pressed by governments such as Mexico and Canada, is supporting increased attention to the issues of demand, treatment, and alternative economic development in the supplying countries.

Drugs: From Natural to Designer

Primitive people, like people today, found a variety of natural drugs to facilitate their desire to escape reality. The use of the coca leaf, peyote, and the opium poppy is thought to have been practiced for at least the last 3,500 years.

Because of the long history of opiates, one of the 1st pharmaceutical derivatives of a natural drug was heroin. In the ensuing years, much was learned about biologically useful derivatives of naturally occurring drugs. This knowledge allowed researchers to unravel many of the structures associated with biological responses, helping them to produce pharmaceutically useful compounds from off-the-shelf chemicals. This body of knowledge, used for personal financial gain, created the so-called designer drug phenomenon.

The technical term for designer drugs is Controlled Substance Analogs. The pharmacology of drugs is enormous and includes such tongue-twisters as hallucinogens, phenylalkylamines, phencyclidines, stimulants, sedatives-depressants, and analgesics. Almost every breakthrough in legitimate medication is mirrored by an illicit cocktail that becomes a part of the UgEcon.

The illicit drug market is the driving force behind many sectors of the UgEcon — money laundering for the traffickers, and prostitution and theft for the users. Canada, once only a channel for drugs bound for the US, is now a drug-producing country. [34]

Free Amy Pofahl!

... age 37, serving 24 years in prison for her ex-husband' drug crimes; convicted of conspiracy to import and distribute Ecstasy (MDMA) and money laundering. [35]

A single Canadian province, British Columbia, produces as much as $1.3 billion in cannabis — a "cash crop," obviously all underground, that is now 7 times the size of its world-famous salmon industry.

Legalized Danger: Alcohol

Alcohol is a dangerous drug and a major public health menace. Studies show that heavy drinkers use medical care at twice the rate of nondrinkers of the same age and gender; drinkers have shorter life expectancies and higher mortality rates; and alcohol consumption increases a person's chances of illness. The associated social costs are enormous.

Inasmuch as alcohol is widely acknowledged to do more harm than all the illegal drugs combined, why is it not illegal? The answer lies in the politics of alcohol policy in the period after Prohibition. By December of 1933, the alcohol industry had managed to convince Americans that drinking was better than the combined merits of abstinence and obedience to the law.

Alcohol and Prohibition

The drinking of alcohol has probably been around almost as long as the human race, and its history holds lessons for today. The Industrial Revolution caused an upsurge in alcohol use, seen as a way to escape the boredom and pain of urban working life. The implications then are clear for our Information Revolution, which comes with at least as many stresses as the Industrial Revolution.[36]

In the US, national prohibition of alcohol (1920-33) was intended to reduce crime and corruption, solve social problems, reduce the need for prisons and poor-houses, and improve health and hygiene. Instead, the results clearly affirm the most basic of economic theories:

The prohibition of mutually beneficial exchanges is doomed to failure.

As a result of Prohibition, alcohol became more dangerous to consume, crime increased and became "organized," courts and prisons were stretched to the breaking point, and corruption of public officials was rampant. No changes were measured in productivity or absenteeism. A significant source of tax revenue was lost, and government spending increased. Many drinkers switched to opium, marijuana, patent medicines, cocaine, or other more dangerous substances.

Legalization of Drugs

"So long as large sums of money are involved – and they are bound to be if drugs are illegal – it is literally impossible to stop the traffic, or even to make a serious reduction in its scope.

"Our emphasis here is based not only on the growing seriousness of drug-related crimes, but also on the belief that relieving our police and our courts from having to fight losing battles against drugs will enable their energies and facilities to be devoted more fully to combatting other forms of crime.

"We would thus strike a double blow: reduce crime activity directly, and at the same time increase the efficacy of law enforcement and crime prevention."

Milton Friedman, *Nobel prize winner*

> *The prestige of government has undoubtedly been lowered considerably by the prohibition law. For nothing is more destructive of respect for the government and the law of the land than passing laws which cannot be enforced. It is an open secret that the dangerous increase of crime in this country is closely connected with this.*
>
> **– Albert Einstein**
> *My First Impression of the U.S.A.,* 1921

Drug Abuse by Prescription

Millions of prescription pills enter the illicit drug market every year, with a double standard in enforcement because of leniency toward doctors and their affluent, drug-abusing clientele.

The US Drug Enforcement Agency estimates that the illegal sale of prescription drugs amounts to about 80% of the money spent on cocaine, including crack. About 10% of the people in the US use prescription drugs for "non-medical reasons" – more than the combined number of users of crack, heroin, and cocaine.[37] Prescription painkillers, sedatives, stimulants, and tranquillizers account for 75% of the top 20 drugs implicated in emergency room episodes each year.[38] And yet the US federal government spends only about 5% of its $13 DEA billion budget to investigate prescription drug offenses.

Part of the problem, according to law enforcement officials, is that medical practitioners are usually charged under laws that carry short prison penalties. In one infamous case, a California physician issued 15,000 questionable prescriptions for the stimulants Preludin and Dilaudid ("drugstore heroin"). The doctor pleaded guilty to 2 felony counts and lost his medical license, but was sentenced to 8 days in jail.

In contrast, a "regular Joe" who was arrested with 2 ounces of crack at the same time in the same city was sentenced to a year in prison. Prosecutors say that the laws allow health care professionals to escape serious drug-trafficking charges as long as they have written a prescription, no matter how fraudulent.

Curbing Drug Traffic

Efforts to greatly reduce the flow of illicit drugs have been a dismal failure everywhere in the world. Over the past decade, worldwide production of illicit drugs has increased dramatically: Opium and marijuana production has roughly doubled, and coca production tripled.[39]

Despite the illusion of a national political resolve to deal with the drug problem, contradictions continue between US anti-drug policy and other policies. US narcotics policy seeks reduction of the supply of illicit drugs and reduction of user demand within the US. On the other hand, important aspects of US foreign policy aim at promoting the political and economic stability of US friends and allies and avoiding excessive involvement in their internal affairs.

Background and Analysis

More than 11 million Americans buy and use illicit drugs more than once per month, annually spending by most conservative estimates over $50 billion – and perhaps as much as $150 billion or more – in a diverse and fragmented criminal market. The US illicit drug market generates enormous profits that enable the growth of diversified international criminal organizations, extending their reach into local neighborhoods, legitimate businesses, and even national governments. Measured in dollar value, at least 80% of all the illicit drugs consumed in the US are of foreign origin, including virtually all of the cocaine and heroin. Of the marijuana consumed in the US, 25-35% is domestically produced, and virtually all of the hallucinogens, psychotherapeutic drugs, and "designer" drugs are of domestic origin.

Eradication of Narcotic Crops

A long-standing US official policy for international narcotics control strategy is to reduce cultivation and production of illicit narcotics through eradication. The US supports programs to eradicate coca, opium, and marijuana by providing chemical herbicides, technical assistance, specialized equipment, and spray aircraft. It also funds programs designed to promote economic growth and to provide alternative sources of employment for the people currently growing, producing, or processing illicit drugs, as well as to help offset the loss of foreign exchange from diminished drug exports.

Interdiction and Law Enforcement

A 2nd element of US international narcotics control strategy is to help host governments seize illicit narcotics before they reach America's borders. Therefore, the US funds anti-narcotics law enforcement training programs for foreign personnel. In addition, it provides host country anti-narcotics personnel with equipment, and US Drug Enforcement Administration (DEA) agents regularly assist foreign police forces in their efforts to destabilize trafficking networks.

International Cooperation

In an address commemorating the 50th anniversary of the UN, President Clinton stressed the importance of international cooperation in combatting organized crime and drug smuggling.

Diplomatic initiatives by the US State Department, both bilateral and multilateral, encourage

Jade and Heroin Trades Overlap in Myanmar

Myanmar, formerly Burma, remains the world's largest opium producer and is seeing an intermingling of the drug and jade trades. Myanmar is the only source of gem-quality jade. The jade trade has traditionally been a government monopoly, but smugglers and insurgents conduct a huge, semi-sanctioned trade in the stone, which is technically illegal within Myanmar, but legal outside the country.

Some heroin smugglers are using hollowed out jade boulders to transport the drug. Myanmar's opium production has boomed since a junta seized power in 1962 and is now estimated in excess of 3 million kilos a year. Heroin and jade each generate hundreds of millions of dollars yearly in illicit revenue, a prosperity for many that is far in excess of official per capita income figures.[40]

and assist nations in reducing cultivation, production, and trafficking in illicit drugs. These bilateral agreements and international conventions have thus far been largely ineffective in reversing the growth of international narcotics trafficking.

Sanctions/Economic Assistance

A 4th element of US international narcotics control strategy involves sanctions against drug producing or trafficking nations. These range from suspension of US foreign assistance to curtailment of air transportation. Current law requires the President to submit to Congress by March 1 each year a list of major illicit drug-producing and transit countries that are eligible to receive US foreign aid and other economic and trade benefits. This sets in motion a 30-day review process in which Congress can override the President's certification and stop US foreign aid from going to specific countries.

For example, in 1996, President Clinton certified the following countries as fully cooperating and deserving of US assistance: Bahamas, Belize, Bolivia, Cambodia, China, Dominican Republic, Ecuador, Guatemala, Haiti, Hong Kong, India, Jamaica, Laos, Malaysia, Mexico, Panama, Peru, Taiwan, Thailand, Venezuela, and Vietnam. The President decertified and denied assistance to Afghanistan, Myanmar (Burma), Colombia, Iran, Nigeria, and Syria.

Conclusion

The primary goal of US narcotics control policy is to stem the flow of foreign drugs into the US. A number of options have been proposed to reshape and more effectively implement US international narcotics control policy. Whatever options are selected will likely require funding on an enormous scale, because it is estimated that the illicit drug industry generates as much as $500 billion a year for criminal organizations.

No single enterprise drives the UgEcon as powerfully as the production of and trafficking in illicit drugs. No multinational program offers as little prospect for success as does the US-led anti-drug struggle. *Only a change in laws that viscerates the profit motive will have a significant impact on this major engine of the UgEcon.*

Evading & Non-Evading Sectors

An empirical fact about tax evasion is that the extent to which a person evades taxes is strongly correlated with the *source* of that person's income. Opportunities for evasion differ among occupations, and these differences in opportunity may, in fact, influence labor market behavior.[41] In other words, an individual may base his or her occupation, in part, on the opportunity to evade taxes; e.g., tax evasion is easier when income is received from self-employment.[42]

In some occupations, a delicate balance exists between the evading sector and the non-evading sector. The wage earned in each sector depends, in part, on the relative allocation of workers between the 2 sectors. An increase of workers in one sector drives down the wages in that sector. Because workers freely choose the sector in which to be employed, wages therefore reflect the law of supply and demand.

Forces that Increase and Decrease UgEcon Participation

Even in occupations that lend themselves to tax evasion, individuals choose the degree to which they report income to tax authorities. In much the same way, "moonlighting" allows workers to divide their efforts, fully reporting income on their "registered" jobs and fully (or partly) evading taxes on their "unregistered" jobs.

However, risk orientation is a primary factor that influences participation in the UgEcon. One seminal study demonstrated that a rise in the tax rate increases participation in the UgEcon if, and only if, the workers also become more willing to take risks. Therefore, an increase in the probability of being caught reduces the size of the evading sector because it increases risk aversion.

This simple two-sector model of the economy demonstrates that the size of the evading sector will decrease when workers are less willing to take risks; the size of the UgEcon will increase when workers exhibit more risk taking. This holds key implications for the design of tax policy.[43]

The Rise & Rise of Tax Compliance Costs

As recently as 20 years ago, the term "tax compliance costs" was unknown. Now the accepted definition is that **tax compliance costs are the costs incurred by taxpayers in meeting the requirements laid on them by the tax law and the revenue authorities.** These are costs over and above the actual taxes and over and above distortion costs inherent in the nature of the taxes. These costs would disappear if any tax were abolished.

For individuals, tax compliance costs include the costs of acquiring sufficient knowledge to meet their legal obligations; the time taken to complete their personal tax returns and to obtain, file, and store the data to enable them to complete their returns; the fees paid to any advisers or tax agents; incidental expenses, such as travel costs to visit a tax adviser or the revenue authorities; and, more difficult to measure, psychic or psychological costs – the stress and anxiety experienced by some taxpayers in dealing with their tax affairs. Besides the costs individuals incur in relation to their own tax returns, many incur substantial time costs in helping other family members or friends who are less able to cope.

For businesses, tax compliance costs include the costs of collecting, remitting, and accounting for tax on the products and profits of the business and on the wages and salaries of employees; and also the costs of acquiring and updating the knowledge to enable this work to be done, including knowledge of legal obligations and penalties.

The term "administrative costs" can be used for the public sector costs of running the tax system – principally the costs incurred by the taxing authority. "Operating costs" is a convenient term to embrace the total costs of running a tax or the tax system, *i.e., both the compliance and administrative costs* .

From relative obscurity, tax compliance costs have become a matter of real significance and high priority in tax policy making.

The key findings of the research from a dozen economically developed countries can be summarized as follows:

- Research studies, whatever the methodology, find the compliance costs of the main central government taxes (personal income taxes, corporate income taxes, and sales taxes), are a multiple of the administrative costs. All countries, whatever their systems, have compliance costs higher than administrative costs.
- Large tax compliance costs reduce global competitiveness.
- Tax compliance costs have undesirable distributional effects. They are capricious and, especially for businesses, regressive, in that they fall disproportionately on small firms.
- Tax compliance costs fall much more heavily on the self-employed than on employees.
- Tax compliance costs generate resentment, adversely affecting voluntary compliance.
- Sales taxes are transaction-based, and the tax compliance costs are necessarily high.
- For a variety of reasons, in recent years in many countries, tax systems have become more complicated; also, an increasing proportion of taxpayers have faced more complex tax situations.
- Since the 1960s, public expenditure has increased greatly in virtually all OECD countries, and with it came an increase in taxation. Between 1965 and 1985, as a percentage of GDP at market prices, total taxation (including social security contributions) rose by an average of 40% in OECD countries.
- Tax systems have become more complex as governments have sought to restrict evasion and, more particularly, tax avoidance. Both have been stimulated by tax increases, aided and abetted by increasingly sophisticated taxpayers employing increasingly sophisticated tax advisers.
- Higher living standards have generated more tax compliance costs because many more taxpayers have widened their sources of income.
- The increasing globalization of the world economy has created many additional opportunities for creative tax avoidance. [44] (See Chapter 6, "Expatriation," for examples.)

Home-Based Business and the UgEcon

It's a little bit like the old chicken-and-egg question, "Does the UgEcon encourage the growth of home-based businesses or do home-based businesses, by their very nature, encourage participation in the UgEcon?"

The answer, not surprisingly, is "yes." The growth of self-employment and the growth of the UgEcon are interactive. Someone working for a regular employer has trouble hiding income. Self-employed people have an easier time hiding income and inflating expenses. Anecdotal data abound that tell us that *most, if not all, small businesses hide income by routinely skimming receipts and camouflaging personal expenses as business activities.* It is more the nature of the opportunity than the nature of the tax.

Competitive Advantages and Disadvantages of Home-Based Business

Today, many individuals are fully or partly employed by producing and/or selling a product or service from home. These entrepreneurs face many of the same hurdles as other small businesses and also face another set of issues that are unique.

Home-based businesses are increasingly the focus of media and public policy attention. While academics squabble about the definition of a home-based business, we use the obvious notion that it "maintains its primary facility in the residence of its owner or in surrounding buildings."[45]

Characteristics of Home-Based Business

Our definition makes no distinction among businesses on the basis of either size, industry, owner commitment to the business, or extent to which the business operations use the owner's residence. Although home-based business, in theory, could include enterprises of any size, in fact, the overwhelming majority are single

JANE DOE

FOUNDER, PRESIDENT & CEO OF

ME, INC.

proprietorships – the ideal climate for the UgEcon to flourish. *Home-based businesses are the hothouses of the UgEcon.* A large Canadian survey found an average employment figure of only 2.28 employees (including the owner) in those home-based businesses that received the owner's full-time employed efforts.[46] (The average employment figure was less in businesses that provided part-time employment to the owner.) For example, a survey of 530 female home-based business owners found that 67% have no employees other than the owner, 21% employed only casual labor in addition to the owner, and only 12% employed one or more full-time employees. The trend in home-based business is so well-ingrained into the North American economy that new homes are being designed and wired to accommodate this phenomenon. Many municipalities are relaxing planning and zoning restrictions, thereby minimizing constraints on the types of business that can be carried on in residential areas.

A Natural Entry into the UgEcon

Operating an enterprise out of the residence not only reduces much of the incremental overhead associated with operating a business; it also creates an inviting opportunity to bury personal expenses in the business. All computer equipment is, of course, solely for business purposes – even phone calls to your sister in Paris or Saskatoon are channelled through your business phone and folded into your business. Providing pizza for friends watching a sporting event on TV becomes business entertainment. The potential for manipulating expenses is limited only by the creativity of the entrepreneur. As we identified elsewhere, a high risk-orientation correlates positively with UgEcon activity; entrepreneurs are, by definition, high risk-takers. It's the perfect combination for an explosion – gasoline and fire.

The Legacy of Corruption

Ferdinand Marcos

Who: Sixth President of the 3rd Republic

When: December 30, 1965 - February 25, 1986

Born: September 11, 1917

Died: September 28, 1989 in exile in Hawaii

Education: Lawyer, Cum Laude, UP College of Law

Miscellaneous: Very colorful life, both real and imagine[d], Philippine Dictator unt[il] the 1986 People Pow[er] Revolt brought him do[wn]

Why Is the Philippines So Poor?

It is true that the Marcos regime plundered the economy to *world record levels*. However, the causes of poverty were more deeply rooted in the interplay of politics and policy. One could say that the dictatorship was an extreme form of crony capitalism. Over the last 25 years, the fall in Filipino poverty was slower than that seen among her Asian neighbors. Among Asian countries, the Philippines spent the least, relatively, on public education. The Filipino ratio of public education spending as a percentage of total government spending was lower than that of Thailand.

Land to the Few

A related issue is land ownership. A World Bank study found that the distribution of income in the Philippines was among the most unequal in middle-income countries. For example, in 1994, the richest 20% got 11 times the share of the poorest 20%. A key reason for this was the sharp inequity in land ownership.

Tax Evasion Squeezes the Poor

Another arena where the poor are hard hit is taxation. Even though income tax rates take more from the rich than from the poor, embarrassing levels of income tax evasion cause the government to rely on indirect taxes. These value- added tax and tariffs make up 70% of tax revenue.

Corruption is not new. During the Spanish rule, officials rewarded their local friends by awarding them huge tracts of land through what was called the encomienda system. Later on, the friends of high officials got cargo space on the galleon trade and thus became rich.[47]

The Richest Woman in the World

In the early 1980's the richest woman in the world was the first lady of the Philippines, Imelda Marcos. She would often go on elaborate shopping sprees, spending hundreds of thousands of dollars. Once she spent $2 million in a day and accumulated nearly 3,000 pairs of shoes, 68 pairs of gloves, dozens of hand-embroidered ornamental gowns, 1,000 packages of stockings, and enough jewelry, paintings, vases, icons, and carpets to fill 300 wooden crates. She often travelled in a specially outfitted B-747 with 300 personal suitcases and 100 servants. When travelling to New York City, Mrs. Marcos often chose to stay at the Waldorf Tower in groups of suites costing more than $600 each per day. "It didn't matter if it fit, or if it worked, or if it looked good, she wanted just everything."[48]

Imelda Marcos

Shop, Shop, and Shop Some More

The Philippines: Every economic report says it is dirt poor. The Marcos' government absconded with billions in public funds. The average Filipino worker earns less than US poverty level, and the value of the peso has intermittent free falls. But certain parts of the country seem to be very prosperous.

Shops are well-stocked and busy. Restaurants, businesses, and offices cram every space; mom-and-pop stores are everywhere. For an economically downtrodden group, Filipinos shop, eat, and play a lot in the countless malls, eateries, golf courses, day and night clubs, sing-along bars, resorts, and casinos that continue to sprout all over the Islands.

Nothing symbolizes this socioeconomic schizo-phrenia more than the latest trend: "mega-malls."

Three Different Philippines

1. **Urban areas.** Although their slums rival the worst in the world, a great many people live in relative comfort and many of them in prosperity.
2. **Agrarian rural areas.** Most people live at a subsistence level.
3. **The governmental sector.** The infrastructure is crumbling, the national institutions are short of cash, and the government, deeply in debt, is critically wounded.

But the UgEcon is booming. Small businesses mean informal workers earn a reasonable living but do not pay taxes. The Filipino twist is that they pay tax inspectors a little under the table either to not pay the full tax or to not pay any tax at all. Through the years, more businesses and more people have copied this idea. Today, more Filipinos are in the UgEcon than in the formal economy.

For the Philippines, if taxes would be collected efficiently and honestly, and if corrupt politicians would quit stealing the tax revenues, the country would be richer than any other nation in Southeast Asia.

Most are 5 or 6 stories high, offering every kind of store, restaurant, supermarket, gallery, theatre, and playground imaginable, all under a single roof. The newest one, still being built along Manila Bay, is already too big to be called a mere mega-mall – it's being called a city. And all of these malls are packed with customers – the whole day long.

Gen. Douglas MacArthur wades ashore for his promised return to the Philippines, OCTOBER 1944.

Tax Amnesty with a Hook

President Estrada started 1999 with a tax amnesty. Although OECD does not support tax amnesty as a viable means of stimulating tax collection, and successive amnesty programs have had declining effects in Pakistan (see page 88), this particular program merits attention.

Tax amnesty in the Philippines puts a different twist on an old, largely unsuccessful tactic. This amnesty program is designed to attract not only those taxpayers who under-report income, but, more importantly, to encourage those operating purely in the UgEcon to *surface* and pay taxes. The twist comes in that the amnesty program data will be used to build an updated taxpayer database as the basis for a computerized tax system.

The UgEcon includes large numbers of workers who pay self-employed social security taxes in order to avail themselves of the substantial benefits. These same workers withhold all or part of their income taxes; since the 2 systems are separate and unsophisticated there is no way to compare social security payer rolls and taxpayer rolls. The basis for computerized cross-checking between the 2 systems is being laid by this amnesty program.

Economic Darwinism

Charles Darwin: In 1859, he authored *The Origin of Species by Means of Natural Selection*

*I*n economically developed countries, baby boomers (and the cohorts before them) grew up believing in a specific path to financial security: a steady job with a large corporation or the government, providing the security of a regular pay check with fringe benefits and retirement plans.

However, the reality of today's global economy is quite different. A steady career with a large company, despite persistent mythical echos, is no longer either rewarding or secure.

We are at the end of a century that has seen the life expectancy in OECD countries skyrocket from about 50 years to about 80 years. In the fall of 1999, we "celebrated" the birth of the world's 6 billionth inhabitant – an astounding 4-fold increase in population in the last 100 years. Our population is probably double what the earth can handle on a sustainable basis – half the people live on less than $2 a day and half of those on about $1 per day.

Counterfeit Morality

The 1990's brought few *inter*state wars, but 61 *intra*state conflicts. Increased ethnic and religious tension has altered the behaviors of insurgent groups. With rapid globalization, international terrorism is fast emerging as the new threat to world order and economic parity.

India, with its billion people, and Pakistan, with its mere 140 million people, have been fighting a religious war since the British Indian Empire was partitioned in 1947. Both countries have stridently ultra-nationalist governments and many of the poorest people in the world. Yet they are both nuclear powers with long-range ballistic missiles. The recent military coup in Pakistan can only further increase tensions with India.

The Liberation Tigers of Tamil are fighting for a separate ethnically cleansed Tamil enclave in Sri Lanka. China asserts nationalistic claims over Taiwan and holds Tibet by force. Estimates go as high as a million people killed in the tribal

violence in Africa's Great Lakes area. The Balkans are ethnic nightmares. Protestants and Catholics fought forever in Northern Ireland. Extremists on both sides are blocking resolution of the Israel-Palestine epic. The media has all but forgotten the 30-year-old civil war in Angola.

Mexico and Guatemala are struggling with indigenous rebels. The Koreas still have not signed a peace accord. North Korea, one of the poorest countries in the world and currently mired in an epic famine, wants nuclear warheads for its long-range missiles. Peru's Shining Path is just a fraction of the anarchy in the Andes. More than 100,000 people have been killed in Algeria's civil war. Basque, Catalan, Kurdish, Scottish, and Quebec separatists are challenging central governments.

Congo-Brazzaville, Congo-Kinshasa, Eritrea, Freetown, Asmara, and Khartoum are yesterday's news. Dili, Chechnya, and Grozny are today's news. Tomorrow's news will be about insurrection in Wadi Hadharamawt, refugees in Huay Kalok, xenophobia against asylum seekers and illegal immigrants in Bloemfontein, and reuniting the Anjouan separatists with the Moroni government. Many are places that only a few people could even find on a map; most are places that even the computer's spell check does not recognize.

Although developed countries intervene slowly and very selectively in some of the ethnic and religious conflicts, they are mainly satisfied to make and sell the armaments that nurture these little wars. In most cases, they sell "hand-me-down" military equipment so they can buy the newer models. Rich nations, with declining birth rates, get richer; poor nations, with escalating birth rates, get poorer, despite population reductions from wars, famine, and the pestilence of AIDS.

Economic Darwinism at its finest.

Underground Immigrants

The smuggling of human beings in the form of illegal immigration is rapidly growing and may be one of the most profitable of all the UgEcon activities. The going price to be smuggled into a 1st-world country is $25,000 to $40,000 – a $10-15 billion-a-year worldwide industry.

Easy Credit Available

Financing entry into an industrialized country is not difficult. Smugglers around the world have created a modern form of slavery or indentured servitude; they will advance the money in return for various kinds of repayment. They will pay the airfare, pick you up at the border or airport, coach you on what to say and what not to say, and counsel you on how to exploit the refugee and welfare systems.

In return, the smuggled aliens are often forced to work 7 days a week for meager pay. The fortunate ones endure dangerous conditions doing legitimate work in such places as restaurants and garment factories. In many cases, smuggled immigrants are forced to engage in such criminal activities as drug and arms trafficking, prostitution, smurfing – a form of money laundering – and/or by handing over their welfare checks.[49]

Relaying desperate people into North America and Europe has become such a lucrative – and relatively risk-free – racket that organized crime has taken control of the industry. The kingpins of these sophisticated human smuggling operations

are known as "snakeheads." Decrepit boats with cargoes of illegal immigrants arrive with increasing regularity in Australia, the Pacific island of Guam (a US territory), Mexico, and Canada.[50]

In contrast, the US has taken a more aggressive stance and does not allow ships with suspected refugees into its territorial waters. France and many other European countries require people to carry identity cards. In these countries, national police can ask anyone for proof of identity and immediately imprison those who are unable to produce such proof. Illegal aliens and organized crime are countering these developments by the more sophisticated manufacture and use of fraudulent travel documents.[51]

However, as long as the quality of life is seen as substantially better in the target countries, the incentives for illegal migration will be present. It is estimated that as many as 15 million illegal aliens have moved to new countries over the past decade with the help of smugglers.[52]

...PLE SMUGGLING LATEST TREND...

Millions of Refugees

Refugees are a symptom of the turbulence of war or persecution. Since 1993, an average of nearly 10,000 new refugees a day has raised the total of refugees worldwide to over 20 million. "Non-refoulement" is the principle under international law that guarantees that people shall not be forced to return to countries where their lives or freedom would be endangered because of "race, religion, nationality, membership of a particular social group, or political opinion."

Sweatshops and Child Labour

New York City is the Mecca for illegal immigrants; it is anonymous and flourishing, and sweatshops abound, especially in the garment district. No experience – or documents – necessary. These kinds of sweatshops flourished early in this century, but were thought to have been largely eliminated. Despite constant revisions of laws and crackdown pledges by government and business leaders, their remarkable comeback reflects fundamental changes in the garment industry. Although the pattern is repeated in most major cities of developed countries around the world, making it in New York is making it in the big leagues.

Child Labour: *Some boys and girls were so small they had to climb up on to the spinning frame to mend broken threads and to put back the empty bobbins – Georgia, USA, circa 1912.*

Immigrants Exploiting Immigrants

Most such sweatshops are owned or managed by newcomers from Asia, who exploit other immigrants, often illegals from Asia or Latin America. For example, many sweatshops owned by Chinese will hire only other Chinese; many of these workers are believed to be indentured servants toiling under a form of debt bondage to pay off the heavy cost of being smuggled into the country.[53]

Typically, both the workers and the employers see themselves as victims of a system dominated by increasingly powerful major retailers. Tales of brutal treatment are frequent and persistent. Whether operating openly in decrepit buildings in New York or Los Angeles or hidden illegally in people's homes in Toronto, sweatshops violate labor and tax laws in cut-throat global competition.

Workers do not tell authorities about labor violations and physical abuse out of fear that their shops will then be raided by immigration agents. An experienced garment maker said that she works in constant fear, not only of her temperamental boss but of the "big rats and mice" that continually crawl over her feet. "I get paid off the books. Even though I am working legally, my boss doesn't pay any taxes or Social Security... I never get a vacation. I never even get a whole weekend off." The workers are afraid, because they do not want to lose their jobs.[54]

Shops at the bottom of the industry often go out of business, relocate, and open under new names. Some fail altogether, never to reappear. But despite decades of lawmaking, the systems designed to eradicate the sweatshops have largely failed, union activists say. Local, state, and federal agencies charged with enforcing labor, immigration, and tax laws have often failed to work together, allowing shop owners and workers to slip through the cracks of the system.

How Did This Happen?

The shops clearly have evolved from an aberration to a tolerable, presumably an essential, part of the garment industry. Thus, they have become part of a vast UgEcon, shielded by an overlay of laissez-faire practices and tacit accommodations:

- Clothing designers and retailers depend on the sweatshops for fast delivery and big profit margins.
- Unions, hopeful of eventually organizing these workers, appear to be more interested in preserving manufacturing jobs than driving sweatshops out of business.
- Large pools of illegal immigrants are so anxious for work that they accept the shops' meager wages and are often afraid to complain.
- Consumers gravitate toward the lowest prices they can find.
- Government agencies do not field enough investigators or cooperate sufficiently among themselves to enforce the laws that would eradicate these shops.

Support the Sweatshop Accountability Campaign

- Sweatshops are thriving because of computerized inventory methods that allow retailers to determine instantly what is selling and to order more of it.

Yet there is no shortage of workers for these jobs because of the increasing waves of legal and illegal immigration into the world's major cities since the 1970's. What is frequently overlooked is that even a sub-minimum wage in a developed country generally surpasses what immigrants can earn in their homelands.

The Food Chain

Sweatshops are at the bottom of what is described as the garment industry "food chain," beneath layers of suppliers, designers, and middlemen, who compete fiercely for orders from the big retailers at the top. It is a system that effectively insulates the big-name stores and fashion labels, allowing them to profess shock and ignorance about the sweatshop conditions in which their clothes were sewn.

The National Retail Federation, which represents 2,000 major US retailers, blames sweatshop conditions on subcontractors. "The retailers don't employ these workers," said a spokeswoman for the Federation. "The retailers many times are at least 2 or 3 steps removed from the problem." She asserted, "It's not the retailers who are reaping the benefits from these criminal activities. It's the greedy subcontractors."

A sweatshop is defined by several parameters, 2 of which prevail in this industry: violations of minimum wage laws and of overtime regulations. It is common to pay workers "off the books" to avoid various local, state, and federal taxes.

Retailers say too many variables go into the final price of a garment to generalize about any of them, but government and union officials estimate that labor typically accounts for less than 3% of the US retail price of clothing made in domestic sweatshops and as little as .5% for those garments sewn abroad.

Any prohibition of mutually beneficial exchanges is doomed to failure.

How a Garment Gets to the Rack

Before a piece of clothing reaches the sales rack, it passes through several steps. At the bottom are the sweatshop workers in sewing shops. Tracing back, here is the path garments take:

Retailers: Sell to the public garments received from manufacturers. As fewer and fewer retailers control a larger share of the market, they have more power to demand low prices and fast delivery from their suppliers, the manufacturers.

Manufacturers: Design garments, market them under a variety of labels, and sell them to the retailers. They fill their orders by using contractors and subcontractors.

Contractors and subcontractors: Cut and sew materials. In the US alone, 22,000 contracting and subcontracting shops are needed to support 1,000 manufacturers. Most employ illegal immigrants, and most violate minimum wage and overtime laws.[54]

Cross-Border Shopping

High tax rates mean greater incentives to evade taxes or to use tax avoidance schemes, thus contributing to slower growth in income tax revenue. Higher tax rates also affect personal decisions about work and leisure: More people are refusing to work long hours because the extra income, after high taxes, is too little to compensate for lost leisure.

The evolution of the EU, with a common excise (sales) tax, is the end of duty-free shopping – a major business at airports, seaports, and many border crossing points. EU members now see it as a loss of tax revenues – a gap that can be closed.

In Canada, more than 80% of the population lives within 120 miles of the US border. The loss in tax revenue from cross-border shopping is mainly in taxes on fuel, tobacco, and alcoholic beverages. During 1992 alone, 3,179 persons were charged with customs and excise offences; this figure increased to 3,389 in 1993. In 1992, there were 505 liquor seizures with a retail value of $2.7 million, while in 1993 it rose to 631 seizures having a retail value of $7.5 million.

Trade Unions and the UgEcon

The explosive growth of the UgEcon, in many ways a by-product of globalization, will hasten the destruction of the trade union movement, particularly in developing and transitional economies. While multi-billon dollar consolidations seem to happen almost everyday, the real growth in jobs is in smaller and more mobile businesses. Trade unions are for the most part, dinosaurs led by Neanderthals; they are reluctant to face reality. Much freer trade means that wages will rise only with productivity increases, on a globally competitive basis. The union argument that the removal of labor constraints and legislation will lead to slave wages is pure economic nonsense; workers outside unionized industries regularly compete in the global marketplace like their non-unionized brothers and sisters. Trade unions must reinvent themselves in order to stay alive.

Prior to the globalization of business, unions exerted power over employers to achieve their goals, particularly when a high concentration of a natural resource anchored them geographically. Economies of scale led to very large businesses, which are, by their nature, vulnerable to union coercion. As quarterly profits continue to drive most large business, the need for short-term performance has made them targets of union extortion. These big businesses inevitably became management-driven, rather than entrepreneur-driven, which cost them an important edge.[57]

Because assembly-line technologies are inherently sequential, they are vulnerable to disruption. At the same time, they remove recognition of individual skills. Assembly lines were designed to accommodate morons and geniuses equally. Globalization has changed many of the characteristics of business. For example, information technology has a negligible natural resource content, and the result has been a lowering of the scale of enterprises.

More of the workforce being employed in fewer factories led to impersonal workplaces; this made it easier for workers and their unions to dismiss the importance of owners' property rights — shareholders became simply stakeholders, which implied that their claims were "no more than those of other stakeholders, such as workers." Capital costs have, in many cases, been lowered dramatically and the production cycle has been both shortened and dispersed. IT-based production means that employers can better measure, and therefore properly reward, individual employees' outputs. This means that skill and mental ability have again become more crucial variables in economic output.

Cost of European Social Welfare

Dr. Gary Becker won the 1992 Nobel prize in economics for applying economic theory to the everyday, average family relationships, welfare, racial discrimination, and crime. His major writings, spanning a 20-year period are *Human Capital, The Economic Approach to Family Behaviour,* and *Treatise on the Family.* Dr. Becker has very practical views about very practical matters.

He estimates that about half of average labor costs in France and Germany are taxes to fund state welfare programs – social security, unemployment insurance, disability, health, and other taxes on labour.

These high labor costs are the reason much of Europe stumbles along with extraordinarily high rates of unemployment. The lost output of unemployed workers amounts to nearly 14% of Spanish GDP, 7.5% of French GDP, and nearly 5% of the Belgian and German GDP.[55]

Domestic output and income also decline when firms shift production to lower-cost foreign locations, when workers move into the UgEcon, and when tax avoidance becomes widespread – all to escape the voracious appetite for revenues common among social welfare economies.[56]

Unfunded Government Pensions

> *One study – frequently mentioned in North America – shows that more young people believe in UFO's than believe they will get their government pensions when the time comes.*

Recently, federal pension schemes have been continually compared to Ponzi schemes (named after a legendary fraud on investors orchestrated by the 1920's Boston con man Charles Ponzi).

The "official historian" of the US pension system challenged this charge in a well-circulated paper called "History Myths." His major point was that Ponzi's schemes are based on *geometric* progressions, which "work only so long as an ever-increasing number of new investors come into the scheme." The US pension system (and all other pension systems not based on the Chilean model), he pointed out, was a simple *arithmetic* progression: One person pays in, another takes out. "There is nothing unsavory about such a system and it is sustainable forever, provided that the number of people entering the system maintains a balance with the number of people collecting from the system." True, if economy and demography cooperate.[58]

Surprise! Surprise! The stark reality is that neither the economy nor demography has cooperated. That is what makes the US and all other countries' non-funded pension plans truly Ponzi schemes.

For young workers, the government pension plan represents a job tax; for many, it is *the* job tax, the major tax cost in the 1st decade of their careers. This problem is not confined to entry-level workers; in the US, for an astounding 7 out of 10 households, payroll tax is the greatest tax they pay.

Part of the reason that this has gone unchallenged is that in many countries at least half of the payroll tax is hidden from workers' view. The pay stub says that payroll taxes equal, for example, 8%.

But that 8% that the employee sees represents only half his burden. Employers must match the employee contribution with another equal amount (8% in our example), which they pay on their employees' behalf. As we have repeated at several points, it is our view that businesses do not pay taxes: They are mere sieves through which monies flow. Ultimately the businesses do not pay "their" share; the employees are the ones who pay because they forgo that amount in additional wages.

In most industrialized countries, the structure of pension contributions also has a regressive dimension, because there is a cap on the amount of income assessed for pensions. Every dollar earned after the cap limit is a dollar not subjected to the Ponzi scheme.

When Roosevelt signed the Federal Insurance Contributions Act in 1935, he explained that help was needed because of the retreat of the old agricultural order. "The civilization of the past hundred years with its startling industrial changes has tended more and more to make life insecure. Young people have come to wonder what would be their lot when they came to old age."

Even Milton Friedman, one of the earliest US Social Security cynics, observed that the "apparent" direct link between the taxation and the benefits was very powerful. "The two combined have become a sacred cow," he said in 1971. "What a triumph of imaginative packaging and Madison Avenue advertising."

TEST YOUR BLOOD PRESSURE

VOTE

FIGLEBY

ABSOLUTELY WORST PLACE TO HANG CAMPAIGN POSTER.

Pork-Barrel Legislation

"Pork-barrel" came into use as a political term in the US post-Civil War era. It recalls the practice of plantation owners who would often hand out rations of salt pork to their slaves, distributing them from wooden barrels. When used in reference to legislation, it implies that a bill is loaded with goodies for Members of Congress to distribute to their constituents as acts of largesse, courtesy of the federal taxpayer.

But what defines a pork-barrel project? What one Member perceives as an important improvement, another might view as an unfair distribution of federal funds. Criticism for pork-barrel projects often reflects the fact that they fund programs without the need first being demonstrated on a competitive basis. However, just because a project only benefits one district or state does not automatically mean that the project has no merit.

Not all Members are equally able to "bring home the bacon." Pork-barrel benefits are not distributed based on a merit-based or national formula. Rather, funding is obtained through adroit political negotiations and advantageous committee assignments. Pork-barrel projects often involve improvements to the infrastructure (highways, waterways, public works projects, etc.), which generate jobs, thereby helping the local economy and bringing political credit to the Member.

Some argue that the fiscal impact of pork-barrel spending is overstated. For example, in 1993, the President's Council of Economic Advisers estimated that pork-barrel programs were no more than 1% of the entire federal budget. However, based on a US Federal Budget for FY2000 of $2.5 trillion, even a 1% spending on pork-barrel programs amounts to *$25 billion.*

In reality it represents significantly more than 1% of the US budget. Although the derivation of the term comes from the US, the practice is universal among politicans who try to set the stage for re-election by making it clear that they know how to take care of their consitituents.

While the politicians tend to take the heat for pork-barrel spending, it is often the entrenched bureaucrats that are the real instruments of waste.

The Grace

The Grace Commission (also known as the President's Private Sector Survey on Cost Control) was inaugurated in 1982 and directed by President Reagan to "work like tireless bloodhounds to root out government inefficiency and waste of tax dollars." We believe that this imaginative model should be adopted in all countries – developed, transitional, and developing.

For 2 years, 161 corporate executives and community leaders led an army of 2,000 volunteers on a waste hunt through the federal government. The search was funded entirely by $76 million of voluntary contributions from the private sector; it cost taxpayers nothing. The Grace Commission made 2,478 recommendations, which, if implemented, would have saved over $424 billion over 3 years (an average of over $142 billion a year) – all without eliminating essential services. The 47 volumes and 21,000 pages of the Grace Report constitute a vision of an efficient, well-managed government that is accountable to the taxpayers.

Citizens Against Government Waste

The legacy of the Grace Commission is CAGW, founded in 1984 by the late industrialist J. Peter Grace and syndicated political columnist Jack Anderson. Its mission is to make the Grace Report's vision a reality. In a little more than a decade, CAGW has helped save taxpayers $486 billion through implementation of Grace Commission findings and other recommendations.

From a base of 5,000 members in 1988, CAGW membership has grown to more than 600,000 in 1999. It is a private, non-partisan, non-profit

CAGW researches and identifies the most blatant waste in government and shows how it can be eliminated. CAGW has a long and successful record of winning major cuts in wasteful spending without sacrificing America's defenses.
– Bob Dole, Former Senate Majority Leader

Commission

Where US Income Taxes Really Go

organization dedicated to educating Americans about waste, mismanagement, and inefficiency in the federal government. Its growth reflects taxpayers' increasing frustration with the government's squandering of their hard-earned money.

Representatives of CAGW appear frequently on commercial and public television, radio talk shows, and in print. From its vantage point as a nationally recognized source of information, CAGW produces numerous publications highlighting wasteful government spending. *Government Waste Watch*, its quarterly newspaper, is distributed to members of CAGW, members of Congress, and members of the media nationwide. *The Annual Congressional Pig Book* is an exposé of the most glaring and irresponsible uses of taxpayer dollars for pork-barrel spending. CAGW's lobbying arm, the Council for Citizens Against Government Waste, tabulates its annual Congressional Ratings, measuring the willingness of each member of Congress to fight government waste and reduce the federal deficit.

Policy Manual

CAGW has published its Policy Manual every election year since 1990; it is a response to demands for the most up-to-date information on government waste. It does not pull punches about a Social Security system approaching insolvency, a Medicare program going broke, and a bloated bureaucracy that squeezes out personal freedom in favor of government control. Instead, it is a blueprint for a smaller and more efficient government and the map of the road to financial responsibility.

Key excerpts from the President's Private Sector Survey on Cost Control were submitted to President Reagan and his executive committee for consideration at its meeting on January 15,1984.

Importantly, any meaningful increase in taxes from personal income would have to come from lower- and middle-income families, as 90% of all personal taxable income is generated below the taxable income level of $35,000.

Further, there isn't much more that can be extracted from high income brackets. If the Government took 100% of all taxable income beyond the $75,000 tax bracket not already taxed, it would get only $17 billion, and this confiscation, which would destroy productive enterprise, would only be sufficient to run the Government for 7 days.

Resistance to additional income taxes would be even more widespread if people were aware that 1/3 of all their taxes is consumed by waste and inefficiency in the Federal Government as shown in the survey.

Another 1/3 of all their taxes escapes collection as the UgEcon blossoms in direct proportion to tax increases and places even more pressure on law-abiding taxpayers, promoting still more UgEcon – a vicious circle that must be broken.

With 2/3 of everyone's personal income taxes wasted or not collected, 100% of what is collected is absorbed solely by interest on the Federal debt and by Federal Government contributions to transfer payments. **In other words, all individual income tax revenues are gone before one nickel is spent on the services which taxpayers expect from their Government.**[59]

CAGW has fought side-by-side with us for welfare reform and massive cuts in wasteful spending to shrink the size of government and the deficit. It is the premier waste-fighting organization in America.

– Christopher Cox,
House Republican Policy Committee Chairman

A study by The International Metalworkers Federation in Geneva predicts that within the next 30 years, 2 or 3% of the world's population will be able to produce everything we need on the planet.
Even if they're off by a factor of 10, we still have a question of what will 80% of humanity do?

China's Mi$$ing Billions

Moody's, one of the world's most respected bond rating services, estimates that bailing out China's banks could easily cost $115 billion. And China's Auditor-General has announced that about $14 billion was stolen by government bureaucrats in the 1st 6 months of 1999.

Moody's statement sets targets for the asset-management companies being established for the country's 4 state-owned "pillar" banks. It believes the recovery rate will be "extremely low."

While praising efforts to overhaul the country's finances, Moody's also noted that these efforts fell short of addressing "structural impediments in the system." Such impediments include the requirement to continue loans to failing state companies.

Even the Communist Party's own flagship newspaper, the *People's Daily*, highlighted the massive corruption unearthed by the national auditors, which was *equivalent to 20% of the annual national tax receipts*. Much of the missing money was from special projects, such as those to improve infrastructure or to combat floods.

The public prosecution office added that more than 1,000 senior bureaucrats were investigated on corruption charges in the 1st half of 1999.

In all, 280,000 people were charged with bribery during this 6-month period, but the prosecutors have recovered less than $100 million of the cash stolen from the state – a tiny portion of the total amount taken.[82]

Collateral Victims

An ethical maxim in NATO's extensive bombing of Yugoslavia:
It is OK to kill and maim innocent civilians as long as there was no intention to harm them.

Consider that at the beginning of the century,
10% of the casualties of war were civilians.
At the end of the century, 90% were civilians...
When do the ends justify the means?

In the economic war against the UgEcon,
the collateral victims are the poor.

The Gray Area Phenomenon

The "gray area phenomenon" (GAP) is defined as the existence of threats to the stability of nation states by non-state groups and organizations. The strength of these assailants depends largely on the existence of areas that governments cannot govern. The GAP exists in the many parts of Andean countries that are controlled by narco-traffickers and/or terrorists. It also exists in many parts of Afghanistan, especially along its Pakistan border. Throughout Russia and many CIS countries, real control rests with the mafia. Although the GAP is a particular problem for weaker nation states that are overwhelmed by the tightening noose of international disorder, 1st-world countries are also

vulnerable. These large and relatively well-to-do markets operate as magnets for criminals dealing in illegal aliens, narcotics, arms, stolen art, plutonium, and prostitutes. Once the money is made, the US economy is a natural target for laundering it.

Some dangerous groups in the non-industrialized, non-democratic Southern world oppose all things Northern and have embarked on a kind of fundamentalist jihad against "McWorld," which is their concept of modern society. The new "bad guys" include terrorists, insurgents, drug traffickers, rogue states, neo-Luddite ecoterrorists, xenophobes, and fundamentalists.[51]

Conclusion
Wasted Tax Money

Everyone knows that tax dollars are being misspent. The right complains about socialist wealth redistribution policies and money wasted on welfare. The left believes that money spent on military hardware is plagued with rampant waste and frequent boondoggles. And, sadly, both are right.

Taxpayers around the world realize that politicians are not going to lower taxes, regardless of their promises. So more people are lowering their own taxes through participation in the UgEcon. The tax revolution has become covert because people do not see much reason to petition the government for redress of their grievances, because it is the government itself which is the cause. So, without waiting for government to respond, taxpayers are taking action, often illegal action, to reduce their own taxes.

Some how-to guides to the UgEcon have attempted to romanticize tax evaders by calling them "Guerilla Capitalists"– everyday Robin Hoods with a little Bonnie and Clyde mixed into the blend. They argue that tax evaders are just everyday people who have spontaneously decided to take more control of their own lives, "even if it means violating a few tax laws."[61]

Nincompoops in Power

The real problem is deeper than the mediocre quality of elected officials. It is even deeper than the self-serving, lackluster performance of bureaucrats. For the most part, politicians and bureaucrats are not evil people; they are, however, just marginally competent workers, lost in minutiae and unable to understand the larger issues. Taxpayers end up paying increasing amounts for incompetently delivered government functions that they do not even want or need.

Sadly, everyday in almost every country of the world, economically uninformed voters receive the pathetic governments that they deserve.

Tax collection and enforcement agencies are, by and large, made up of yokels of the same ilk. They are tethered to their jobs by a package of salary, perks, fringe benefits, and the frequently outlandish pensions that go with many government jobs. This often leads to avoiding any action – the "don't make waves" mentality. An employee will strive to avoid taking any risks, even in pursuit of the agency's unambiguous objectives, because taking risks can be dangerous to his career. Little spirit of bold entrepreneurship exists or is wanted in bureaucracies, merely dull and plodding adherence to procedures.

Tax Regulations

The 1st income tax return in the US is shown on page 76 – a single page. Even more remarkable is the tax code (shown on the facing page), which is also 1 page . Today the US tax code is pushing 10,000 pages with almost another 100,000 pages of regulations. In contrast, the Canadian tax code is a modest 1,500 pages. What is important to keep in mind is that these thousands of changes were not created to make paying taxes easier for the average taxpayer or to make the rules and forms easier to understand, but rather to create loopholes for the friends and supporters of the governments of the day.

The issue of voluminous tax codes designed for businesses and wealthy individuals is a pattern present in every developed economy. In less developed economies, it is more simplistic – selective enforcement. In these situations, who you know and who you pay off determines your tax liability.

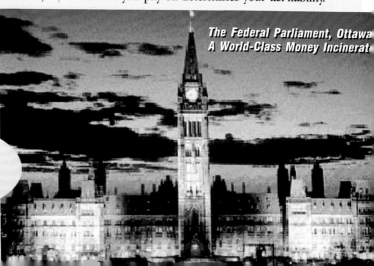

*The Federal Parliament, Ottawa
A World-Class Money Incinerat*

Dickens in the Andes [63]

Lima, the capital of Peru, resembles Charles Dickens' descriptions of London at the beginning of the Industrial Revolution 200 years ago: overcrowded, bustling, packed with street vendors and beggars. Micro-business activities happen everywhere. Not unlike London at the end of the 18th century, an air of frivolity persists among the decaying bourgeoisie and tiny aristocracy.

The Informal Economy

To the native Quechua Indians, Peru means "land of abundance." And yet, in Peru at the end of the 20th century, each poor person is living face-to-face with the economic shambles created by a series of corrupt, interventionist federal and state regimes. Most poor people are, by necessity, full-time or part-time private entrepreneurs struggling in a complex and unregulated economy. For the poor, informality is synonymous with survival through small businesses.

Despite rich stores of natural resources (silver, copper, lead, zinc, and petroleum), it is estimated that at least half of Peru's economy is ensnared in the UgEcon. This informal economy does not exist to avoid taxes, as is the case in more developed countries; it exists because it is the only viable alternative for the poor to survive.

Most of the economically active population operates without licenses, permits, or records, ignoring burdensome regulations, buying and selling for cash. In terms of transportation alone, the informal economy accounts for more than 90% of the services. [62]

Causes of Informality

The underlying cause of informality in Lima is that the formal systems are inadequate to meet the needs of the emerging economy. A simulation conducted a few years ago demonstrated that the official steps for opening a small grocery store theoretically took 40 days at a cost of $400. A study of 5 actual cases revealed an average time frame of 18 years. In another case, starting a business legally took 289 days to get the 11 required permits, at a total cost of $821. Graft was demanded about 10 times and had to

STARVE THE BEAST!

be paid on 2 occasions. Thus, in spite of compliance with regulations, bribery to some officials could not be avoided.

Given that people are inclined by nature to do what is cheapest and avoid what is most expensive, compliance with the law – materially speaking – depends on whether its costs are lower than its benefits. Individuals making this evaluation will naturally pursue their own objectives and not those of the state. If the costs of access are such that they either become unaffordable for people with fewer resources or exceed the benefits of legal access, people will choose to stay in the informal economy. Likewise, if the costs of "staying formal" exceed the benefits, people will decide to go back to the informal system. This demonstrates why there are 2 different types of informal workers: those who never joined the formal system because they could not afford the costs of access, and those who, having entered, leave it because of the high costs of belonging.

Obviously, deregulation would favor not only new businesses but also existing ones, because it guarantees faster movement of production factors. Bureaucracy has to be rooted out in order for Peru to take the next step in economic development. It must be easier and less expensive to enter the formal economy and the cost of membership in the formal economy must be lowered to correspond to the benefits of participation. A formal market cannot operate at full capacity unless it can reduce its costs, stabilize its contractual relations, and guarantee property rights.

Certainly Peru, like much of Latin America, is throttled by inefficient government. The executive processes are mired in a tradition of corruption and cronyism, and they lack the prerequisite transparency. Regulations are "cooked up" in government offices and surreptitiously approved, making it impossible for anybody to oppose them until they are published as already mandatory.

Formal Name:	**Republic of Peru**
Local Name:	Peru
Local Formal Name:	Republica del Peru
Location:	South America
Status:	**UN Country**
Capital City:	**Lima**
Main Cities:	Arequipa, Lambayeque, Trujillo, Chiclayo
Population:	**23,381,000**
Area [sq.km]:	**1,285,220**
Currency:	**1 nuevo sol = 100 centimos**
Main Languages:	Spanish, Quechua, Aymara
Main Religions:	Roman Catholic

Lessons From the Informal Sector

Activities that become illegal as a result of excessive government regulation are, nevertheless, still illegal. Therefore, in a rule-compliant society, informality and illegality are equivalent concepts.

There are 3 main areas of illegality:
- Taxation, reflecting the extent that a business is not a registered tax unit and/or is not paying taxes;
- Environmental and health issues, reflecting noncompliance with regulations, particularly important for food establishments, and noncompliance with an urban master plan in following zoning and building regulations;
- Labor, reflecting the absence, not only of contracts, but also of social security and health insurance for workers.

The Accessing Cost of Legalizing Informal Production

Country	Economic Sector	Time (days work)	Financial Costs			
			No Improvements		Alterations Required	
			Amount $	% Annual Profits	Amount $	% Annual Profits
Bolivia	Commerce	15-30	14	2.8		
	Industry	15-30	13	0.25-1.6		
	Services	15-30	26	0.25-1.6		
Brazil	Commerce	31-60	44	3.5-7.5		
	Industry	44	84	17.7		
	Services	32	99	–		
Chile	Commerce	12	110	–	5,308	128.3
	Industry	65	222	2.8-5.4	11,135	147.8
Ecuador	Commerce	60-75	32	15.5	70	33.8
	Industry	180-240	239	23.4	70	6.8
Guatemala	Commerce	179	216	4.2		
	Industry	525	894	8.6		
Mexico	Commerce	83-240	212-368	–		
	Industry	83-240	210-368	–		
	Services	83-240	212-368	–		
Uruguay	Industry	75-90	337	159.5	613	290.5
	Services	75-90	405	6.1-13	613-675	1.97-10.2
Venezuela	Commerce	170-310	–	5.1	–	21.5
	Industry	170-310	–	23.5	–	181.5

All figures in US dollars.

The Context of Expatriation

*E*xpatriation is the loss of nationality. Such a loss today is usually, although not necessarily, voluntary. Generally, the term applies to those who renounce nationality and citizenship in one country to become citizens or subjects of another.

Times of war add special conditions to expatriation. For example, most countries forbid voluntary expatriation in time of war. In contrast, wars also can lead to a more general type of involuntary expatriation: the loss of nationality that occurs with the cession or conquest of a territory.

Migration: A Natural Process

From a demographic perspective, migration is an important social process: Along with birth and death, the outward and inward movement of individuals are the only ways that population can increase or decrease. However, it is the political organization of world space into mutually exclusive sovereignties that delineates international migration. The distinctive feature of international migration arises not from the nature of the movement, but rather from the fact that it entails a transfer from the jurisdiction of one sovereign to another.

This section addresses the historical backdrop against which modern immigration policy must be viewed, beginning with a discussion of pre-monarchist Europe and the early US, then moving to the dramatic developments of the 20th century, including decolonization. Several contemporary issues are examined which, taken together, lead to the conclusion that though many nations may want to close their borders, new immigration will persist.

The Rules of Modern Migration

Internal movement within most European States was generally free, as opposed to other conditions of serfdom or in slave colonies. Concomitantly, with the drastic reduction of overlapping networks of authority to a single hierarchy, the distinction between mutually exclusive subjects was sharpened.

Modern notions of sovereignty reflect the idea that strength equals human capital. Because human capital was essential to the mercantilist state, the most important control pertained to the outward movement of the populace. The State sought to retain its human capital for economic production and war. Accordingly, in the early centuries of the modern State's existence, unauthorized emigration was tantamount to treason and was punishable by death or enslavement. The resilience of this concept is confirmed by its persistence, in more recent times, as the hallmark of "totalitarian" states such as The Soviet Union before its fall.

These mechanisms are historically bound. Seventeenth-century Europe was clearly divided into mutually exclusive State-like territories, ranging from large kingdoms to small principalities. Much of the overseas world was organized similarly, where territory was either part of established non-European empires (e.g., the Ottoman Empire or China) or under the colonial control of Europeans. The "frontier" was Africa. Movement from Europe to the colonies was by and large regulated by the controlling sovereign in accordance with changing assessments of the interests and relative strengths of the contending parties. Under prevailing socioeconomic conditions, reinforced by regulations, little emigration

Over and over again courts have said that there is nothing sinister in so arranging one's affairs as to keep taxes as low as possible – *Judge Learned Hand, US Supreme Court*

The 1896 statutory preamble of the US Congress [say]s that "the right of expatriation is a natural and [in]herent right of all people, indispensable to the [en]joyment of the rights of life, liberty, and the [pu]rsuit of happiness." It left open what means or [cir]cumstances would terminate US citizenship. In [the] same year, the Department of State, acting on [the] opinion of the Attorney General, declared that [US] citizenship could be lost by renunciation or by [nat]uralization in another country.

[I]t was not until 1907 that the US enacted [legi]slation effectively specifying that certain acts [wou]ld result in the loss of US citizenship, including [nat]uralization in a foreign state or taking an oath [of al]legiance to a foreign state. Naturalized citizens [wer]e presumed to have expatriated after residing [2] years in the foreign country from which they [cam]e, or 5 years in any other country, but the [pres]umption was rebuttable. Consistent with the [unsett]led attitude toward women during this [peri]od, an American woman who married a [forei]gner took her husband's nationality (and lost [her] own when she went abroad), but could [recla]im her US citizenship if the marriage ended.

[...] declared a doctrine of perpetual allegiance, which denied a subject the right to sever his allegiance with the place of his birth. That rule was widely recognized, even in the US at first, where the legal opinion was that "a citizen cannot renounce his allegiance to the US without the permission of government to be declared by law, in the absence of which the perpetual allegiance rule of English common law prevails."

This common legal view prevailed until 1868, when the US challenged this doctrine to protect naturalized immigrants against the claims of their native states, the majority of which did not recognize the right of subjects to expatriate themselves.

The US Congress declared voluntary expatriation to be "a natural and inherent right of all people," and announced US protection for naturalized citizens abroad, even in their native countries. Great Britain abandoned the common-law interpretation in 1870. But many other nations, including France and Russia, still do not recognize expatriation.

The Wealthiest People in the World

Nationals of Switzerland, Norway, and Denmark are the wealthiest people in the world, with 1998 per capita gross GDP in each exceeding $40,000. The Japanese ranked 4th, with per capita GDP of $32,380, followed by Singaporeans at $30,060.

The recently released World Bank report ranked the following countries as 6th through 10th: the US, Austria, Germany, Sweden, and Belgium.

France, the Netherlands, Finland, Hong Kong, Britain, Australia, Italy, Canada, Ireland, and Israel, in that order, finished in the 11th through 20th places.

Taiwan was listed as 23rd highest in the world, ranking between Spain ($14,080) and Greece ($11,650). In contrast, Mainland China had a per capita GDP of $750, ranking it 149th.[65]

*Remember the point we have been stressing throughout the book: These numbers are based on each country's national accounts, which are based on **reported** rather than **actual** income.*

Changing Sovereignty Games and International Migration

Despite development of borderless markets and communication infrastructures, much remains to be done to build a truly global community. The "right of expatriation" potentially sabotages sovereignty: What "sovereignty" remains if individuals exercise an unlimited right to move out? The obvious result would be "sovereignty" over an empty land – as almost happened in East Germany (GDR) when Hungary opened its border to Austria 2 months before the Berlin Wall came down in October of 1989.

Although the right to leave a country – except in repressive dictatorships – has been well-established since the mid-19th century, there is no reciprocal right to enter another country. This limitation is the basis of the thriving UgEcon enterprise of people smuggling. (See page 43.)

Racial bigotry was at the root of many of the anti-immigration laws that have been enforced in the last 200 years. In the US, "the land of the free," the very 1st Congress enacted a naturalization law restricting candidates to the "free and white." The most significant development arose during the first 30 or 40 years of the 19th century. The US leaders sharpened 2 related objectives: (1) to promote the freedom of movement of individuals living in other countries so they could emigrate to the US, and (2) to regulate entry to exclude the undesirables, i.e., anyone who was not a white Protestant. The prevailing yet strained logic of the day was that a nation could not prevent the entry of potential invaders posing as immigrants without restricting the movement of people across its borders.

Immigrants by definition are considered to be foreigners or aliens. This is confirmed by the distinction in the laws of many countries between such aliens and outsiders who are members of a national tribe by reason of their ancestral origin, a distinction explicitly espoused in recent times by Germany and Israel and also practised by other countries, including the UK, Ireland, Italy, and Spain.[67]

Despite contentions that US nationality is political rather than ethnic, racist conceptions of citizenship prevailed until the mid-20th century, and was also present in the "national origins" system established to regulate immigration in the 1920's. Similar policies prevailed in Canada and Australia. Today, these policies persist in Canada, where within the "point" system, positive weight is given to language competence in one of the 2 languages of the "founding" nationalities, British and French.

The desire of countries to achieve control of population movement was substantially achieved only in the wake of World War I, with the establishment of a worldwide system of border controls based on "zero immigration." Sovereignty became absolute in matters of immigration and naturalization.

Reflecting the dynamics of our global markets, economic factors worldwide are challenging boundaries and have already achieved significant successes in creating transnational institutions, such as the various regional "common markets."[66]

IN THE NEWS TONIGHT... ANOTHER BOATLOAD OF TAX IMMIGRANTS HAS BEEN SPOTTED OFF OUR COAST...

STARVE THE BEAST!

Dual and Multiple Nationalities

Related to this is the vast expansion of the authorization to travel with only minimal regulation. Those concerned with controlling unauthorized immigration are well aware that a large proportion of it is attributable not so much to surreptitious entry as it is to legal entry followed by *over*staying. Thus, by extending tourist facilities, States in effect acquiesce to some reduction in their policing capacity. An extreme form of this is the right of "First World" citizens to travel just about anywhere on the authority of their passports alone, without any special permission in the form of an advance visa from the States they enter.

The most dramatic instances involve direct challenges to the State by alternative national identities, such as the Catalans and Basques in Spain, the Flemish in Belgium, the Russians in the Baltics, or the Ukrainians in Russia. More new States have been admitted to the UN in the current decade than at any time since the great wave of African decolonization in the early 1960's. However, as one might expect, the newcomers are particularly vigilant regarding their sovereignty claims, so that the trend is to be more restrictive of individual rights.

Occupational affiliations and employment by multinational corporations transcend national borders. The emergence of transnational communities (Mexicans, Central Americans, and Caribbean islanders in the US, Turks in Germany, and Algerians in France) tends to reduce individuals' commitments to their countries of origin as their commitments to their host countries increase.

The proliferation of marriages among nationals of different countries has resulted in a growing number of formal holders of dual nationality. Moreover, many recent immigrants who would like to become citizens of the host country are reluctant to give up their nationality of origin, often on practical grounds, such as the desire to maintain eligibility for land ownership and inheritance. Despite their traditional insistence on the mutually exclusive nature of citizenship, many States appear willing to quietly accommodate the changing needs of their citizens or prospective citizens, so long as it does not involve problems of security.

Transcending Nationality

This accommodation is in striking contrast to the sovereign world that has evolved over the past 4 centuries. Although formal citizenship remains vested at the level of the States, there has been considerable movement toward the formation of a European "quasi-citizenship," denoted symbolically and practically by the adoption of uniform passports by all the Member States and by the institution of European Union entry gates at airports. Citizens of member countries can move freely throughout the region and can work in any country without special permits. To this has now been added the right to vote in municipal elections in the country of residence. Although the experience of the EU is so far unique, it portends possible developments in other regional common markets, including NAFTA. Canadian and US citizens are already admitted as visitors in each other's countries on the basis of ordinary identification, without visas or passports; only the economic gap is blocking similar rights for Mexicans.

Counterpoint to Globalism

Elsewhere, however, a trend is emerging in the other direction, particularly in countries where federalism is based on the persistence of identifiable cultural or national characteristics. The most indicative case is that of Canada, where Quebec's special status is shown by establishing what amounts to unofficial diplomatic representation abroad and the incorporation of provincial considerations into Canadian immigration policy. Immigration is of special importance because the province seeks to avoid immigrants who are more likely to become English-speaking than to become French-speaking. Although this might seem theoretically unenforceable (once newcomers have settled in any Canadian province they are free to change residence at will), the process of initial screening has apparently been largely effective in bringing about the desired result.

—— The UgEcon ——
is to government sovereignty
what AIDS is to public health.

The Unique Issues of Immigrants

Except in the extreme examples of wars, pogroms, persecution, and dire poverty, the decision to leave one's native country is complex. It usually means leaving family, friends, and a way of life that is at least familiar. People have always moved about, but modern means of transportation make migration much less difficult. Although the most common reason for migration is so that the relatively poor can better themselves, it is increasingly the case that well-to-do people are now immigrating to other countries solely for tax reasons. A booming industry of tax avoidance and tax evasion exists in more than 50 tax-haven countries, such as the Cayman Islands. One tax-haven publication lists 128 different tax jurisdictions that have advantages to certain groups of taxpayers. For example, more than 100 current and former world-ranking tennis players claim the tiny principality of Monaco as home. Through a complex of offshore companies, trusts, and bank accounts, an increasing number of people are becoming tax refugees, often without ever leaving a high-tax jurisdiction home.

Our interest here is not in the unique aspects of off-shore jurisdictions, but in their impact on the world's underground economy.

Studies have shown consistently that immigrants outperform native-born citizens in most measurable categories. They tend to do better with educational opportunities, require fewer social benefits, and earn above-average incomes. The obvious explanation is that most immigrants choose to leave their homes in search of better opportunities; because they have made this sacrifice, they work harder to succeed.

However, many of these immigrants come from lesser-developed countries, with well-established informal economies and without a history of self-motivated tax compliance. Therefore, UgEcon activity also tends to be more prevalent.

The scale and scope of international immigration is growing, its pattern is also becoming more complex — more than 100 states are categorized as countries of major inward or outward immigration.

The Expatriation Trend

America has long been a promised land and will attract almost a million *legal* immigrants in 2000. In sharp contrast, many US citizens have had enough of the American dream and are finding other dreams in Canada, New Zealand, Mexico, Israel, Taiwan, and a growing list of other countries that are attracting record numbers of immigrants from the US.

Experts estimate that roughly 250,000 to 300,000 Americans move overseas each year. Of these, most are former immigrants returning to their native countries, but as many as 100,000 are native-born. Why are they leaving? The globalization of the world's economy and the breakdown of national barriers have facilitated a freer flow of goods, ideas, and people – it will be a major trend of the 21st century. The land of real opportunity is now a land without borders.

Who is leaving? The majority tend to be university-educated professionals; it is often the best and brightest, the innovators, who are choosing to leave. Why are they leaving? People applying to foreign embassies cite fear of crime, racial tensions, and the lack of morality in the US as reasons for their desire to leave the country, but increasing numbers of wealthy Americans are leaving to obtain a tax advantage. Currently, 3.2 million Americans are living abroad, an increase of more than a million in the last decade.

We are seeing rampant tribalism in many areas; on the whole, various economic and political forces are leading to the reduction of traditional sovereignty and a relaxation of national borders. [68]

Expatriation from the US

US citizens have more difficulties getting free of the tax man than citizens of other countries. It may seem to most non-US citizens that their own country's tax authority is oppressive, but the US comparatively has some of the most draconian tax collection laws in the world.

Most countries adhere to an established financial convention of international law, and they tax people purely on the basis of residence; if you do not live there, you do not pay taxes there. Taxation usually has little to do with one's citizenship, which is why Canadians, British, French, Germans, Australians, Mexicans, and most other countries' nationals can wave a fond farewell to their national revenue authorities once they choose to permanently leave their homelands to live in a country with a more favorable tax climate.

Not so with US citizens. The IRS extends tax jurisdiction over its residents AND its citizens worldwide, even if those citizens have never lived in the US! This unusual situation exists in only 2 other countries: the Philippines and South Korea, whose tax laws were written with strong US input.

Currently, the US allows non-citizens to avoid taxes on capital gains and estates. That, critics point out, has permitted a handful of very wealthy Americans who have renounced their citizenship to save millions – some say billions – in taxes. The tax provisions in question continue a person's liability for income and transfer tax for 10 years beyond the loss of US citizenship, unless the taxpayer can establish that tax avoidance was not a main reason for giving up citizenship.

A Voluntary, Deliberate Act

Since 1990, under the US government's official policy, if a US citizen (1) is naturalized in a foreign country, (2) takes a routine oath of allegiance, or (3) accepts non-policy-level employment with a foreign government, the intent to retain US citizenship is presumed, in the absence of a statement or other evidence to the contrary. When such a case comes to the attention of a US consular officer, the person is asked by questionnaire whether he or she intended by the act to give up US citizenship. If the person had no such intent,

the consul certifies that position. Evidence that expatriation was intended, including the individual's statement to that effect, will ordinarily result in the issuance of a certificate of loss of nationality, an administrative finding that registers the loss of nationality as of the date of the expatriating act. Dual or multiple nationalities have become very commonplace in the last decade.

In 1995, US Senator Patrick Moynihan introduced an Administration bill, with certain revisions to tax the unrealized gains of wealthy individuals at the time they give up their US citizenship. The bill also imposed such a tax on aliens who give up a status of lawful permanent resident of the US ("green card" status) that was held for at least 8 of the preceding 15 years. Now, such residents can immediately escape being automatically taxed on their worldwide income as resident aliens by turning in their green cards.

Tax Havens for Cyber Businesses

The 1st major problem with taxing cyber businesses surfaced in the summer of 1999. British bookies, including mega-operations like Hilton's Ladbroke and William Hill, announced plans to move their operations to tax havens – Gibralter and the Channel Islands – to avoid paying the 9% surcharge levied by the British government.

This is the tip of a very big iceberg. As consumers begin seriously to download music and video over the Internet, it is hard to imagine why the large corporate vendors would not create subsidiaries and "operate" through tax havens.

 Case in point: In a very noteworthy case, Canadian officials raided the Vancouver offices of a financially successful purveyor of Internet pornography and gambling. Within a week, the company announced plans to move operations *(computers)* to the Caribbean Island of Antigua, a tiny tax haven with sophisticated telecommunication systems.

*AdultCheck® currently has over **65,000** participating sites!*
(Nov99)

Expatriation to Avoid Tax

Under regulations that became effective March 8, 1965, every former US citizen, now a nonresident alien, who lost US citizenship within the 10 years preceding the close of a tax year, is liable for income taxes for that year. The only exception is in cases where the avoidance of taxes was not one of the principal purposes for the loss of citizenship. However, the burden of that proof is on the individual.[69]

The following items of gross income shall be treated as taxable income if they are from sources within the US:

*(1) **Sale of property.** Gains on the sale or exchange of property located in the US.*

*(2) **Stock or debt obligations.** Gains on the sale or exchange of stock issued by a domestic corporation or debt obligations of US persons or of the United States or political subdivision thereof.*

Defining Expatriation Rules for Aliens

Taxpayers will go to great lengths to avoid taxes; expatriation, although somewhat extreme, is becoming more common. The US government does not like to lose revenue, particularly from individuals who are abandoning US citizenship or long-term residency. In general, expatriation recapture rules apply to US citizens who abandon their citizenship with the intention of avoiding US tax. These rules provide that those individuals may be subject to US taxation regardless of the fact that they have renounced their US citizenship. The recapture provisions extend the application of expatriation tax to certain nonresident aliens as well.

US Citizens

Former citizens may be assessed expatriation tax on income, capital gains, gifts, and estate transactions that occur before the end of the 10th calendar year following expatriation. To avoid the expatriation tax, the taxpayer must prove that tax evasion was not a principal purpose for his renunciation of citizenship, and the law places the burden of proof on the taxpayer.

Former Residents

Former residents are subject to expatriation tax if the following circumstances apply, *regardless of their*

intent: the alien was treated as a US resident during at least 3 consecutive calendar years (referred to as the "initial residency period") beginning after December 31, 1984; the period of residence for each of the 3 consecutive years includes at least 183 days in the US; the alien once again becomes a nonresident (including a dual resident who is treated as a nonresident under an income tax treaty); and the alien again becomes a US resident before the end of the 3rd calendar year beginning after his residency termination date for the initial residency period. Former residents are subject to expatriation tax only on income transactions that occur during the intervening period between residencies.

Expatriate Income Tax

The former citizen or former resident will be taxed on US source income and any foreign source income effectively connected with a trade or business within the US, whichever results in the higher tax. The normal nonresident alien taxation is set at 30% or, in the alternative, the treaty rate. In computing the alternative tax, deductions are allowable to the extent they are connected with gross income subject to alternative tax. Deductions must be allocated if they are connected with both taxable and non-taxable gross income.[70]

Taxing E-Commerce

As soon as Internet shopping began to boom in the mid-1990s, state revenue departments in the US started to find ways to tax it. The appearance of taxing agencies in cyberspace was not a welcome one, because this arena had previously been free of government intervention. Eventually, the Internet Freedom Bill passed the US Congress and was signed into law, severely curtailing Web taxation. This early capitulation by the US set a worldwide expectation that governments everywhere will keep their hands off e-commerce.

In Canada, the Federal Minister of Revenue appointed an advisory committee on e-commerce, in the belief that Canada, relative to other countries in the world, is better positioned to monitor and tax e-commerce.

All taxing authorities are very concerned about e-commerce, from both compliance and loss of revenue perspectives. E-commerce raises issues that can be quite profound, such as the definition of a permanent establishment, which is 1 of the most common tests of whether or not an individual or company is subject to taxes in a particular jurisdiction. The question then becomes: Does a server located in a particular country qualify as a permanent establishment?

Obviously, e-commerce makes it possible to hide and manipulate books and records. Many kinds of transactions would become difficult to audit. Already, the salespersons for the major providers of software for the hospitality industry – restaurants, bars and hotels – have been convicted of selling electronic skimming software that can dig back through the electronic transactions for the day and remove a defined percentage of the transactions, particularly those that are in cash or other items not traceable to detailed invoices.

New York City Street Vendors

New York's world-famous Fifth Avenue is a 15-block stretch of ultra-exclusive boutiques – Versace, Tiffany, and Gucci – side-by-side with 30 hot dog vendors, 10 roasted nuts vendors, and a Middle-Eastern food vendor. That is not counting candy, books, toys, paintings, portraits, baseball cards, and counterfeited designer watches and scarfs, all of which also are available on Fifth Avenue. Sunday is the best day for business, because people are not as rushed and have time to stop and look at the merchandise. A New York street vendor can earn from $50 to $150 on a good day – perhaps even $300 on an exceptional day.

The arcane, frustrating bureaucracy of city regulation drives many

Middle-class Russians hawking cigarettes on the streets of Moscow

vendors underground to earn a living. (See Mexico and Peru, pages 30 and 52 for similarities.) Most vendors seem indifferent to the requirement of the NYC Department of Consumer Affairs that all general merchandise vendors have permits to operate on city streets. Few worry about the under-manned New York City Peddler Squad, the unit in every precinct that enforces street vendor laws. In total, the City has fewer than 100 inspectors.

Although *what* general vendors can sell is not restricted, strict regulations dictate *where* they can sell. Besides being restricted to specific streets, vendor tables must meet certain criteria in terms of size, placement on the sidewalks, and non-obstruction. The New York City Department of Health regulates food vendors, who are required to purchase a licence and register their food carts with the city.

In 1979, the City Council froze the number of food cart permits; the permits, which were issued free, now have soared in value to more than $6,000.

Europe's Underground Economies[71]

Much of the UgEcon in Europe has its roots in the black market that was an essential ingredient of survival in wartime and postwar Europe. The UgEcon flourishes wherever governments tax excessively or regulate economic activity unreasonably. As we have discussed elsewhere, the UgEcon includes criminal activity, such as drug dealing; however, a very significant component consists of the sale and distribution of ordinary goods and services which would be perfectly legal and legitimate if taxes were paid.[71]

The growth of the UgEcon is a matter of increasing concern throughout Europe. An unpublished report by the EU acknowledges that UgEcon activities account for between 7% and 16% of the total GDP of its member nations. In addition, the UgEcon employs 10 to 28 million workers and accounts for 7-19% of employment. The problem is especially acute in transitional economies in Eastern Europe, but it is a growing epidemic everywhere.

The UK: The UgEcon has been a heated topic since 1979, when Sir William Pile, chairman of the British Revenue Board, declared with great attention to the politics of the moment, "it was not implausible" that untaxed earnings equalled 7.5 % of GDP. This led academics to try measuring the UgEcon by various methods. The noted American economist Edgar Feige believed that Sir William was half-right and put the true figure in 1979 at closer to 15% of GDP. (See page 84 for more on Dr. Feige.)

In 1997, a study by the accounting firm of Deloitte & Touche estimated that the UgEcon amounted to 12% of Britain's GDP and reduced income tax revenues by one-third. The latest study, by a prominent Austrian economist, put the UgEcon in Britain at 12.4 % of GDP in 1994.[72]

Italy: Twenty years ago Fiat Chairman Giovanni Agnelli reckoned that Italy's true output was 25% larger than official figures indicated, due to vast off-the-books economic activity. Academics generally agreed.[73]

Bolstered by such studies, the Italian government raised its official GDP statistics by 15% to account for all the unrecorded economic activity. This caused an uproar in Britain, because the recalculation propelled Italy ahead of it to be named the world's 5th largest economy. Whatever the truth statistically, tax evasion in Italy is pervasive. Even luminaries such as fashion designer Giorgio Armani have admitted bribing officials for favorable audits.

Germany: It is tempting to blame Italy's large UgEcon on the traditional Italian contempt for authority. But even Germany, with its long tradition of obedience to the law, has faced growing problems with tax evasion and illicit economic activity. In 1986, a senior government official said that the UgEcon had risen to 10% of GDP, employing between 100,000 and 600,000 people. Lost revenues equalled 50 billion German marks, or twice the federal deficit that year.[74] Tax evasion in Germany appears to have escalated in the 1990's. In 1993, the government imposed a new tax on investment income that greatly increased the incentive to hide such income in accounts in Luxembourg and Switzerland. As a result, the government took in less than half the revenue it anticipated from the new tax. Recently, a number of senior officials at Germany's largest banks were implicated in tax evasion activities, and the government instituted payments for tax informants, despite widespread misgivings by civil libertarians. A poll in August of 1997 found 46% of Germans agreed with the statement that "those who don't cheat on taxes deserve only pity."

Spain, Portugal, and Greece: Not surprisingly, problems with the UgEcon and tax evasion escalate as one moves to Europe's periphery. In Spain, 1/3 of those officially classified as unemployed are thought to be employed in UgEcon activities. In Portugal, several top government officials have been forced to resign in recent years after being caught evading taxes. Greece's efforts to crack down on tax evasion have led to nationwide strikes.

Eastern Europe: The largest UgEcon problems unquestionably exist in the former Communist countries. Tax evasion is so rampant that it has caused financial crises for the central governments of almost every former Soviet republic, including **Georgia** and **Moldova**. The situation is little better in the former Communist Bloc. A 1996 study by the prime minister's office in **Hungary** found that 17- 25% of the average family's expenditures were in the UgEcon. Earlier this year, **Serbia** demanded that all property and vehicle sales be transacted through the banks, in an effort to stop tax-evading cash-only sales.

The UgEcon is a large and growing problem in every single country in Europe. Although authorities frequently attack the problem with arrests and prosecutions, such methods have had little impact. In the end, successful efforts to reduce the UgEcon must involve market-oriented tax reduction, deregulation, and privatization.

In most transition countries, growth of the UgEcon has characterized the initial process of change. Yet it is a significant loss of revenue for government and distorts indicators of economic development. In the **Ukraine,** most estimates put the size of the UgEcon as high as 40-50% of GDP.

The Ukraine, at present, relies too much on audits to counteract tax avoidance and evasion. More emphasis needs to be put on information to taxpayers; the most efficient way to collect revenue from the UgEcon is by increasing taxpayers' voluntary compliance. The current financial penalties for tax evasion are very excessive and a new, less harsh, penalty system for tax evaders needs to be established. The Ukraine's government is presently working on a simplified tax system for small businesses that would limit the possibilities for tax evasion and reduce compliance costs. [75]

Improving to a Lighter Shade of Gray

POLAND

The black-market economy in **Poland** is known as the gray zone. According to the Central Statistical Office, the gray zone peaked in 1993, at 19% of the official reported economic activity. However current estimates indicate that the UgEcon is still 30-40% of GDP. Like most countries, Poland's definition of the UgEcon excludes all illegal activities, even its vibrant smuggling sector. Therefore, despite improvements, German marks and US dollars still finance much of Poland's economic activity.

The government attributes the decrease in the UgEcon in the last 7 years to the VAT tax. As visible and as unpopular as value-added taxes may be, they are effective in taxing consumption. (See page 112 for the case for consumption taxes.)

In Poland, the UgEcon comprises elements of both transitional and developed economies. Small and medium-sized businesses hire workers illegally and pay them without making the 48% surcharge payment to the Social Insurance Company. Unregistered businesses still operate, but this practice is declining as collection efficiency increases and penalties become at least a moderate deterrent. Polish companies operate in the UgEcon for universal reasons: greed which is expressed through direct tax evasion and a reduction of costs to keep or gain a competitive edge.

As in all transitional economies the UgEcon acts as a shock absorber during recessions. In 1989-91, for instance, when recession was at its worst, many Poles staved off financial ruin by working illegally. The UgEcon also supplements income for the poorer segments of society – the unemployed, retirees, students, and service workers. [55]

Knowledgeable observers criticize direct attacks on the UgEcon. Instead they suggest targeting its root causes and encouraging businesses to operate in compliance with the law. The same voices argue that heavy sanctions will not enhance state revenues because they can kill beneficial economic activity; in some cases, if pressed too aggressively, targeted businesses may adopt the structures of organized crime.

The **Offshore Option**

For years, the rich have used offshore trusts to shelter income and assets, which is one of the major ways that they manage to pay little or no taxes. Now it is becoming easier for everyone in higher tax brackets to do the same, particularly those who work in the often borderless world – for example, tennis and golf pros, movie makers and actors, information technologists, and call center operators, as well as the increasing array of run-of-the-mill knowledge workers, from stock specialists to investment counselors.[60]

An increasing number of businesses exist only in cyberspace, including tens of thousands of pornographic websites, cyber casinos, and betting shops that all dispense services that are not dependent on their locations.

A recent book explaining offshore options is James Davidson's *The Sovereign Individual*. Gordon Laight's *Offshore Advantage* begins with a chapter about the emergence of the global citizen, and it is written specifically for Canadians by a Canadian expatriate financial consultant. Because each industrialized country has unique tax problems and solutions, books abound that have been written specifically for every country with an expatriate market.

Which hand *really* owns the money?

The suspicion and fear that used to surround offshore banking emanated from a lack of knowledge and information. Very few people, including those who condemned it and those who promoted it, really knew what offshore banking was all about. However, the governments, the tax authorities, and the domestic bankers (who were losing business) did know that money held outside the domestic economy was money that could not be legally controlled, taxed, or accessed.

In the past, offshore middlemen advertised only occasionally in the *International Edition of* the Herald Tribune or in low-key ways in investment newsletters. Today they are everywhere – thousands advertise on the Internet and in local newspapers, and they hold "education" (marketing) seminars throughout the world.

It is not just England's truly international *Economist* that carries articles on the "offshore advantage." So too do other magazines such as Canada's staid *Maclean's*. Walking though the business districts of Panama City (Panama), Nassau (Bahamas), Georgetown (Cayman Islands), or Gibraltar is like walking through Wall Street in New York or "The City" in London. Almost every major bank in the world has a branch in each of these offshore money centers, just to handle the tidal waves of money from high-tax jurisdictions.

Increasing numbers of over-taxed high-wage earners are looking offshore for relief. In most cases, the only true means by which an individual can achieve tax-free status is to abandon residency in his or her country of origin and take permanent residence in a tax haven. This "non-residency" remains a valid option for most aspiring expatriates. Non-residency, in general, means creating a primary residence outside your tax residence and spending more than half of your time there to exempt yourself from the taxes of your "home" jurisdiction.

This works because *most* industrialized nations tax on the basis of residency. Anyone who is a tax resident *must* report all international income, including income from foreign bank accounts, offshore trusts, investment accounts. *By contrast, US citizens are taxed on the basis of citizenship and are therefore obliged to pay US taxes regardless of source and regardless of residency.* Americans who abandoned their citizenship can now be barred from even visiting the US.

Globalizing Investment Portfolios

Those who are not ready to physically move out of the country have the option of creating a fictional move. Offshore middlemen quickly explain that this is usually a combination of a foreign donor trust in one tax haven jurisdiction and a shell company in

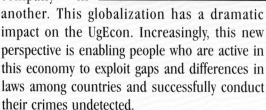

another. This globalization has a dramatic impact on the UgEcon. Increasingly, this new perspective is enabling people who are active in this economy to exploit gaps and differences in laws among countries and successfully conduct their crimes undetected.

IMF Threats to Tax Havens

More than 50 countries are actively involved in offshore tax avoidance (and evasion) manoeuvers. Luxembourg and Liechtenstein dominate as European tax-haven countries, but Austria and Switzerland have equally strict bank secrecy legislation; virtually every island in the Caribbean offers some form of tax haven benefit. The esoteric jurisdictions range from Guernsey, Jersey, and Sark (The Channel Islands in the English Channel between England and France) to Vanuatu and the Cook Islands, specks in the South Pacific.

The IMF is trying to institute heavy sanction pressure on these countries to discontinue their practices of assisting tax avoidance/evasion. However, for many of these countries, the offshore financial industry represents their primary source of hard currency, so the pressure is futile. It's possible that a few countries may be coerced out of the business, but it is impossible to imagine a world where offshore options cease to exist for an ever-increasing group of haggard and unhappy taxpayers.

The Long Arm of the Tax Collector

The already long arm of taxing authorities is getting longer because of bilateral cooperation between governments — a disconcerting trend for geographically mobile workers. In 1999, the Canadian Mounties (RCMP) arrested prominent German-Canadian businessman Karlheinz Schreiber on behalf of German officials, who wanted him extradited to face tax charges. Schreiber, a well-connected "middle man," had been linked to kickback schemes in deals for tanks to Saudi Arabia and European airplanes to Air Canada. An RCMP spokesman denied that the arrest was connected to the investigation of the Airbus scandal. "There is absolutely no connection between the two. He was arrested by the RCMP on behalf of German authorities and it relates to [his] failing to pay trade and income taxes."[76]

Getting Your Money Offshore

Offshore adventures come in 1000's of varieties. A general search of the Internet will offer every gadget and gimmick out there. How rich do you have to be to "play" this game? Most offshore services will tell you that you need to have accumulated between $35,000 and $65,000, or be able to make an annual "contribution" of about $15,000 to make it worth the costs involved.

Following is a sample "infomercial" that was picked, at random, from the net:

A Typical Internet Ad

As Governments are pirating more and more money from overtaxed citizens around the world, they are also becoming more and more zealous in attempting to obtain information on individual and corporate holdings both domestically and overseas. As a result, individuals have become much more resourceful in structuring offshore entities that avoid reporting requirements. One such structure is the "British Virgin Islands Non-Disclosure Structure," a structure that combines 2 British Virgin Islands International Business Companies (IBC2).

Generally, the idea of holding assets inside a corporate shell is a popular protection mechanism, providing both ongoing tax relief and protection from seizure. The idea of holding assets inside a corporate structure that is not subject to disclosure is a further refinement of a time-proven concept. Offshore companies present you with opportunities you would not otherwise have. For instance, through the effective use of an offshore structure, you may be able to:

- eliminate reporting and paying income tax on earnings, interest, dividends, and investments;
- protect against high capital gains taxes and reporting requirements;
- prevent inheritance taxes, estate taxes, executor's fees, and probate fees;
- protect assets from creditors, malpractice claims, judgments, liens, and bankruptcy, and deter the initiation of civil litigation;
- prevent the erosion of assets as a result of divorce or separation; and

- protect the privacy of your involvement with investment houses, brokers, and securities markets.

The key is to make use of an effective structure, one that allows you to prevent any knowledge of your assets or affairs from becoming public due to domestic disclosure legislation. An effective structure can seamlessly work with a confidential offshore broker, maximizing your rate of return on stocks, bonds, and mutual funds around the world.

Trading Securities

If a fictitious client, Dr. Smith, buys and sells a stock at a profit, he pays capital gains taxes. In some cases, the marginal tax rate on capital gains is higher than the rate on passive interest investments, even though the risk of success is higher. If Dr. Smith instead placed some funds into an IBC2 Structure and did the same trade, his gain would be tax free because the British Virgin Islands do not have any income taxes whatsoever on IBC's.

The share structure of the company must conform to Dr. Smith's local government tax system, or he runs the risk of tax evasion charges. To accomplish this, the IBC2 Structure prevents Dr. Smith from appearing as a shareholder, officer, or director of any offshore corporation.

After the IBC2 Structure is formed, a securities trading account must be set up for the structure. Dr. Smith is able to direct and control the trading activities, and he is protected in that the IBC2 structure may be controlled only by himself or those he designates – it cannot be controlled by an unknown trustee. Therefore, he knows that no one can access his funds without his consent. The portfolio grows tax free within the IBC2 structure, allowing Dr. Smith to attain his goals of ongoing tax relief and asset protection.[77]

The Internet offers 1000's of alternative investment schemes that are designed to help you get your money offshore. Many cross the line from avoidance to evasion.

Rational Anarchists in the UgEcon

have special credit (actually debit) cards from offshore banks that give the illusion of a normal transaction but are buried in the millions of credit transactions that occur each day.

2. Those who seek RA status, but have not accumulated enough wealth, resort to low- or medium-income jobs that allow flexibility in working hours, such as owning a small store or doing contract work. Authorities assume that these individuals are harmless drones, allowing them to earn other undocumented income in the UgEcon. This keeps taxable income to a minimum and avoids the paper trail.

In the complex economic systems of today's developed societies, individuals of means who consciously do not leave a paper trail of credit and debit cards and checks are very rare individuals. Such behavior is a pattern that fits the definition of what most expatriate literature refers to as rational anarchists (RA's).

By leaving no paper trail, RA's make it difficult for the economic observers of the world to detect their existence – precisely their aim. The intent is to be invisible to the system, so that they can be free to live a life that is emancipated from routine economic monitoring.

The differences among the breeds of RA's are primarily related to the amount of money they have accumulated and its sources:

1. Relatively well-off RA's often live outside of their "normal" country of residence. Elaborate networks, with their own newsletters and books, cater to this class of "Perpetual Tourists." This class of RA's has often accumulated an appreciable amount of wealth and has found a way – either legally or quasi-illegally – to expatriate money.

Another part of this group earns a significant livelihood from foreign, UgEcon, or hard-to-trace sources. In this electronic era, these individuals

3. The more paranoid or fanatical RA's or ones who live in politically volatile countries recommend a covert identity that is used only if the individual has to suddenly become a non-person. This is unlikely to be needed in fully developed countries, but may be needed if political chaos occurs. Extremist forms of governments, either a paternalistic socialist/communist government or a militarist/fascist dictatorship, might take harsh action against RA's who threaten the stability of the government.

The mechanics of these forms of invisibility are quite simple yet very effective. Whole industries have grown up around the need for alternative identities, creating legal and semi-legal passports and identification cards. RA's do not use "normal" credit and often do not have domestic checking accounts. Some RA's avoid the mainstream economy by doing business in the UgEcon; they often prefer the barter system, but in all cases avoid having their transactions leave paper or electronic tracks.[78]

A Land of Hidden Blessings

In Macedonia, the UgEcon means "profitable and healthy," and this economic sector has kept the country alive during the transition period. If Macedonia had to rely only on its official/formal economy, it would have gone bankrupt long ago.

Although always hard to estimate, it is probably reasonable to say that as much as 50% of the GDP in Macedonia is underground. The money generated by these activities is largely held in foreign exchange outside the banking system or smuggled abroad. Experience in other countries shows that only about 15% of the money "float" is actually needed for commercial transactions; this means that billions in hard currencies are transferred outside the country. A trickle of money comes back and is "laundered" through the opening of small legal businesses.

This is solid evidence of a pending economic boom when the macroeconomic, geopolitical, and

Over-Regulation
by governmental agencies often stifles business activity which then escapes partially or completely into the UgEcon.

(especially) the micro-economic climates change – billions of US dollars will flow back into Macedonia. People will bring their money back to open businesses, to support family members, and just to spend it. It all depends on the atmosphere and on how much people feel that they can rely on political stability and rational governments.

Similar enormous flows of returning capital happened in Argentina after the Generals and their corrupt regime were ousted by civilians, in Israel when the peace process started in earnest, and in Mexico following the signing of NAFTA. Given the right political and economic climate, these reserves can be lured back quickly, and they will rapidly transform the economy.

Important Functions of the UgEcon

The UgEcon is a cash economy. Because it is liquid and fast, it increases the velocity of money. It injects much needed foreign exchange to the economy and inadvertently increases the effective money supply and the resulting money aggregates. In this sense, it defies the dictates of "we know better" transnational institutions such as the IMF. It fosters economic activity and employs people.

It encourages labor mobility and international trade – *it can be very positive.* With the exception of illegal activities, it does everything that the official economy does – and, not surprisingly, much more efficiently.

This puts us back to one of our basic questions, "If the UgEcon is doing such a good job in Macedonia, is there anything morally wrong with it?" The answer is, "Yes, because it is exploitative." The formal parts of the economy, which are not hidden (though they might like to be), are penalized for their visibility. They pay taxes. Captive taxpayers who are workers in factories owned by the state or in the government service cannot avoid paying taxes.

At least in theory, the money that the state collects from its captive and compliant taxpayers is invested in infrastructure (roads, telephones, electricity) or used to pay for public services (education, defense, policing). The workers in the UgEcon benefit from these services without paying their fair share of the costs.

Macedonia, with its industrious and creative people, offers us an insight into the difference between a *theoretical* market economy and a highly efficient *practical* market economy. Unfortunately, our societies are regulated by bureaucracies that are controlled, in theory, by politicians. These nincompoops have a tendency to misuse and to abuse resources and to allocate them inefficiently. Virtually all economic theories assert that a dollar left in the hands of the private sector is much more efficiently used than the same dollar in the hands of even the most well-meaning and competent civil servants. Governments all over the world delude themselves about their economic decisions and waste scarce human and economic resources.

The upside potential of the UgEcon, from the perspective of a rational anarchist, is thought provoking. Economist Dr. Sam Vaknin, the most well-known expert on Macedonia, asserts that if the goals are to encourage employment and economic growth – the black economy should be welcomed. *The fewer tax dollars a government has – the*

Alexander the Great...

...was king of Macedonia and one of the greatest generals in history. He conquered much of what was then the civilized world – from Egypt to India. Though Alexander also spoke Greek, loved Homer, and respected his tutor Aristotle, much evidence indicates that he hated the Greeks of his day. He thoroughly destroyed Thebes. His Asian empire is correctly called Macedonian, not Greek, for he won it with an army of 35,000 Macedonians and only 7,600 Greeks.

Nevertheless, Alexander brought Greek ideas and ways of doing things to all the countries he conquered. This great general and king made possible the broadly developed culture of the Hellenistic Age. He died at the age of 33, in 323 BCE.

less damage it does. This is an opinion shared by most progressive economists in the world today.

The UgEcon is especially important in times of economic hardships. It plays an essential role in countries in transition or in those with developing economies – what used to be called (in less politically correct times) "Third World Countries." The UgEcon is a perfect solution until the dust of transition and development settles.

Location:	**Europe**
Status:	**UN Country**
Capital City:	**Skopje**
Main Cities:	**Bitola, Prilep, Kumanovo**
Population:	**2,034,000**
Area [sq.km]:	**25,710**
Currency:	**Macedonian denar**
Main Languages:	**Macedonian, Albanian**
Main Religions:	**Macedonian Orthodox, Muslim**

A Nation of Tax Revolters

America is a nation born of a tax revolt. The American credo, "In God We Trust," is not a statement of religious belief, but a clever piece of irony saying the founders did not trust any *government*.

Colonists in America paid taxes under the Molasses Act, which was modified in 1764 to include import duties on foreign molasses, sugar, wine, and other commodities. The new act, known as the Sugar Act, did not raise substantial revenue. Therefore, the Stamp Act was added in 1765, which imposed a direct tax on all newspapers printed in the colonies and on most commercial and legal documents. The stamp tax was the direct cause of the famous Boston Tea Party and the start of the revolution against England.

> **Americans have had many overt tax revolts, and actually seem to enjoy them: It was no accident that the Boston Tea Party was called a party.**

Americans think of their founders as individualists who rebelled against the British Crown for imposing taxes without their consent. But the founding fathers did try to figure out which taxes the new citizens would tolerate, giving serious consideration to excise taxes. Alexander Hamilton, a principal thinker in formulating American tax policy, favored excise (consumption) taxes because they were obvious. The amount to be contributed by each citizen was, to a degree, at his own option and could be regulated by attention to his resources. The rich might be extravagant, but the poor could decide to be frugal.

However, early Americans wanted to challenge the "greedy hand," even in the form of an excise tax. When the founding fathers levied taxes on spirits, America's early citizens fought back – with a vengeance. During the Whiskey Rebellion, they used whatever weapons they had available – muskets and pitchforks. It was a bloody exchange between the people and their taxers. However, even that unenlightened government listened, and by 1800, the US, led by Thomas Jefferson, had abandoned internal taxes altogether.

This tea chest was constructed and painted in China during the second half of the 18th century. It was used by the East India Company for the exportation of tea from China to the American colonies.

A Boston Tea Party Ch

The Boston Tea Party

On May 10, 1773, Parliament authorized the East India Company to export a half a million pounds of tea to the American colonies for the purpose of selling it without the usual duties and tariffs. It was its intention to try to save the corrupt and mismanaged company from bankruptcy. The effect was that the company could undersell any other tea available in the colonies, including smuggled tea. The disruption to American commerce was unacceptable to many, including Samuel Adams of Boston.

On November 27, 1773, three ships loaded with such tea landed at Boston and were prevented from unloading their cargo. Fearing that the tea would be seized for failure to pay customs duties and eventually become available for sale, Adams and the Boston Whigs arranged a solution. On the night of December 16, 1773, a group of colonists, thinly disguised as Mohawk Indians, sneaked aboard the ships and dumped 342 chests of tea into Boston Harbor.

The sabotage was denounced by Boston's less radical population and applauded by those more radical. England's response was the passing of the Intolerable Acts, which precipitated the formation of the First Continental Congress to consider a united resistance.

Stop Me Before I Collect More

In 1976, *The Wall Street Journal* published my "Letter From a Pensioner," which told of my ballooning federal pension, and how I felt younger taxpayers were being had by retirees on the collecting end, like me. Much to my consternation, my civil service pension had grown from $1,560 a month to $2,205 a month, a 41.5% increase in just 3 years.

Now, more than 20 years after retirement, my bewilderment has only grown. Today I receive 4 pensions – civil service, military, widower's, and Social Security. Since 1973, my total pension has skyrocketed by 603%, to a total of $9,410 per month. The increase is due, first, to the compounding cost-of-living adjustments (COLA's) and second to "double-dipping" – I can credit my years of military service on both my civil service and military pensions.

Since I retired in 1973, I have received more than $1.2 million from the government. At age 78, according to actuarial tables, I am expected to live another 8 years. If I survive those extra years and laws do not change, I will receive an additional $1 million from Uncle Sam. But I personally paid less than $50,000 toward my federal pension – American taxpayers pay the rest.

This reminds me of President Eisenhower's warning: "As we peer into society's future, we must avoid the impulse to live only for today, plundering for our own ease and convenience the precious resources of tomorrow." While federal pensioners watch the taxpayer's money flood their bank accounts, their children may discover government coffers empty by the time they are ready to retire.[79]

Hastings Keith, a Republican Congressional Representative (Massachusetts, 1958 -1972), is co-chairman of the National Committee on Public Employee Pension Systems, which is lobbying to limit retirees' cost-of-living-adjustments.

In 1995, the IRS assessed over 34 million civil penalties on American taxpayers in an effort to force compliance with the tax system.[80]

Do Governments Waste Taxpayers' Money?

The Age-Old Questions: Popes and Wild Bears

"Is the Pope Catholic? Do wild bears poop in the woods? However much people of different political persuasions disagree about which parts of the budget constitute waste, hardly anyone will deny that the government throws money around like a drunken sailor with only one weekend left to live."[61]

Bureaucracies Are the Real Roots of Government Waste

The 1983 Grace Commission Report, "The President's Private Sector Survey on Cost Control," gave great insight about how US tax dollars were being wasted. The head of the commission, J. Peter Grace, a very successful industrialist, used sound business analysis in reaching the conclusions. As offensive as its findings may be, they probably are fairly typical for developed countries. The compelling issue is, however, "Did this excellent document change government behaviour?"

The answer is, of course, a resounding, "No!" *Apparently bureaucracies are impervious to facts.* The Grace Commission (see page 48) pointed out that "100% of what is collected" in US personal income taxes "is absorbed solely by interest on the federal debt and by federal government contributions to transfer payments."

As long as the government continues to pursue its present preposterous policies, individuals will no doubt continue to seek means of protecting themselves from the effects of those policies.

US Tax Evasion Today

Under today's income tax system, tax evasion is a major, continuing, and growing problem. Notwithstanding a much larger IRS, more burdensome information-reporting requirements, increasingly stiff and numerous penalties, and a host of legislative initiatives, the problem is getting worse. Tax evasion has increased by 67% during the past 11 years. [80]

– Based on IRS figures

The History of the 16th Amendment to the US Constitution [81]

Taxes on Income

1862: The Tax Act of 1862: The rates were 3% on income above $600 and 5% on income above $10,000. Citizens accepted the tax "with cheerfulness," according to the Commissioner of Revenue. This acceptance was primarily due to the need for revenue to finance the Civil War. However, despite the apparent acceptance of the tax, compliance was not high. Figures released later indicated that 276,661 people actually filed tax returns in 1870, when the country's population was approximately 38 million.

1864: The Tax Act of 1864: To raise additional revenue to support the Civil War, tax rates rose to 5% for income between $600 and $5,000; 7.5% for income between $5,001 and $10,000; 10% on income above $10,000.

1870: The rate was a flat 2.5% and the exemption amount was raised to $2,000.

1872: Income tax was repealed and replaced with significant tariff restrictions, which served as the major revenue source for the United States until 1913.

1913: 16th Amendment: Congress was given the authority to tax the citizenry on income, regardless of its source.

Background

Ironically, the 16th Amendment that created income taxes was never supposed to have passed. It was introduced by the Republicans as a political scheme to trick the Democrats, but it backfired.

The US had always raised national revenue by tariffs on imported goods, but during wars this source dried up. Hence, during the war against Britain in 1812 and again in the American Civil War (1861-65), forms of income tax and estate duty were imposed but they were repealed as soon as hostilities ceased.

However, at the start of the 1900's, in the midst of great social unrest, the idea of a new tax that would "soak the rich" began to have a growing appeal to liberals in both major parties. Several times the Democrats introduced bills to provide a tax on higher incomes, but each time the conservative branch of the Republican party killed it in the Senate. The Democrats used this as evidence that the Republicans were the "party of the rich" and should be thrown out of power. In April 1909, Senator Joseph W. Bailey, a conservative Texas Democrat who personally opposed income taxes, decided to further embarrass the Republicans by forcing them to openly oppose another income tax bill. However, to his amazement, Teddy Roosevelt and a growing element of liberals in the Republican party came out in favor of the bill.

Republican leader Senator Nelson W. Aldrich frantically met with Senator Henry Cabot Lodge and President Taft to plan a strategy for a political end run. They decided to favor income tax only as an amendment to the Constitution, which they were quite certain would be defeated by the states — 3/4 of which need to ratify any Constitutional amendment.

Reaction to the Amendment

Democratic Congressman Cordell Hull saw exactly what was happening and went on to expose this political trick. He needn't have been so concerned. The slogan of "soak the rich" automatically aroused

Pavlovian salivation among politicians, both in Washington and the states. The Senate approved the 16th Amendment with an astonishing unanimity of 77-0, and the House approved it by a vote of 318-14. The end run of the Republican leadership did indeed backfire. State after state ratified this "soak the rich" amendment until it went into full force and effect on February 12, 1913.

The Cute Little Monkey that Grew into a Gorilla

At the time, Congress chortled confidently that "all good citizens will willingly and cheerfully support and sustain this, the fairest and cheapest of all taxes." That was the cute little monkey part. After all, the tax ranged from merely 1% of the 1st $20,000 of taxable income to only 7% on incomes above $500,000. Who could complain? (Note: In 1999 dollars, $20,000 became $300,000 and $500,000 became almost $7.5 million!)

At first, scarcely anyone did – because the tax did not apply to the vast majority of citizens. Even in 1939, 26 years after the amendment was adopted, only 5% of the population was required to file returns. Today, more than 80% of the population is under income tax regulations. By the time the tinkering was finished in Washington, this system would be described by many Americans as the most unfair and expensive tax in the history of the nation.

Weaknesses of the System

The most damaging aspect of the 16th Amendment is the fact that it violates the unalienable rights provided in the 4th Amendment: Privacy – privacy of the home, business, personal papers, and personal affairs of the private citizen. When taxes are based on income, the IRS must make certain that everyone pays his or her fair share, which is impossible without violating the privacy of individual citizens.

Even the prosecution of tax cases is unfair to individual citizens. Appeals are heard through a system of tax courts, which are without juries. In order to get a tax case into a regular court with a jury, the citizen must pay the tax and then sue the government.

FDR Needs Help

Do you occasionally have problems completing your income tax return? Well, you are in excellent company. More than 50 years ago – when tax regulations were much simpler – the president of the US, educated at Groton and Harvard, could not figure out how much he owed. Maybe every American taxpayer should adopt the Roosevelt strategy and ask the IRS to compute how much we owe. On 2nd thought, that is not such a good idea.

From the Desk of
The President of the United States

... March 15, 1938 ...

My dear Commissioner Helvering:

I am enclosing my income tax return for the calendar year 1937, together with my check for $15,000.

I am wholly unable to figure out the amount of the tax for the following reason:

The first twenty days of January, 1937, were a part of my first term of office and to these twenty days the income tax rates as of March 4, 1933, apply. To the other 345 days of the year 1937, the income tax rates as they existed on January 30, 1937 apply.

As this is a problem in higher mathematics, may I ask that the Bureau let me know the amount of the balance due? The payment of $15,000 doubtless represents a good deal more than half what the eventual tax will prove to be.

Franklin Delano Roosevelt
President of the United States

The Birth of Charitable Foundations

Although some naive political hacks rejoiced that this amendment shifted the tax burden to the wealthy, nothing could be further from the truth!

The wealthy, especially the super-wealthy, had anticipated this development and had created a clever device to protect their riches: a charitable foundation. The idea was to assign all of their wealth, including stocks and securities, to a foundation, and then get Congress and the state legislatures to declare all such charitable institutions exempt from taxes. By setting up boards that were themselves under the control of these wealthy benefactors, they could escape the tax and still maintain control over the disposition of these fabulous fortunes.

Long before the federal income tax was in place, multimillionaires such as John D. Rockefeller (who once said, "I want to own nothing and control everything"), J.P. Morgan, and Andrew Carnegie had foundations set up and operating.

The tax bill authorized by the 16th Amendment was introduced as House Resolution 3321 on October 3, 1913. It turned out to be a legislative potpourri for tax attorneys, accountants, and the federal courts. In the ensuing years, billions of dollars have been spent trying to figure out exactly what this tax law, and those that followed it, were intended to provide. However, tucked away under Section 2, Paragraph G was that precious key to protect the riches of the super wealthy: "Provided, however, that nothing in this section shall apply... to any corporation or association organized and operated exclusively for religious, charitable, scientific or educational purposes."

Is There a Better Way?

T. Coleman Andrews served as Commissioner of IRS for nearly 3 years during the early 1950's. Following his resignation, he made the following statement:

"Congress [with the 16th Amendment] went beyond merely enacting an income tax law, and repealed Article IV [the absolute right to privacy] of the Bill of Rights, by empowering the tax collector to do the very things from which that article says we were to be secure.

"It opened up our homes, our papers, and our effects to the prying eyes of government agents and set the stage for searches of our books and vaults and for inquiries into our private affairs whenever the tax men might decide, even though there might not be any justification beyond mere cynical suspicion.

"I believe that a better way to raise revenue not only can be found but must be found because I am convinced that the present system is leading us right back to the very tyranny from which those, who established this land of freedom, risked their lives, their fortunes, and their sacred honor to forever free themselves and other citizens."

Taxing the Poor

Collecting taxes from the poor is a completely different situation. The welfare poor and the working poor have the equivalent of the Monopoly game's "get out of jail free" card if they are caught evading taxes, typically low levels of benefit fraud. The reality is that governments and their taxing agencies can do almost nothing against poor tax evaders. The poor do not own anything of value, which leaves nothing to attach. We occasionally see cases of benefit fraud in the media, but these tend to be elaborate and systematic scams involving flagrant violations of the laws.

Soak It to the Rich

One of the greatest scams that governments have ever run on the masses is that income taxes "soak it to the rich." As we have seen in this section and in a variety of other places in this book, the reason that tax codes are so complex (9,000 pages in the US and 1,500 pages in Canada) is that they are full of loopholes designed to shield the rich from taxes. If there is no loophole, they go offshore. If the poor *cannot* pay the taxes and the rich *do not*, who does pay the taxes? The middle class, of course.

We need true tax reform that will at least make a start toward restoring for our children the American Dream that wealth is denied to no one, that each individual has the right to fly as high as his strength and ability will take him. But we cannot have such reform while our tax policy is engineered by people who view the tax as a means of achieving changes in our social structure.
— **Ronald Reagan,** 40th US President and Former Governor of California

was astounded at the results of a 1996 survey done of the major corporations in Europe and Japan. They were asked, "If the US abolished s income tax and went to a sales tax, would that have any impact on ur decisions?" More than 80% of the corporations said they would uild their factories in the US; 20% said they would move their international headquarters to the US.
— **Bill Archer,** US Congressman and Chairman, House Ways and Means Committee

In my opinion our challenge will do no less than pull the current income tax code out by its roots and throw it away so that it can never grow back.
— **Bill Archer,** US Congressman and Chairman, House Ways and Means Committee

In principle, income tax, at this time, is incompatible with freedom.
— **Alan Keyes,** US Ambassador and 2000 US presidential candidate

Have we the courage and the will to face up to the immorality and discrimination of the progressive tax, and demand a return to traditional proportionate taxation?...
Today in our country the tax collector's share is 37 cents of every US dollar earned. Freedom has never been so fragile, so close to slipping from our grasp. Our income tax system is an international embarrassment.
— **Jimmy Carter,** 39th US President

I will be the first member of Congress to vote to scrap the federal income tax.
— **Billy Tauzin,** US Congressman and Co-author, The National Retail Sales Tax Act of 1996

We, in Congress, need to recognize that the income tax has failed. It is now time to look at a totally different way of financing spending, before it is too late. I propose that we replace the current system with a National Sales Tax.
— **Dan Schaefer,** US Congressman and Co-author, The National Retail Sales Tax Act of 1996

I favor abolishing the federal income tax. I propose the states be responsible for collection of the national sales tax so the IRS can be dismantled properly. Replacing the federal income tax is the right thing to do and this is the right time to do it.
— **Richard Lugar,** US Senator

The income tax is a discriminatory tax. It discriminates against success and subsidizes failure. It discriminates against saving and investment and subsidizes consumption. It discriminates against work and subsidizes leisure. There is nothing good that can be said about the income tax.
— **Paul Craig Roberts,** President of the US Institute for Political Economy

The American People have had ample opportunity to consider the Income Tax and they have found it sorely wanting. It deserves to die. I wish you Godspeed in your efforts, Mr. Chairman.
— **Christopher Cox,** US Congressman

I want to get back to an America free from the IRS.
— **Newt Gingrich,** US Congressman and Speaker of the House, 104th & 105th Congress

A hand from Washington will be stretched out and placed upon every man's business; the eye of the Federal inspector will be in every man's counting house. The law will of necessity have inquisitorial features. It will provide penalties. It will create a complicated machinery. Under it, businessmen will be hauled into courts distant from their homes. Heavy fines imposed by distant and unfamiliar tribunals will constantly menace the taxpayer. An army of Federal inspectors, spies, and detectives will descend upon the state. They will compel men of business to show their books and disclose the secrets of their affairs. They will dictate forms of bookkeeping. They will require statements and affidavits ...
— **Richard E. Byrd,** Speaker of the Virginia House of Delegates, March 3, 1910, speaking against the ratification of the 16th Amendment

Get the federal government out of the collecting business and bring the tax collecting back to the state level.
— **Robert Dornan,** US Congressman

Thomas Jefferson ran for office in 1799 on a plan to ban all internal taxes – and won. One of Jefferson's most famous promises was that a "wise and frugal government" would not "take from the mouth of the labor the bread it has earned."

1913

TO BE FILLED IN BY COLLECTOR.

Form 1040

TO BE FILLED IN BY INTERNAL REVENUE BUREAU

List No. . . . .

. . . . District of . . . . . .

Date Received . . . .

INCOME TAX

THE PENALTY

FOR FAILURE TO HAVE THIS RETURN IN THE HANDS OF THE COLLECTOR OF INTERNAL REVENUE ON OR BEFORE MARCH 1 IS $20 TO $1,000 (SEE INSTRUCTIONS ON PAGE 4)

File No . . . .

Assessment List . . . .

Page . . . . Line . . . .

UNITED STATES INTERNAL REVENUE

RETURN OF ANNUAL INCOME OF INDIVIDUALS.

(As provided by act of Congress approved October 1, 1913.)

RETURN OF NET INCOME RECEIVED OR ACCRUED DURING THE YEAR ENDED DECEMBER 31, 191 . . . .

(FOR THE YEAR 1913, FROM MARCH 1, TO DECEMBER 31.)

Filed by (or for) . . . . of . . . .
(Full name of individual) — (Street and No.)

in the City, Town, or Post Office of . . . . State of . . . .
(Fill in pages 2 and 3 before mailing entries below)

1. GROSS INCOME (see page 2, line 12) . . . . $

2. GENERAL DEDUCTIONS (see page 3, line 7) . . . . $

3. NET INCOME . . . . $

Deductions and exemptions allowed in competing income subject to the normal tax of 1 per cent.

4. Dividends and net earnings received or accrued, of corporation, etc. subject to like tax. (See page 2, line 9, column A) . . . . . $

5. Amount of income on which the normal tax has been deducted and withheld at the source. (See page 2, line 9, column A) . . . . . .

6. Specific exemptions of $3,000 or $4,000, as the case may be. (See Instructions 3 and 19) . . . .

Total deductions and exemptions (lines 4, 5 and 6) . . . . . . $

7. TAXABLE INCOME on which the normal tax of 3 per cent is to be calculated. (See instruction 3) . . $

8. When the net income shown above on line 3 exceeds $30,000, the additional tax thereon must be calculated as per schedule below:

		INCOME	TAX
1	per cent on amount over $20,000 and not exceeding $50,000 . . . $	$	
2	" " 50,000 " " 75,000		
3.	" " 75,000 " " 100,000		
4	" " 100,000 " " 250,000		
5	" " 250,000 " " 500,000		
6	" " 500,000		

Total additional or super tax . . . . $

Total normal tax (1 per cent of amount entered on line 7) . . . . $

Total tax liability . . . . $

As simple as the 1913 income tax was, it turned out to be the thin edge of the wedge that has created a monster of inequity that, in turn, created the climate for the rapid development of the UgEcon and the disrespect for government that goes with it.

INSTRUCTIONS

1 This return shall be made by every citizen of the United States, whether residing at home or abroad, and by every person residing in the United States, though not a citizen thereof, having a *net income* of $3,000 or over for the taxable year, and *also* by every *nonresident alien* deriving income from property owned and business, trade or profession carried on *in the Unites States* by him.

2 When an individual by reason of minority, sickness or other disability, or absence from the United States, is unable to make his own return, it may be made for him by his *duly authorized* representative.

3 The normal tax of 1 per cent shall be assessed on the total net income less the specific exemption of $3,000 or $4,000 as the case may be. For the year 1913, the specific exemption allowable is $2,500 or $3,333.33, as the case may be. If, however, the normal tax has been deducted and withheld on any part of the income at the source, or if any part of the income is received as dividends upon the stock or from the net earnings of any corporation, etc. which is taxable upon its net income, such income shall be deducted from the individual's total *net income* for the purpose of calculating the amount of income on which the individual is liable for the normal tax of 1 per cent by virtue of this return. (See page 1, line 7)

4 The *additional or super tax* shall be calculated as stated on page 1.

5 This return shall be filed with the Collector of Internal Revenue for the district in which the individual resides if he has no other place of business, otherwise in the district in which he has his *principal place of business,* or in case the person resides in a foreign country, then with the collector for the district in which his principal business is carried on in the United States.

6 This return must be filed on or before the first day of March succeeding the close of the calendar year for which return is made.

7 The *penalty* for *failure to file the return within the time specified by law* is $20 to $2,000. In case of refusal or neglect to render the return within the required time (except in cases of sickness or absence), 50 per cent shall be added to amount of tax assessed. In case of *false or fraudulent return,* 100 per cent shall be added to such tax, and any person required by law to make, render, sign, or verify any return who makes any false or fraudulent return or statement with intent to defeat or evade the assessment required by this section to be made shall be guilty of a misdemeanor, and shall be fined not exceeding $2,000 or be imprisoned not exceeding one year, or both, at the discretion of the court, with the costs of the prosecutor.

8 When the return is not filed within the required time by reason of sickness or absence of the individual, an extension of time, not exceeding 30 days from March 1, within which to file such return *may be* granted by the collector, *provided* an application therefore is made by the individual within the period for which such extension is desired.

9 This return properly filled out must be made under oath or affirmation. Affidavits may be made before any officer *authorized by law* to administer oaths. If before a justice of the peace or magistrate, not using a seal, a *certificate of the clerk of the court as to the authority* of such officer to administer oaths should be *attached to the return.*

10 Expense for medical attendance, store accounts, family supplies, wages of domestic servants, cost of board, room or, or house rent for family or personal use, *are not expenses that can be deducted from gross income.* In case an individual owns his own residence he can not deduct the estimated value of rent, neither shall he be required to include such estimated rental of his home as income.

11 The farmer, in computing the net income from his farm for his annual return, shall include all moneys received for produce and animals sold, and for the wool and hides of animals slaughtered, provided such wool and hides are sold, and he shall deduct therefrom the sums actually paid as purchase money for the animals sold or slaughtered during the year.

When animals were raised by the owner and are sold or slaughtered he shall *not* deduct their value as expenses or loss. He may deduct the amount of money actually paid as expense for producing any farm products, live stock, etc. In deducting expenses for repairs on farm property the amount deducted must not exceed the amount actually expended for such repairs during the year for which the return is made. (See page 3, item 6) The cost of replacing tools or machinery is a deductible expense to the extent that the cost of the new articles does not exceed the value of the old.

12 In calculating losses, only such losses as shall have been actually sustained and the amount of which has been definitely ascertained during the year covered by the return can be deducted.

13 Persons receiving fees or emoluments for professional or other services, as in the case of physicians or lawyers, should include all actual receipts for services rendered in the year for which return is made, together with all unpaid accounts, charges for services, or contingent income due for that year, if good and collectible.

14 Debts which were contracted during the year for which return is made, but found in said year to be worthless, may be deducted from gross income for said year, but such debts can not be regarded as worthless until after legal proceedings to recover the same have proved fruitless, or it clearly appears that the debtor is insolvent. If debts contracted prior to the year for which return is made were included as income in return for year in which said debts were contracted, and such debts shall subsequently prove to be worthless, they may be deducted under the head of losses in the return for the year in which such debts were charged off as worthless.

15 Amounts due or accrued to the individual members of a partnership from the net earnings of the partnership, whether apportioned and distributed or not, shall be included in the annual return of the individual.

16 United States pensions shall be included as income.

17 Estimated advance in value of real estate is not required to be reported as income, unless the increased value is taken up on the books of the individual as an increase of assets.

18 Costs of suits and other legal proceedings arising from ordinary business may be treated as an expense of such business, and may be deducted from gross income for the year in which such costs were paid.

19 An unmarried individual or a married individual not living with wife or husband shall be allowed an exemption of $3,000. When husband and wife live together they shall be allowed jointly a total exemption of $4,000 on their aggregate income. They may make a joint return, both subscribing thereto, or if they have separate incomes, they may make separate returns, but in no case shall they jointly claim more than $4,000 exemption on their aggregate income.

20 In computing net income there shall be excluded the compensation of all officers and employees of a State or any political subdivision thereof, except when such compensation is paid by the United States Government.

The **Birth** of **Withholding Taxes**

Bad, Bad Beardsley [Ruml]

One of the greatest villains in tax history was Beardsley Ruml, treasurer of a New York retailing giant, who served as chairman of the board of directors of the Federal Reserve Bank of New York and was an adviser to President Franklin Roosevelt during World War II.

Faced with an immediate need to double taxes to finance participation in World War II, the US government imposed an income tax on tens of millions of Americans who had never been taxed this way before – the "class tax" became a "mass tax." Remember that up until this time in 1939, 26 years after the constitutional amendment that authorized income taxes, only 5% of the population earned enough to be required to file returns.

Ruml's insidious contribution was packaging this unpalatable concept. From his experience in retailing, he had learned that customers preferred making a series of small installment payments rather than paying a big bill all at once. Therefore, he recommended that the government get businesses to do the work of collecting the taxes. Employers would be required to retain an income tax of approximately 20% from workers every week and forward it directly to Washington. Workers would no longer even need to see the money they were forgoing; government could now put its hands directly into the taxpayer's pocket and take whatever it wanted – without asking. This manoeuver effectively camouflaged the size of the new taxes being taken from the workers. Withholding, as we know it today, was born.

The packaging was masterfully designed. The program was not labelled "collected at source" or "withholding," both accurate and descriptive technical terms for what was being done, but rather used the wily phrase: "pay as you go."

Other factors came into play:

- Ordinarily Americans, with their history of recurrent tax revolts, would not have tolerated

BEARDSLEY RUML – The Most Fiendish Man of the 20th Century

this blatant invasion of their economic privacy, but the government caught them at a time when their defenses were down. They were wounded by the Japanese assault on Pearl Harbor, and were, at that moment, willing to sacrifice more than at any other point in memory.

- The federal government had 6 successful years of withholding and administering Social Security which demonstrated that, for the first time ever, it was able to handle such a massive program of revenue collection.
- Keynesians said that high taxes were crucial to controlling inflation and saw withholding as the right tool for getting them.
- Conservatives also played their part. Among withholding's backers was the man who was later to become the world's leading free-market economist, Milton Friedman. Decades after the war, Friedman called for the abolition of the withholding system. In his memoirs he wrote, "We concentrated single-mindedly on promoting the war effort. We gave next to no consideration to any longer-run consequences. It never occurred to me at the time that I was helping to develop machinery that would make possible a government that I would come to criticize severely as too large, too intrusive, too destructive of freedom. Yet, that was precisely what I was doing." With an almost audible sigh, Friedman added: "There is an important lesson here. It is far easier to introduce a government program than to get rid of it."

The US Federal Debt [83]

The recent explosion of federal debt in the US belies a history in which holding down or reducing the debt in peacetime was the norm. Until the Republican "revolution" of 1994, responsibility for creating the debt was in the hands of members of the US Congress, who stood to gain politically by increasing government spending without applying off-setting taxes.

In 1792, the federal government was still in the process of establishing itself, and its budget deficit amounted to fully 38% of revenues. The next year, however, the government sharply reduced expenses while enjoying increased tax receipts and showed its 1st budget surplus. Except during periods of grave economic or military crisis, the government would never again run up so large an annual deficit in terms of a percentage of total revenues.

That is, until the peaceful and relatively prosperous year of 1992. That year the federal government had revenues of $1.076 trillion and outlays of $1.475 trillion, a budget deficit equalling 37% of revenues. In fact, the last 18 years of the nation's history have been marked by a more than 25% increase in federal revenues (in constant dollars) and the collapse of the only significant external military threat. Yet in those years, the US spent as much of tomorrow's money as it would have spent fighting a major war or new Great Depression. That will have significant consequences if it actually has to fight a major war or a depression.

How did the world's oldest continuously constituted republic lose control of so fundamental a responsibility as its own budget? Over the last 60 years, 5 trends have increasingly affected government fiscal policy:

- First, a powerful but fundamentally flawed concept in economics (Keynesianism) has changed the way economists and politicians view the national economy as well as their responsibilities.
- Second, the responsibilities of government in general and the federal government in particular, as viewed by the public, have greatly increased.
- Third, a shift in power from the executive branch to Congress has fragmented the budget process

by sharply limiting the influence of the single politician whose constituency is national in scope, the President.
- Fourth, the decay of party discipline and the seniority system within Congress has further balkanized the budget process, dividing it among innumerable committees.
- Finally, the PAC system of financing congressional elections has given increased influence to special interests while sharply reducing that of the electorate as a whole.

The result is a budget system that has become ever more heavily biased toward spending. As a consequence, the national debt has been spiralling upward, not only in absolute numbers but as a percentage of the GDP as well. Today it stands at about 68% of the annual GDP, higher than it has ever been in peacetime except in the immediate aftermath of a great war.

To be sure, a country as rich and productive as the US can afford to service its present debt. But the current trend is ominous. Just consider: In the first 204 years of independence, the nation took on the burden of a trillion-dollar debt mostly to fight the wars that made and preserved the nation. The last 15 years, however, have added $4 trillion more for no better reason than to spare people in Washington the political inconvenience of having to say no to one constituent or another.

US Tax Freedom Day

Calendar Days 1980-1999

Taxpayer Relief Act of 1997:

aka the Accountant and Tax Lawyers Full-Employment Act

Tax professionals are an integral part of tax compliance in most well-developed countries. They exert bizarre dominance over all taxpayers because the complexity of the tax codes and various compliance requirements are beyond all but the most simple tax filings. Americans pay $40 billion a year to tax professionals for counsel, advice, or protection of some sort. The US Taxpayer Relief Act of 1997 was the country's 1st real cut in taxes in more than 10 years, but significant drawbacks included 800 new amendments, 290 new sections, and 36 new retroactive provisions added to the Internal Revenue Code.

Tax preparers H&R Block are one of the backbones of US tax compliance, specializing in handling the "shoebox" filings of unsophisticated taxpayers. "The passage of the 1997 Act marked a bright and happy day for any tax preparer, tax adviser, or tax publisher. This bill creates the most relief and causes the most confusion," burbled an October press release, before detailing the 11 rates the law visited on capital gains.

Henry Bloch, the firm's 75-year-old founder, offered some thoughts on the matter. "Every year a few more people throw up their hands and say, 'I can't prepare my return any more,'" he said. "Every time government changes things, business does increase." More complex changes mean more business for tax experts. Call it "Bloch's Law."

When the *H&R Block Income Tax Guide* was 1st published in the 1960s, it had 196 pages. By 1988, it was up to 317 pages; in 1998, its pages numbered 574. "Change is good for tax preparers" is an important corollary of Bloch's Law.

Today Block is so big that the federal government relies on the firm to get through the blizzard of 120 million individual returns filed each year. In March – at the high point of tax season – Block and its franchises had raked in $685 million from taxpayers in exchange for preparing and filing their returns. Even Wall Street has demonstrated its faith in Bloch's Law in dramatic fashion. In 1997, as the damage of the new tax law became clear, it bought up millions of shares in the nation's tax preparers. An economist with a Chicago bond house actually created a special Index of Complexity made up of the stock of the 3 publicly traded tax preparers.

Of course, it must be true that a complex code is good for the industry. Who has time to analyze the theory when sales volume goes up 10%?

What's the difference between the short and long income tax forms?

- If you use the short form, the government gets your money.
- If you use the long form, the accountant gets it.

The Clotfelter Rule of Thumb

Once every 10 years, the US Internal Revenue Service (IRS) conducts audits of 50,000 randomly selected taxpayers to build a statistically valid tax evasion profile. The random nature of this procedure is important: Ordinarily, tax audits concentrate on the highest income earners, in expectation of higher returns in taxes recovered.

On one of these decennial occasions, Charles Clotfelter, with access to the individual data points of the IRS data set, conducted an econometric study on the effects that the marginal tax rates were likely to have on individual rates of evasion.

Clotfelter found that marginal income tax rates influenced evasion significantly. His preferred estimate implied that unreported income went up 0.2% for each % increase in the income tax rate.

At higher income levels, presumably individuals do not resort to outright income tax evasion as much as to legal avoidance through tax reduction schemes. **The evidence from the IRS studies of tax compliance suggests that the bulk of tax evasion occurs among the independent business owners with relatively modest incomes.**

IRS Statistics (in US Dollars)[84]

Who Pays The Income Tax?

Income		Share of Income	Share of Taxes
Top 1%	(above $209,105)	14.6%	30.2%
5%	(above $96,104)	28.8%	48.8%
Top 10%	(above $72,092)	40.2%	60.5%
25%	(above $44,147)	63.4%	80.3%
Top 50%	(above $22,361)	85.5%	95.4%
Bottom 50%	(below $22,361)	14.5%	4.6%

Federal Tax Revenues

Total Taxes Paid (Fiscal Year 1998): $1.665 trillion

Individual Income Taxes	$768 billion	(46%)
Social Insurance Taxes	$573 billion	(34%)
Corporate Income Taxes	$197 billion	(12%)
(Excise, estate, and others)	$127 billion	(8%)

Filers Using Professional Preparers

1040EZ	1.8 million	(8% of EZ filers)
1040A	4.8 million	(19% of 1040A filers)
1040	52.4 million	(81% of 1040 filers)

Deductions Taken (in millions)

Filers who **Itemize**	35.3	(29%)
Filers with **Charitable Deductions**	31.6	(26%)
Filers with **Home Mortgage Deductions**	29.4	(24%)
Filers with **Medical Deductions**	5.4	(4%)

Estimated Preparation Time (TY '97)

1040	10.0 hr
Schedule A (Itemized Deductions)	4.5 hr
Schedule B (Interest and Dividend Income)	1.3 hr
Schedule C (Profit or Loss from a Business)	10.3 hr
Schedule D (Capital gains and losses)	4.3 hr

Which Agency Is Larger?

	IRS	FBI	Border Patrol
Annual Budget (Billions)	$7.8	$3.0	$0.7
Number of Employees/Agents	100,551	11,271	6,848

IRS

Department of the Treasury
Internal Revenue Service

IRS WANTS YOU

Income Taxes Due

	Single Filer	Joint Filer
$10,000	$1,504	$1,504
$20,000	$3,004	$3,004
$30,000	$5,203	$4,504
$40,000	$8,003	$6,004
$50,000	$10,803	$8,651
$60,000	$13,611	$11,451
$70,000	$16,711	$14,251
$80,000	$19,811	$17,051
$90,000	$22,911	$19,851
$100,000	$26,002	$22,656

How Big Is the Tax Code?

	Number of Pages	Number of Words
Internal Revenue Code	9,471	5.75 million
Tax Code Regulations	91,824	13.00 million
Total Tax Law	101,295	18.75 million
War and Peace	1,444	660,000
The Bible	1,291	774,746

Americans waste 5.5 billion person-hours of non-productive time each year just in complying with this onerous tax system.

Reliance Defence[85]

Upwards of 10 million working Americans do not file income tax returns or pay income tax. The numbers are growing exponentially each year as the tax revolt spreads, fuelled in part by the Reliance Defense.

How It Works

The 1st step is to acquire a set of legal opinion letters from licensed attorneys, CPA's, and other professionals who hold that no law requires you to file an income tax return and/or pay income taxes. Such letters are written on their letterheads, personally addressed to you, listing their legal and professional credentials. In general, courts have held that reliance on professional advice absolutely shows good faith as a matter of law.

Following receipt of such letters, make several copies and keep each in a separate place to guard against loss. Then stop filing tax returns. The Reliance Defense is effective only forward in time from the date of the letters. Therefore, obtain the legal opinions *in advance* of the deadline for filing.

Who Is Required to File

No one has yet found a law requiring filing an individual income tax return. One seminar offers a $50,000 reward to anyone who can find such a law; to date, no one has earned the reward. An officer of a corporation legally must file the corporation's tax return and pay corporate income taxes, but the requirement is for corporate, not personal income.

In the case of the infamous mobster Al Capone, common belief is that the IRS put Capone in jail for tax evasion back in the 1940's. Capone was a major mob leader who had murdered and stolen and violated Prohibition laws, but the government was unable to prove it. The public thought what the IRS wanted them to think: If Al Capone, who had the money, the clever strategies, and the best attorneys, could not escape the IRS, then no one could. But Capone was not convicted for failure to file an income tax return . . . he was convicted of perjury for submitting false information on his return. If he had not filed the return, he could not have been convicted.

Some argue that Article I, Section 8 of the US Constitution gives Congress the "power to lay and collect taxes . . ." but this refers to excises, customs, and corporate taxes, not taxes on an individual's earnings. The IRS claims that the 16th Amendment gives the authority to collect individual income tax; however, many attorneys advise that the 16th Amendment is invalid because it was never properly ratified. In addition, at the time the 16th Amendment was proposed, Webster's dictionary defined "income" as corporate profit. Furthermore, additional legal opinions convincingly confirm that citizens of the 50 states are not under the jurisdiction of the US government.

Therefore, no individual American has any legal obligation to file or pay income taxes, with the exception, perhaps, of those who profit from alcohol, tobacco, or firearms; officers of corporations on behalf of the corporation; federal employees; and inhabitants of Washington, DC, federal military bases, and US territories like Guam.

HISTORY OF SOCIAL SECURITY OLD AGE SURVIVORS INSURANCE (OASI) TAXES

Year	OASI Rate	Medicare (Hospital Ins. Rate)	Max. Taxable Wage Base	Maximum Contribution
1937	1.00 %	—	$3,000	$ 30
1949	1.00	—	3,000	30
1959	2.50	—	4,800	120
1969	4.20	0.60 *	7,800	374
1979	5.08	1.05	22,900	1,404
1989	6.06	1.45	48,000	3,605
1999	6.20	1.45	72,600 **	5,554 **

*Introduced at 0.35% in 1966   **An example: Wage base limit removed on 1.45% Medicare contribution in 1994

American Tax Compliance

Although 40% of Americans are not in compliance with the income tax code, the reasons for non-compliance are enlightening and have general application to all industrialized countries: (1) taxpayers lack the requisite knowledge of the tax law – of course, even tax lawyers and revenue agents cannot grasp the entire tax code these days; (2) taxpayers interpret the law differently than the revenue service (you can usually depend on most revenue services to inevitably make aggressive interpretations in favor of the government); (3) taxpayers lack record keeping sufficient to satisfy tax codes and (4) taxpayers make math errors or they rely on professional return preparers who make errors – if professional tax preparers cannot complete the tax returns accurately, it is very unlikely that ordinary taxpayers will be able to so.

Periodically, the US tax authority conducts a series of extremely intrusive audits of taxpayers selected at random and requires those taxpayers to document every item on their tax returns to the most minute detail. These audits are part of the Taxpayer Compliance Measurement Program (TCMP). The General Accounting Office, the US federal government's chief auditing authority, in a recent tax gap report said: "The TCMP data showed that 82% of those audited were not assessed fraud or negligence penalties, data that suggest that most of their noncompliance was unintentional."

The Cost of Tax Compliance

Despite an estimated $300 billion spent by the private sector trying to comply with the Federal income tax system, 40% of the US taxpayers are not in compliance with the current tax system. Money spent on complex tax compliance does not add to national productivity; it is only an overhead that real productivity has to cover. These data lend credence to the argument that complicated tax laws create great waste in compliance even among well-intentioned and generally compliant taxpayers.

A Time for Change

After almost 80 years of amendments, revisions, exceptions, loopholes, extenders, and the occasional overhaul, the current US tax code is a monument to complexity. Working Americans currently spend 5.5 billion person hours learning tax laws, finding the right forms, gathering receipts and cancelled checks, completing returns, and dealing with IRS problems. That is more time than is spent producing every car, truck, and van manufactured in the US! By one estimate, the needless time and paperwork costs the US economy a staggering $200 billion a year, calculated at minimum wage.

The current tax code is not only confusing to the average American, it is even confusing to professional tax preparers. In November of 1998, Money magazine asked 45 tax professionals to prepare a return for a fictional family. The results: No two came up with the same tax total and not one preparer calculated what the magazine believed to be the correct federal income tax. Fewer than 1 in 4 came within $1,000 of that figure.

According to the Tax Foundation, a flat tax would reduce compliance costs by 94%, freeing up resources that are currently wasted on record keeping, filing forms, learning the tax code, litigation, and tax avoidance.

No longer will families have to maintain shoe boxes filled with receipts and cancelled checks. In a flat tax world, instead of fighting with your spouse about who lost what receipt, you would be able to spend quiet evenings and long weekends together enjoying a peaceful spring.

The current tax code fosters not only resentment toward the government, but toward our fellow citizens. One reason is that our nation's capital is dominated by 67,000 lobbyists who seek to advance the agenda of special interests rather than the broader public interest. Not surprisingly, more lobbyists work on taxes than any other issue.[86]

– Dick Armey, *106th US Congress*
Excerpted from Flat Tax – Not Just a Distant Dream

A dog who thinks he is man's best friend is a dog who obviously has never met a tax lawyer. – Fran Lebowitz

Digging into the UgEcon

The *types* of UgEcon activities in the US are very similar to those experienced in other developed economies, but the *level* has traditionally been significantly below the average of the OECD countries. Americans have a strong tradition of being tax compliant, and a large portion of the taxpayers is captive to the withholding tax system.

However, tax experts acknowledge that billions of dollars in potential tax revenues go unreported and uncollected, largely **because Americans are dissatisfied with government.** The "tax gap" – the difference between what is due and what is paid – is rising sharply. The IRS, notoriously conservative in its estimates, concedes the current gap has more than doubled in the last 10 years.

Drug dealers and hit men are not the only ones who swap products and services for good old untraceable cash. Air-charter operators, babysitters, lawyers, innkeepers, construction workers, salespeople, and morticians also evade the taxes in this way, as do cab companies, gas-station owners, truckers, and musicians. Experts estimate that legal, but unreported, underground income has quadrupled in the last 20 years. It is calculated that 75% of the individual tax gap comes from unreported income, mainly from self-employment.[71]

The UgEcon is an unquestionably fast-growth sector – increasing about 8% a year, compared with 3% for legitimate businesses, and these figures do not include activity in the truly criminal world.[87]

More tax compliance guidelines are on the way, as the IRS hones in on businesses likely to be able to hide income. It is also beefing up efforts to ensure that taxpayers understand their obligations.

In an interesting contradiction of facts, IRS spokespersons recently said that about 83% of the taxes Americans owe their federal government come in voluntarily. Audits and other enforcement methods yield another 4%. But they acknowledge that 13% of taxes slip through the cracks, a share that has been roughly the same for the past 20 years.

Note the major discrepancy between data showing that the UgEcon has grown 4-fold in the last 20 years and other data contending that tax evasion behavior has not changed in 20 years. It is our position that the 1st estimate is probably fairly accurate and the later statements attributed to IRS spokespersons are no more than wishful thinking on the part of the bureaucrats.

The UgEcon is a traditional way to avoid taxes, and the temptation to cheat is growing as taxes take bigger bites out of Americans' incomes. According to the National Taxpayers Union, average Americans in 1964 had to work until April 13 to earn enough to pay their taxes. By 1994, the break-even date was May 5, and by 1999, the date slipped to May 11. As the burden gets heavier, the burrows of hidden coffers can only get deeper.[20]

The UgEcon Is Nothing New

The 1990 census reports a 1989 per-capita income of $12,200 in the rural Bakersfield, California, "metropolitan area." But the Bureau of Economic Analysis (BEA) reports that Bakersfield residents' average personal income that year was 21% higher ($14,800). Such differences show up whenever data from different sources are compared. Even a decade ago, BEA figures ranged 10-25% higher than census data.

BEA reports are based on administrative records combined with a macroeconomic model. They include transfer payments, in-kind contributions, and non-cash income. They do not presume to capture the entire underground economy, but they do show that households' self-reporting of money income does not tell the whole story.

Edgar Feige,

University of Wisconsin economist, is the father of US UgEcon analysis. He is responsible for conducting the most careful analysis ever of the issue of the UgEcon. Professor Feige concludes that based on the amount of US currency held abroad, **an UgEcon equal to the size of the US economy is hidden among the unreported economic activities in the world's** *other countries.*

The US Criminal Prosecution of Foreign Nationals

Growth of the UgEcon in the US has been fueled by the sharp increase in applying extra-territorial criminal sanctions under US export legislation. As a result, foreign nationals are being prosecuted using law enforcement practices that often are at odds with prevailing international law. For example, purchases of non-arms goods and services can be considered criminal because they will eventually reach embargoed countries such as Cuba, Iran, Iraq, and Libya. One consequence has been inordinately complex and often contradictory laws and regulations that defy fair application.

This high-handed, unilateral, and overzealous use of economic sanctions has made criminals out of many unknowing individuals and driven many more to trade in the UgEcon. To limit the increasingly detrimental effects of its international export control policy, from the perspective of diplomacy as well as criminal justice, the US must take the following actions: exercise restraint in extra-territorial jurisdiction; limit the scope of its investigations; select cases carefully; respect the sovereignty of other countries; and pay attention to international human rights laws, including laws regarding apprehension and pre-trial treatment of foreigners and fairness throughout the criminal justice process as it is applied to foreigners. Because these cases involve large foreign and inter-national legal entities, the failure to cooperate closely with foreign governments will continue to have adverse short- and long-term con-sequences for curtailing the activities the US is trying to stop. In addition, this failure to cooperate will continue to increase the already negative US reputation for encroach-ing on the sovereignty of other friendly nations.

> Our system of taxation is based upon voluntary assessment and payment, not upon distraint.
> – Supreme Court,
> US v. Flora, 362 US 145

California's UgEcon Strike Force

California usually leads the US – and often the rest of the world – in innovation. In 1994, its governor created a joint strike force on the UgEcon, consisting of agencies from labor and employment to justice and taxation. The strike force is modeled after a program that conducted sweeps of businesses throughout the state to inspect for compliance with labor and unemployment insurance tax laws.

Businesses operating in the UgEcon avoid payroll and sales taxes by not reporting activities or by paying for goods and services in cash. In California alone, these tax shortfalls run an estimated $2 billion per year. Such businesses frequently are unlicensed and also cut corners by violating labor laws regarding minimum wage, paying in cash without proper records or withholding of taxes, or failing to have workers' compensation insurance. These actions not only cost the state tax revenues, but undercut the competitiveness of employers who obey the law.

The initial program found an 80% correlation between businesses that failed to comply with the unemployment insurance tax laws and businesses that failed to provide mandatory workers' compensation insurance. Industries identified as having the highest incidence of violations were the 1st target of the efforts, beginning with the con-struction industry. In the program's 1st 17 months, a total of 13,604 inspections were conducted in a variety of industries, resulting in 3,738 citations, with penalty assessments of more than $9.5 million.

The sweeps also netted 2,638 tax audit leads, for which the average tax assessment was $3,100.

Conclusion
The **Founding Fathers Need Your Help**

The Protection Racket

In researching the Mafia it is noteworthy to see that it defines its core business as "protection." There is a remarkable similarity to the purpose of governments. Historically taxes were paid to kings in return for the right to use "their" land and to be *protected* in the course of everyday existence.

A Break with Tradition

As we have seen elsewhere in this book, income taxes, including the heinous withholding taxes, were created to pay for wars – on the presumption that wars protect the freedom of the taxpayer.

In most countries the history of war taxes is that they were discontinued once the war debt had been paid. That long-standing tradition was broken by virtually all countries at the end of WWII. Taxpayers of developed countries were blinded by the abundance of the postwar boom, income taxes were reasonably low, and times were prosperous.

After the end of the war, governments, addicted to high revenues and even higher spending habits, decided that wealth redistribution was a justifiable reason to continue income taxes. Not content with spending the rapidly increasing income tax revenues, governments continued to layer on a variety of other taxes, most notably sales taxes, but even these new taxes could not satisfy the profligate spending and enormous deficits that became common practice. In Italy and Canada the interest cost of the debt has grown to about 25% of the tax revenue *stream.* This means taxpayers can receive a maximum of 75¢ worth of services for every dollar paid.

Semi-hidden debts such as massive unfunded pension plans (see page 47) have been ignored in all but a few countries (Chile and the few adherents to the Chilean privatized, free-market model).

The government has invested heavily in social marketing to convince taxpayers that paying high taxes is a solemn obligation. It has gone out of its way to intensify enforcement processes to reinforce the "voluntary" nature of most income tax systems. All of this imperious behavior should raise the founding fathers of the country from their graves. The US has developed the same bad habits of England's King George III that precipitated the American Revolution 225 years ago.

High-Profile Tax Dodgers

Our Tax-Evader Poster Child – Leona Helmsley – is not alone in her tax problems. Other celebrities, famous and infamous, also have got into trouble with the US tax authorities:

In 1998, **Heidi Fleiss**, the notorious Hollywood madam, received a sentence of 37 months in prison. Guilty of tax evasion, laundering prostitution profits, and conspiring to cover up her actions, she was also ordered to serve 300 hours of community service.

Clothing and cosmetics entrepreneur **Gloria Vanderbilt** owes millions of dollars in back taxes and has been forced out of both her Long Island, NY, mansion and Manhattan apartment.

Beatles-era artist **Peter Max** was indicted for neglecting to report over $1.1 million in arts sales.

The triumphant and tragic **Judy Garland,** country singer **Willie Nelson,** and rock-and-roll pianist/singer **Jerry Lee Lewis** also made headlines with their tax woes.

Thomas Paine's Classic

Tax Protests: Sedition or Patriotism

The oppressive stamp tax of George III, drove solid citizens to revolt, and was the precipitating cause of the Revolution.

A Need for Stronger Medicine

Like strains of bacteria that become resistant to formerly effective antibiotics, governments shrug off compelling data and informed opinions and proceed on their self-serving paths.

There are dozens of think tanks all over the political spectrum with good ideas, but most of their information gets shunned by the governments and is often over the head of the average taxpayer. They end up preaching to their own choirs and occasionally to each other. The time has come to actively challenge the publicly accepted scope of government authority.

, from the more wretched parts of the old world, we look at those which are in an advanced stage of improvement, we still find

The Greedy Hand of Government

rusting itself into every corner and evice of industry, and grasping the oil of the multitude. Invention is ontinually exercised, to furnish new retenses for revenues and taxation. watches prosperity as its prey and ermits none to escape without tribute.
— *Thomas Paine, Rights of Man*

You're asking the government to control individual morality.

This is a government that can't buy a toilet seat for under $600.
— Peter McWilliams

Stopping Income Tax Withholding:

Taxes are the backbone of any politico-economic regime and limitations on a government's power to tax are constraints on its power to act. Withholding on income tax at the source, an invention to finance WWII, is the paramount administrative mechanism enabling the federal government to collect, without significant protest, sufficient private resources to fund a vastly expanded welfare state. Governments of all the OECD member countries now view withholding as the cornerstone of administering individual income tax. As a US tax official said in testimony before the US Senate, more than 100 years ago, "Wherever an income tax has been in practice for any time the small incomes as well as the large are taxed; and it is the small incomes which yield the largest revenue to the state.[108]

The history of income tax withholding involves extensive misrepresentation by government officeholders; since withholding itself alters perceptions of private tax burdens, one may legitimately be concerned with use of political deception. The scam used by politicians and bureaucrats is to create the optics that a situation is a crisis. If there is a crisis, actions can be taken, usually without direct opposition, that would otherwise be considered gross violations of regime boundaries.[44]

A Time to Stand and Be Counted

We hope that you will make the choice to become an active force for overt tax redesign and to hold politicians accountable for their economic decisions. Anyone can take the passive course of covert participation in the UgEcon, but it takes knowledge, courage, and a real concern about the future of your country to stand tall and say, "Starve the beast; it is time to slash government spending and chop the tax burden."

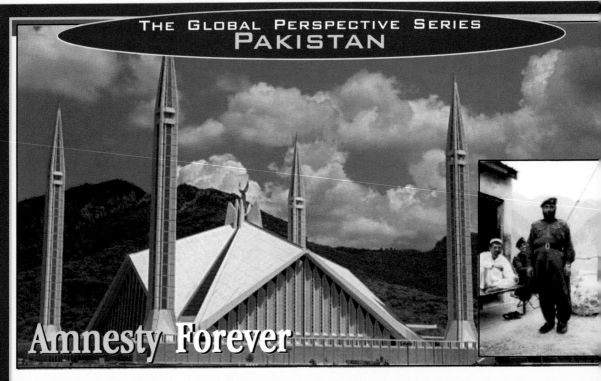

Amnesty Forever

Pakistan's government acknowledges that the UgEcon constitutes 25% of the GDP. However, this estimate, it is quick to qualify, does not include either the informal or the illegal sectors. In a country that spends 80% of its revenues on debt service and defence, little is left to spend on its people. The average per capita expenditure on education, health, and social services is about $10 a year. Like India, Pakistan spends $5 on defence for every $1 it spends on education, health, and social services. Consequently, the people have little motivation to pay taxes when they receive so few tangible benefits.

In a country with no tradition of paying taxes, corruption and smuggling are major industries. Leather, one of the country's main consumer exports, is cursed by a worldwide oversupply. Another major consumer export, textiles (in particular, unbleached cotton fabrics and bed linens), has been severely damaged by anti-dumping sanctions imposed by the EU.

India and Pakistan were once one country. But ever since the partition of the sub-continent more than 50 years ago, they have been arch rivals. Their animosity has its roots in religion, and has recently escalated into a dangerous nuclear arms race.

Tax Amnesties

The OECD argues strongly that tax amnesties are ineffective because people believe that if a government grants amnesty once, it is likely to do so again. Despite this fact, amnesty has played a major role in the various money-whitening schemes that have been introduced in Pakistan in the past 4 decades. With these repeated attempts to use amnesty to bring more activity into the formal economy, Pakistan offers strong empirical proof of its declining impacts:

- The 1958 Amnesty attracted 77,289 new tax filers, with formerly undisclosed income of Rs 1.36 billion.
- The 1969 Amnesty attracted fewer than 10% new taxpayers.
- The 1976-77 Amnesty generated only Rs 450 million.
- The 1985 Amnesty, in the form of Special National Fund Bonds, added 32,000 new tax filers and generated Rs 1.52 billion (measured in bonds at the face value).
- The 1992 Amnesty, in the form of Foreign Currency Account, was introduced with full immunity against any probe. Participation was minimal, and collections were meagre.
- The 1998 Tax Amnesty Scheme attracted only 2,780 new tax filers, and the total revenue generated was Rs 173.4 million.

A Perspective from the IMF

A long-term IMF report (1974-91), *The Underground Economy: Estimation, Economic and Policy Implications – The Case of Pakistan,* presents a more analytical picture. This report shows that while the formal economy was stagnant over this extended period, the UgEcon in Pakistan grew at an estimated annual average of 9%.

The report observes that structural reform program and economic liberalization policies had a dampening effect on the UgEcon. However, high budget deficits and the absence of either expenditure reduction or rapid economic and revenue growth led to a higher tax burden on the formal economy, forcing more activities to go to the underground sector.

The report suggests that a reduction in spending or an increase in revenue-enhancement measures (e.g., widening the tax base and reducing the number of exemptions in the existing tax structure) would be more effective in stimulating the economy. It also suggests that Pakistan should make deficit reduction commitments and maintain them for 5 years in order to have lasting effects on the UgEcon.

Nearly a decade after the report, no positive changes have occurred. Economic expectations are dismal for this country with an irritable government that is locked in a series of military confrontations with India (ostensibly over the control of Kashmir) and seems more focused on a holy war than on enhancing the welfare of its people.

Corruption: The Sport of the Rich

Immediately after the late 1999 coup, the witch hunt, a tradition in Pakistani politics, started. In a massive crackdown on major loan defaulters and those involved in corruption, the civil and military authorities arrested 23 of the country's wealthiest people. The country-wide crackdown against corrupt former rulers, politicians, industrialists, feudals, senior officials, and retired armed-forces personnel, marked the start of across-the-board accountability. More than 350 more people were rounded-up on similar charges.

Pakistan's priority

Formal Name:	**Islamic Republic of Pakistan**
Local Name:	Pakistan
Local Formal Name:	Islamic Republic of Pakistan
Location:	Asia
Status:	**UN Country**
Capital City:	**Islamabad**
Main Cities:	Karachi, Lahore, Faisalabad
Population:	**131,434,000**
Area [sq.km]:	**796,100**
Currency:	**1 Pakistan rupee = 100 paisa**
Main Languages:	Urdu, Punjabi
Main Religions:	Sunni Muslim

Deposed prime minister Nawaz Sharif was accused of being the kingpin in the corruption schemes. His predecessor in the PM's office, Benazir Bhutto, was also convicted of corruption and sentenced to 5 years in jail.

Two businessmen who quickly "repaid" their loans were able to avoid prosecution. Their names were deleted from the list after they repaid their loans. It demonstrates that if you are rich and are well-connected, your punishment for stealing is that you just might have to give the money back.

Coup Leader,
General Pervaiz Mushrraf

Revenue Canada Becomes "The Agency"

*I*n order to "provide better service to the public, the provinces, and Canadian business," 1998's Bill C-43 changed Revenue Canada to The Canada Customs and Revenue Agency — "The Agency." Status as an agency means that the new organization has more flexibility to manage its resources and operations according to its own in-house approaches. The Agency asserts that experience in the UK and Australia has shown that greater managerial autonomy improves the efficiency of administration and service to the public with "the potential to reduce costs for business, taxpayers, and governments."

The Agency claims that it will be able to offer more streamlined services and improved response times. It will also be in a better position to offer provinces and territories new ways to reduce paperwork burdens and expenses for companies, particularly those that are small or medium sized.

The Canada Customs and Revenue Agency carries out its mandate through 4 lines of business:

- **Revenue Generation:** the appropriate assessment and collection of taxes, duties, and levies.
- **Customs Border Services:** a full range of services at Canada's international borders, including processing travellers and commercial goods; and monitoring and controlling the importation of firearms, drugs, and other restricted cargo.
- **Income Redistribution:** delivery of a number of social and economic benefits on behalf of the Government of Canada through the tax system such as GST credits, Child Tax Benefit, and other programs.
- **Trade Administration:** multilateral and bilateral international agreements, such as the NAFTA, APEC and conventions of the WTO and GATT, domestic trade policy agreements, and duties relief programs.

POINT

"The new Canada Customs and Revenu Agency is the springboard our country needs to ensure Canada has the best customs, and trade administration in world. This legislation will provide the necessary framework for change, and will create opportunities to lead us in the next millennium. The Agency provid opportunities for millions of dollars in savings for government, business, and all Canadians."
  — **Herb Dhaliwal,** former Minister of Nat Revenue and MP (Vancouver South-Burnab

COUNTERPOIN

"Creation of the Canada Customs and Revenue Agency will cost taxpayers millions of dollars to 'repackage' what already exists, with no savings. Furthermore, it adds a bureaucratic layer with a Board of Management and secretariat. We are convinced there is no valid business case for the propose agency from either a public or employe perspective. This legislation offers noth ing new to the Canadian public except higher cost and lower accountability. Instead of wasting tax dollars, wouldn taxpayers rather have a tax cut?"
  — **Steve Hindle,** President, The Hill Tim

To doubt the efficacy of this restructuring, you need only know that the plan had the full support of The Professional Institute of the Public Service of Canada, the largest union representing professionals working in the public service of Canada. "As a union representing 7,100 professionals at

The Canadian Income Tax Act is more than 1,500 pages lon

Revenue Canada, we must ensure that our members are not needlessly stripped of important rights that are well established for federal public service employees."

A recent analysis by the *Canadian Tax Journal* concludes that the tax savings projected by Revenue Canada are "relatively modest and depend on the assumption that all provincial taxes in all provinces (or in all except Quebec) will be administered by a single tax authority."

Revenue Canada has misled the Canadian government and taxpayers into thinking that no costs were associated with the creation of The Agency. Instead, Revenue Canada documents reveal a $187 million shortfall this fiscal year for the 1st time in history. Thousands of employees were diverted to work on the agency concept instead of administering Canada's tax laws in a fair and timely manner. Because travel budgets have been cut, tax auditors are limited in their ability to conduct reassessments, and tax "collectors" are being restricted in their ability to collect taxes owing.

The structure proposed for the new agency adds an additional level of bureaucracy, which will require time, money, and staff. It will cost millions of dollars to reprint thousands of forms, publications, letterhead, and business cards; to change signs on all taxation and customs offices and border crossings; to change the identification on customs uniforms and vehicles and to modify the computer systems. This Bill creates a new commissioner, which will be another patronage position to be appointed by the government. In theory, the new agency will remain accountable to Parliament for its activities and performance through the submission of a regular annual report. However, The Agency will have carte blanche with respect to contracts and with respect to the management of property, material, information, and technology. With limited outside oversight, the "optics" of favoritism and abuse of power by bureaucrats is very high.

What Are Fair Taxes?

A *Reader's Digest*/Gallup Canada phone poll was administered to a cross-section of 1,014 Canadians in December, 1998. For each question, respondents were instructed to think about "*not* just federal income taxes, but all the taxes you pay to the federal, provincial, and local governments, including income and sales taxes, and local property taxes." The poll clearly reveals that *the vast majority of the Canadian people feel the present tax burden is unfair* – a sweeping and deeply held belief that we are all overtaxed.

Another crucial finding is extraordinary personal unhappiness with the amount Canadians personally pay in taxes. An astounding 83% of respondents feel their own total tax payments are "too high."

Evaluating their mean responses, we found that respondents underestimated their own and other families' tax burdens by as much as 25%. For example, Canadians think a family earning $67,000 pays only 39% in taxes, when the figure is in reality over 50%. Asked to estimate their own overall tax burden, respondents do better. The mean response of 41.75% is close to the actual national average of 48.2%.

"What is the highest percentage you think would be fair for a family making $134,000 a year to pay when you add all their taxes together?" Canadians earning less than $20,000 think a family of four earning $134,000 should pay no more than 34% a year in taxes. In real life, such a family pays, on average, 51% of its total income in taxes. Nearly 40% of respondents feel those earning $134,000 are paying too much tax.

A perennial claim is that taxpayers are angry because they think other Canadians are not paying enough taxes. "People are especially frustrated when they hear about millionaires and corporations that don't pay their fair share of taxes," says a Liberal MP.[89] But despite the often-heard belief that the poor and middle class resent

*In a stellar example of **innumerate** reporting by the media, the reporter said "Canada's total tax burden is 14% higher than the US rate." In reality, if the Canadian rate is 39% and the US rate is 25%, the Canadian rate is actually 56% higher (39 <u>divided by</u> 25 NOT 39 <u>minus</u> 25).*

"the privileged," the poll found that **Canadians at every income level feel overtaxed.**

To a remarkable degree, different groups of Canadians agree that they themselves pay too much in taxes. The percentage is the same for residents of British Columbia and the Atlantic Provinces (84%), virtually the same for men and women (84%-81%) and for English and French speakers (82% - 84%). Liberals and conservatives differed by a mere 8 points: 87% of self-described conservatives feel their taxes are too high, compared to 79% of liberals.

Canadians with children living at home are especially dissatisfied: An incredible 100% of those with 3 or more children aged between 10 and 17 say they pay too much, versus 81% of those without children at home. Overall, *just 15% of respondents say the taxes they pay are fair.*

This broad dissatisfaction has not always been the case. According to survey research from the Gallup Organization, as recently as 1962, Canadians were almost equally divided between those who thought their taxes were "too high" (47%) and those who thought they were "about right" (43%).

Since then, though, the percentage of dissatisfied Canadians has risen steadily. By 1975, 66% thought their taxes were too high and only 27% were satisfied – a 39-point gap. By 1987, the gap had widened to 49 points, with 72% dissatisfied and 23% thinking their taxes were fair.

The Voice of Experience

Poll participant Doug Thompson, 73, of Amherst, NS, feels strongly that the government does not need to take half of every dollar Canadians make. Thompson, retired from the Department of Transportation where he worked for more than 30 years as a road grader and superintendent, says: "I know. I've seen the waste and the expensive, needless bureaucracy of government first-hand.

"You could easily get the same services for half the cost."

How Much Is Fair?

The poll showed strong consensus on the issue of tax fairness. When asked to name the highest total tax a family of 4 should pay, respondents across economic, ethnic, ideological, and age lines answered with surprising uniformity: 29%.

When the question was worded a little differently, people were asked to consider a family of four "that makes a high income." What is the "highest percentage that you think would be fair for any family to pay in all their taxes combined, no matter how high their income?"

The maximum tax burden Canadians think a family of four should bear is 29%. That's not just federal income tax. That's 29% for all major levies combined – federal, provincial, and local – including income, sales, and property taxes.

The consensus was striking; roughly 29% was suggested by those in their 30's and those over 65, English speakers and French speakers, even conservatives and liberals.

"This consensus is startling and indicates a growing dissatisfaction with the government's taxation policies," says Gary Edwards, vice president and general manager of Gallup Canada. Edwards, who conducted the Reader's Digest poll, has more than a decade of experience in survey research. "It is intriguing that taxpayers across Canada, regardless of their age, politics or class, had such a similar idea of what is the 'ideal' fair tax. It indicates an opinion that is pretty much nationwide."

It's not surprising that so many Canadians in your poll underestimate their own and other families' tax burdens. We are so overtaxed – paying everything from income to liquor to airport departure taxes – that we have become numb to all these taxes. Canadians are suffering from "total tax fatigue."

Walter Robinson, Federal Director, The Canadian Taxpayers Federation

Contract Payment Reporting System

The federal government is providing more data about non-wage payments to The Agency. This move is designed to promote increased "voluntary" compliance by business and individuals who are engaged under contract to provide services to departments, agencies, and crown corporations. It is important to understand the special meaning attached to "voluntary" compliance by taxing authorities; it most typically means, "Is there a systematic way to increase the risk factor associated with tax evasion so that fewer taxpayers and potential taxpayers will elect not to report the income?" Any payments made to the taxing authorities without audit assessments are deemed to have been voluntary. [90]

In January of 1998, federal government departments and agencies resumed reporting the contract payments made to all forms of businesses (individuals, small business, corporations, partnerships, etc.) where the total payments for service contracts are greater than $333. T4A information slips [income reports] are now issued annually. Crown Corporations began to report such contract payments as well, effective January 1, 1999.

Some of the provincial governments have undertaken similar initiatives, and discussions are under way with others.

Enforcement Efforts

The Agency has undertaken several other activities in the construction and home renovation sector, including the following:

- More than 13,000 UgEcon audits have been completed in the sector, resulting in reassessments of $110 million in previously unreported taxes.
- Additional sources of information, including building permits, municipal and provincial licensing, and information from materials suppliers are being used to help identify UgEcon activity.
- A revised GST New Housing Rebate form was introduced in 1997. As part of the form, owner-builders are required to provide information on who did the work and how much was paid.

- The Agency and the Canadian Home Builders' Association established a working group to address areas of mutual concern.
- A consultative framework has been established with the Canadian Construction Association to deal with compliance issues.
- The Agency has held meetings with local and national union representatives.
- The Agency participates in home renovation and industry trade shows to raise industry awareness of UgEcon issues and to provide consumers with information on the pitfalls of dealing with the UgEcon.

Although The Agency has been fairly aggressive in attempting to deal with some of the more blatant aspects of the UgEcon in the home renovation and construction industries, no data support that it has had any measurable impact on the epidemic growth in these industries. Even the $110 million in reassessments is an insignificant amount, given the size of the sectors.

Although enforcement is unlikely to promote compliance, the proper reporting of sub-contract payments will do so. It encourages voluntary compliance and is less intrusive than traditional enforcement actions. Such reporting will help to ensure that those who comply will not face the cost of an audit, while enabling The Agency to focus its enforcement actions on the most non-compliant.

High Filing Compliance

It should be noted that the rate of voluntary compliance among Canadian taxpayers, at 95%, is one of the highest in the world. Every year, the non-filer program deals with some 500,000 Canadians who have not fulfilled their tax obligation to file as required. The Agency's enforcement activities bring the overall rate of filing up to an estimated 98%. With a population of 30 million, Canadians file 21- 22 million tax returns, which is phenomenal. But this is not the same as saying that 98% of the taxes due are reported or even that 98% of the taxes reported are collected.[88]

Measuring Canada's UgEcon

The Agency, Statistics Canada, and the OECD, like most other governmental and international agencies, do not include illicit activities in UgEcon measurements, but include only activities which, other than being clandestine, are legal.

The Standing Committee on Public Accounts is the parliamentary oversight committee of The Agency. The Committee posed a very straightforward question to Barry Lacombe, the former assistant deputy minister of the Verification, Enforcement, and Compliance Research Branch of The Canada Customs and Revenue Agency. The question: "How does The Agency measure the size of the underground economy?" His answer:

Let me explain what we did. We did not, ourselves, go out and start measuring the size; it would have been a phenomenal task. But a lot of studies have been done on the size of the UgEcon. We hired some top-notch economists to come and work with us to review the studies and the methodology used in those studies, and to ask what was the difference in those studies. Some were giving huge numbers, such as 15% or 20%. Other studies, such as the one done by Mr. Drummond, for example, who is now Associate Deputy Minister of Finance, talk about 4.5%, and StatsCan came out with the number of 4.2%.[88] **As all readers of this book know by now, the answer given is utter nonsense.**

How Does the OECD Rate Canada's UgEcon?

Recent OECD reports indicate that the size of the UgEcon in Canada's economy is slightly higher than the average of other major industrialized countries (for 1995, 16%, as opposed to 13%). At the turn of this century, that figure clearly will exceed 18% of GDP, meaning that Canada's UgEcon is growing at one of the fastest rates in the developed world.

Although the OECD data are interesting on a comparative basis, the fairly narrow definition used in collecting them is not particularly helpful in measuring the impact in any single country. One area that is excluded is the fraudulent use of blatantly excessive business deductions (BEBD). This area has a very potent impact on Canada's data because of the disproportionately large number of self-employed workers. (See page 22 for a more on BEBD.)

The Self-Employment Option[91]

In the 1990's, Canadians have embraced self-employment at more than 4 times the rate of Americans. Although the proportion of the work force that is self-employed has grown in Canada over the last 10 years, that rate is unchanged in the US. More than *twice* as many Canadians are self-employed now than there were just 20 years ago; this contributes significantly to tax-evasion,

People have lost confidence in the government – as their taxes went up, up, up. The tax bill for the average Canadian family increased by **139%** (after inflation) between 1961 and 1998.
Michael Walker, President, The Fraser Institu

Are You an Active Participant in the UgEcon?

If you pay your housekeeper, gardener, handyman, or babysitter in cash – without GST – are you participating in the UgEcon?

If you have a reasonable expectation that the total income earned by that individual is less than $30,000, that person would be exempt from collecting GST. So the act of paying an individual in cash without GST is not per se participation in the UgEcon. However, if you have reason to believe

that the individual you are paying is not going to declare your payment as income on his or her tax return, then you *are* an active participant in the UgEcon.

An argument can be made that if you benefit from your participation in an "under the table" transaction, you are guilty of conspiracy to commit tax fraud. Therefore, you would be as culpable as the person who receives the payment and fails to declare it.

Estimated Tax Revenue Lost to the UgEcon

Size of UgEcon (as a % of GDP)	Lost Federal Revenue ($ billions)	Lost Provincial Revenue ($ billions)	Total CPP/QPP Lost Revenue ($ billions)	Total Lost Revenue ($ billions)
5 %	5.3	3.8	0.4	9.5
10 %	10.6	7.6	0.8	19.0
15 %	15.8	11.5	1.3	28.6
20 %	21.1	15.3	1.7	38.1
25 %	26.3	19.2	2.2	47.7
30 %	31.6	23.0	2.6	57.2

[92]

Canada's tax rates are very high. No other G-7 country takes as big a personal income bite out of its economy as Canada does:

Canada's personal tax rate is 47% higher than the average G-7 rate.

because it is more difficult to monitor home businesses than large corporations.

Fewer than 20,000 of the 700,000 self-employed Canadians who started businesses in the last decade have hired staff. Entrepreneurs without employees now account for 66% of all self-employed workers, up from 50% in the 1980's. Canada's taxation system offers the self-employed advantages that are not available to paid employees. Therefore, the costs and bureaucratic burden of having employees discourage entrepreneurs from hiring them; it is much simpler and less costly to use contract support on a project-by-project basis.

More than 2/3 of these new "businesses" are in the service sectors. In terms of education, the new entrepreneurs either are highly educated or have minimal formal education – the highly educated are *choosing* the advantages of self-employment, and the others may not have an alternative.

Canada's UgEcon

Cash businesses, such as taxis, waiters, flower shops, and corner stores, share a strong tradition of under-reporting. Businesses that invoice and are paid for service by check (automotive repair, lawn and garden services, or skilled trades) use a different gimmick: They often maintain 2 bank accounts and 2 or more sets of clients/invoices. The skimming portion of the business is deposited in a bank that is hidden from the accountants who prepare the business financial records and tax returns. Money from these 2nd bank accounts is often used to pay personal credit cards or the costs of 2nd homes.

A prominent Toronto lawyer was recently quoted in a major newspaper as saying, "I see lots of clients who demonstrably have the money to buy a house but can't quite qualify for a mortgage because their T-4's [income statements] don't show how much money they really make."[93]

Regional Differences

In Canada's 4 Atlantic provinces, evidence shows more UgEcon activity than in the rest of the country, particularly in the area of benefit fraud with seasonal workers. This raises a problem when we try to analyze StatsCan data. How do we adjust the employment rates to account for UgEcon? It seems clear that when we have high levels of UgEcon activity, the unemployment rate is a less viable economic indicator.

One of the best examples of this dilemma is British Columbia's booming cannabis crop, which is estimated to be as much as $1.34 billion a year. This would make this particular UgEcon "industry" equal to 7 times the size of the heavily publicized Pacific salmon industry.

The GST: A Canadian Red Herring

Peter Spiro, one of Canada's leading experts on the UgEcon, examined whether the introduction of the Goods and Service Tax (1991) prompted a sharp increase in the UgEcon and concluded, using an econometric equation for money demand, that the covert sector might have increased by 0.8 % of GDP by 1992. This is about the same growth that would have been anticipated without the unpopular tax.

Revenue Canada's UgEcon Initiative

By trying to combat the UgEcon, The Agency asserts that it is committed to ensuring fairness and equity in the tax system to create a level playing field for businesses and taxpayers. Therefore, in 1993, Revenue Canada declared war on the UgEcon, claiming it had a balanced action plan:

- identifying non-filers and GST non-registrants;
- special audit teams for 4 areas of high non-compliance: construction and home renovation, auto sales and repair, jewelry, and hospitality;
- cooperating with other federal departments and the provinces to encourage voluntary compliance ;
- working with key industry groups and professional associations to encourage voluntary compliance to identify UgEcon activities;
- increasing the visibility of compliance and enforcement activities by publicizing convictions for tax evasion and conducting community visits;
- reviewing and acting on public referrals; and
- increasing public awareness of the government's voluntary disclosure policy.

In terms of results, it reported the following:

- voluntary disclosures quadrupled since 1993;
- staff visited 160 communities and met with more than 29,000 businesses;
- more than $1.3 billion in additional taxes were collected from enforcement activities; and
- 480,000 returns from non-filers in 1996/97.[94]

Actual Results of The Initiative

In 1993, the Canadian Taxing Authority hired 1,200 new auditors to help to combat the UgEcon. About 200 staff were assigned to the non-filers and non-registrants programs and 1,000 staff to the auditing of small businesses. More than 35% of the audit staff for small and medium-sized businesses are now involved in the UgEcon initiative audit activities. The success, if any, has been very minimal.

Studies over the last year indicate that the underground economy has reached such staggering proportions that it is at a minimum 15% of the Canadian economy and most likely approaches 25%.
– Joseph Volpe, *Liberal MP*
Parliamentary Secretary to Minister of Health, May, 1993

"In terms of the marginal impact of the extra 1,200 auditors, the program evaluation did indeed break out how much revenue was attributable to those extra 200 who went into non-filers. On a per-auditor basis, the revenue generated was $340,000 per FTE per year."
– Barry Lacombe, *former chief of the Enforcement and Compliance branch of The Agency* [88]

Although it was initially reported that The Initiative had a tax impact of more than $1.3 billion in its first 5 years, further analysis determined that this amount included regular, ongoing enforcement programs. After re-evaluation, estimates were revised to less than $335 million in *reassessments* during that period.

That $335 million attributed to the increase in staff over a 5-year period works out to an average of just over $50,000 per auditor per year, presumably *less than half of that in actual collections.* It is probably accurate to say that each additional field auditor produced a maximum of $25,000 per FTE. When you offset salary, benefits, travel, and office overheads to these amounts, **the auditors, at best, may have covered their costs, but failed to add a single cent of "profit" to the government's treasury.**

Tax Cops Are Losing

Barry Lacombe spent 5 years at the head of the federal government's Underground Economy Initiative. However, most of the tax dodgers he and his 1,200-member team found were of the garden variety.

"The task force has generated very little in the way of results," said University of Victoria Economics professor Peter Giles, a consultant on a recent report to the federal government. *"Canada has had a very poor return on that investment."*

Foreign Reporting Rules [60]

Capital Flight

Much more serious than the occasional tax protest has been the emergence of a very aggressive level of tax avoidance, leading to a flight of investment capital from North America. As a result, in 1994, 2,400 Canadians opened tax avoidance structures in the Cayman Islands.[49] This is only the tip of the iceberg; a check of the Internet yields hundreds of companies that are in the business of selling aggressive tax avoidance schemes. Major newspapers and upscale magazines offer a comprehensive array of offshore alternatives. (This subject is covered in more detail on page 66, "Getting Your Money Offshore.")

The Canadian Tax Foundation shares the concerns raised in many quarters about the growth of these aggressive international tax avoidance arrangements. A particularly thorny issue is that this growth often appears to be fueled by those advocating contentious schemes that depend on tenuous technical arguments and non-disclosure. Voluntary self-assessment will not continue to work if honest taxpayers feel others are beating the system through aggressive tax avoidance and evasion.

Immigration Attorneys Tell Their Clients to Ignore Tax Laws

Section 233.3 of the Income Tax Act requires Canadians to report annually the details of their foreign assets. This provision is designed to ensure that Canadian tax is paid on income earned from such assets and could ensure that those not reporting foreign-source income would be targeted appropriately for audit.[95] Given that Canada has a higher percentage of foreign-born residents than any other developed country and the highest rate of acceptance for refugees and immigrants of any country in the world, *this law is, sadly, an unenforceable joke.* The 1st message that immigrants hear is that the Canadian Government has created tax laws that it really does not expect people to follow – the wrong message to give potential new taxpayers.

Such a measure inspires creative noncompliance. Additionally, this provision has been vigorously criticized on several counts:

- It intrudes unnecessarily into the private affairs of taxpayers.
- It imposes additional complex compliance.
- It adds unnecessary reporting and processing costs for taxpayers and for The Agency.
- It is inconsistent with a system of taxation based on income, as opposed to wealth or changes in wealth.

An Alternative Proposal

The Canadian Tax Foundation advocates the introduction of a new form and the addition of a simple question to a standard tax return. The proposed question would ask if you received income from outside Canada or if income from outside Canada was accrued or collected for your benefit. Those taxpayers who answer yes would be directed to complete and file an additional schedule.

This additional form and the question on the tax return would not address foreign accrual property income (FAPI), which is adequately reported on a variety of other forms, including those required by sections associated with Section 233.3.

Free-Trade Issues

More than 85% of Canadian exports go to the US, yet data from a major national survey suggests that Canadians in every part of the country are *ignoring incontrovertible evidence to the contrary* and are convinced that NAFTA does the country more harm than good. This "brain washing" is the result of trade union propraganda and the biased liberal press.

In January 1999, an Environics poll asked 2,000 people whether they thought NAFTA had helped or hurt the Canadian economy – 43% said the free-trade pact hurt, while only 28% said it helped. The rest said they didn't know.

These data contradict claims made by the Canadian government and then Trade Minister Sergio Marchi, who maintain that Canadians have increasingly supported NAFTA and free-trade initiatives. Hindering free trade depresses the economy and thereby increases UgEcon activity.

Ensuring Fair Tax Administration:
The Government's Side of the Story

Said of Finance Minister Paul Martin:

"It's an important step in the recovery of a taxoholic to admit that he has a problem."
— *Monte Solberg, MP*
Reform Party finance critic

Foreword by the Minister of National Revenue

As Minister of National Revenue, I am responsible for administering a wide range of laws, regulations, treaties, and agreements. These govern collecting and distributing revenue through the tax system, as well as regulating people and goods crossing Canada's borders.

In 1996-1997, Revenue Canada collected more than $115 billion from 22 million individuals and corporations. The Department issued almost 70 million payments for the Child Tax Benefit, goods and services tax credit, and provincial benefits, which helped more than 12 million Canadians. At the border, the Department served almost 110 million travellers and processed about $167 billion in trade for 158,000 importers.

With this responsibility comes the need for accountability. Canadians expect their customs and revenue administration to be professional, responsive, open, and efficient. Above all, people must perceive the system as fair.

The most important measure of how Revenue Canada performs is obtained through the views of the people it serves — Canadians who pay taxes, receive benefits through the tax system, cross Canada's borders, and engage in international trade. In order to fulfill their obligations, Canadians must believe that Revenue Canada is treating them fairly.

... I know that by working together we can make sure that our customs and revenue administration is fair to all.

— **Herb Dhaliwal,** *PC, MP, Minister of National Revenue* [88]

A Commitment to Fairness

Revenue Canada administers matters that significantly touch the lives of every Canadian:
- the requirement to pay taxes and duties;
- the right to receive certain benefits through the tax system; and
- the movement of people and goods across the border.

Our job is to work with individuals and corporations to achieve compliance with the laws, including ensuring that they receive any entitlements that are due under the law. In Canada, our revenue and customs administration operates on the principle of voluntary compliance. This is the belief that most Canadians will abide by the law if they have the information, advice, and other services necessary to help them meet their obligations.

We take responsible and fair enforcement action against the few people who choose not to meet their legal requirements. Their lack of compliance may place more financial burden on, and threaten the safety and security of, the majority of Canadian individuals and businesses who do respect their obligations.

Whether we are providing a service or enforcing the law, fairness must be one of our defining characteristics. We have built our pursuit of fairness around the following 5 commitments:

1. We Will Inform You About Your Rights and Obligations

As a Canadian, you have a number of rights, including being treated fairly, protecting confidential information, and getting service in the official language of your choice. Your obligation is to comply with laws, regulations, and treaties we administer, such as paying taxes, providing information, and declaring imports and exports.

Our Internet address, http://www.rc.gc.ca, provides access to our guides, brochures, forms, and news releases. Each month, there are more than 600,000 hits on our Internet site. In 1996-7, we responded to 1.9 million counter inquiries and 14.9 million telephone inquiries. In addition, we issued more than 2,900 income tax and 6,130 GST/HST rulings and interpretations.

2. We Will Ensure That Our Administrative Processes Support a Fair Outcome

A fair process is one that is clear, timely, flexible, and equitable and reflects the intent of the law. It must suit the needs of the public and be responsive to evolving circumstances. Therefore, we have established processes to help you exercise your rights and fulfil your obligations.

We support a network of volunteers, including many of our retirees, who help people with special needs to complete their income tax returns. In 1996-1997, more than 15,000 volunteers helped 268,000 Canadians complete their returns and get their entitlements. Over the last few years we also have introduced ways to make it easier to meet reporting requirements, such as filing electronically.

A customs goal is to serve travelers in a timely manner. Travelers have a preliminary interview with a customs officer to determine if they can be admitted to Canada and to get a declaration of any goods they have. Travelers also may be referred for a secondary examination, which generally involves a brief baggage examination. There is no user fee for travelers entering Canada, although duties, taxes, and penalties may apply to goods.

3. We Will Respond Effectively to Your Concerns

We completed a comprehensive review of our importing control process in 1994. As a result, we changed the process to ease the use of electronic commerce, streamline reporting and release, and allow offsetting of debits and credits. In 1996-1997, 92% of travelers surveyed entering Canada said they were reasonably to very satisfied with the service they received.

4. We Will Offer You an Impartial Redress Process

If we cannot reach an agreement with you on a tax, duty, or penalty matter, you should have access to impartial redress by professional officers who were not involved in the original decision. In addition, this redress should be accessible, affordable, open, and timely.

Therefore, there is no charge for a review. The non-adversarial nature of the process enables many Canadians to represent themselves and avoid the cost of seeking the help of a lawyer or an accountant. More than 21.3 million income tax returns were filed in 1996-1997, and about 52,000 Canadians asked for an independent review. Of these reviews, about 50% resulted in changes in favor of the client.

We recently surveyed Canadians who had gone through our tax appeals process. They expressed some concerns, which led us to improve its impartiality, timeliness, and fairness. We added steps to monitor the process and to consult Canadians about improving it. These improvements are referred to as the Appeals Renewal Initiative.

5. We Will Provide You with Relief in Extraordinary Circumstances

Beyond everything else that can be done, there may be extraordinary circumstances that call for special consideration, such as fire or flood, postal disruption, serious illness or accident, or death of a close family member. A responsive customs and revenue administration must have the flexibility, supported by the law, to provide relief when these circumstances arise. Relief can take the form of forgiving or remitting all or part of an assessment, or of extending a deadline.

In our case, between 1991 and 1993, new laws referred to as the fairness provisions were introduced for income tax, goods and services tax, and customs matters. Now we have a certain amount of discretion to cancel or waive penalties and interest; extend the time limit to file an objection; refund amounts beyond the usual reassessment period; and accept requests to late file, amend, or revoke certain elections. Beyond all other forms of relief, in cases of extreme hardship, a remission of taxes, penalties, duties, and interest owed may be granted.

Diamonds Are a Smuggler's Best Friend

Excise Tax History

The excise tax was established in 1918 and applied to a range of so-called luxury items to help finance Canada's WWI costs. Over time the tax was dropped on virtually all items except jewelry. There is no excise tax on yachts, furs, or luxury cars.[5]

North American Jewellery Taxes

At least half of all Canadian jewelry sales are "under the table," according to Ernst & Young.[95] This finding, part of a Canadian federal finance department study of the underground jewelry market, is attributed to the 10% excise tax.

Testimony before the Ontario Legislature's Standing Committee pointed out that jewelry sales reported per capita were 33% higher in the US than in Canada. In Quebec, sales were only 60% of Ontario's, despite similar incomes and tastes. The absence of a sales tax on jewelry in the US explains the first finding, and negative attitudes toward taxes in Quebec explain the second. These results indicate that as much as 60% of the Canadian jewelry trade is part of the UgEcon.

Bad Tax Laws Create the UgEcon

Although Canada could easily be producing 10% of the world's diamonds in the next decade, it is probably the worst place in the world to buy one. Canada has the skills, talent, and natural resources to become a major diamond-trading capital, but the current levels of taxation are driving the industry elsewhere. Three layers of taxes (10% excise tax and about 15% in federal and provincial taxes) add 25% to the cost of buying a diamond in Canada.

Consequently, most Canadians buy diamonds elsewhere. The Netherlands, Belgium, and South Africa are favorite shopping places, as are the duty-free shops that abound in the Caribbean islands.

In addition, "diamond smuggling has become endemic in Canada."[96] Gemstones are small and easily carried across borders. Sellers who have acquired stones illegally can offer lower prices. The jewelry association estimates this segment of the UgEcon is valued at about $1 billion annually.

Jean & Paul
Song & Dance Guys

Ottawa Denies Brain Drain Flip, Flop and Plop

As recently as June of 1999, Paul Martin, the Federal Finance Minister, had played down both the urgency of tax cuts and the links among taxes, productivity, and the brain drain. That same month, Prime Minister Chretien announced that the Canadian brain drain was a myth invented by business people to force Ottawa to cut taxes. Echoing the Prime Minister's remarks, Mr. Martin said there was no proof of a brain drain despite dire warnings from Canada's major high technology firms, which threatened to move south of the border unless taxes were reduced.

Just weeks later, after a profound epiphany of economic insight, Mr. Martin told *Time* magazine that personal taxes, capital gains taxes, and corporate taxes must be lowered to make sure Canada becomes more competitive. He said that the federal government must cut taxes "as quickly as we possibly can" because they could be responsible for lagging productivity and a "brain drain" of Canadians to the US.

Canada's M1

The number of times that money "recycles" in a year is referred to as M-1. In countries with freely convertible currencies, money theorists hypothesized that debit and credit cards and other electronic transfer mechanisms should have reduced cash holdings by 10% between 1970 and 1990. It is probably reasonable to assume an additional 10% reduction by 2000. This is a likely extrapolation for Canada, the world's per capita leader in the use of debit cards.

If these hypotheses are accurate, Canada would have almost $7 billion in extra currency by 1999; multiplied by its M-1 (the velocity of its money turnover) of 15 would account for $100 billion in cash-based additional GDP.

The Brain Drain

Highly qualified professionals choose to leave their own countries for many reasons: peace, security, job satisfaction, better pay and conditions, a higher standard of living, etc. In recent years, developing countries have emerged as the biggest suppliers of qualified professionals to the industrialized world. Today more than 1.5 million skilled expatriates from developing countries have settled in Western Europe, the US, Japan, and Canada.

A Fundamental Human Rights Issue

This migration presents the international community with a major dilemma. First, the "brain drain" cannot be stopped by force nor can it be legislated against. It is considered a fundamental human right for individuals to move from one country to another. Second, it is fundamentally a national problem that can only be resolved at the national level by providing enough incentives for qualified nationals to remain at home.

One case in point is Russia: When it appeared that Russia was going to embrace capitalism in the early 1990's, banking analysts, marketing managers, and advertising executives were in demand. But once the bubble burst, they were the first to go. Given the competition, the language barrier, and the fact that most Russian professionals of this type are a relatively new breed, they are not top candidates for jobs abroad, either. And yet 70% of young professionals want to leave.

Although the West does not need people like this, Russia desperately does. How can the country solve its banking crisis without accountants, or build a service economy without marketing executives? The trouble is that the new values that make Russia's young professionals so important to their country's future also make them more prone to leaving.

On a global level, the free movement and interaction of highly skilled people is a positive thing. But the costs to the home countries of losing their professionals is incalculable, both in development opportunities and loss of investment. These migrant professionals intensify the disparities between the world's rich and poor nations. And it is the developing countries that need them most.

Canadian Branch of Doctors* Without Borders
*also academics, scientists, and information technology and business professionals

Only Fools Pay Taxes

Meet a Tenevki

The new Russian term for a shadow-economy entrepreneur

Mikhail is a Russian entrepreneur who owns a woodworking shop employing 10 craftsmen in blue overalls who make tables and chairs – knock-offs of modern Italian designs. Business is booming, and he plans to start a 2nd workshop with a staff of 20.

Mikhail does not advertise, hold any business licences, or list his company in the local equivalent of the yellow pages. Of course, he also does not report his income to the tax authorities. His customers, suppliers, and employees are happy to deal in cash. After all, they do not want to pay taxes either. Invisible to the authorities, Mikhail's business is part of Russia's vibrant "shadow economy."

The Shadow Economy That Keeps the Country Running

Two new studies conclude that the untaxed shadow economy in Russia accounts for at least half of Russia's GDP.[97] That astounding figure, double what the Russian government had guessed, helps answer a political enigma: Why aren't Russians taking to the streets in massive protests when millions of workers have not received salaries in months? The answer is that Russians hide significant parts of their incomes and that they are much better off than they appear on paper.

From Overestimating to Underestimating the Economy

For decades, Soviet statistics exaggerated the size of the communist economy. Today, the reverse is true: Official figures underestimate Russia's economic vitality. Using independent surveys of household spending from 1994 to 1997, new research shows that the uncounted shadow economy peaked in early 1995 at 56% of Russia's GDP and declined to 49.5% by June 1997. "There isn't a Russian who isn't involved or whose family member isn't involved one way or another in the informal economy," says a researcher at Rand in Washington. Russians have

even coined a word for underground entrepreneurs – tenevki, or "shadow people."

Most businesses in the shadow economy provide legitimate goods and services. Despite the publicity that Russian gangsters have received, racketeering represents only about 3% of GDP.[98] The biggest hidden sectors are retail trade and agriculture, with millions of small farmers quietly selling produce from kitchen gardens. Goskomstat, the State Committee on Statistics, estimates that 46% of Russia's agricultural income is unreported.

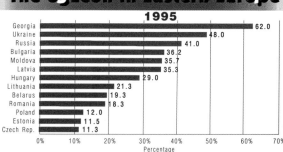

The UgEcon in Eastern Europe

1995

Country	Percentage
Georgia	62.0
Ukraine	48.0
Russia	41.0
Bulgaria	36.2
Moldova	35.7
Latvia	35.3
Hungary	29.0
Lithuania	21.3
Belarus	19.3
Romania	18.3
Poland	12.0
Estonia	11.5
Czech Rep.	11.3

Source: Simon Johnson, Daniel Hoffman "The Unofficial Economy in Transition," Program Economic Activity, No. 2, 1997.

Unofficial Russian Prosperity

In a study funded by the US Treasury Department, two Moscow economists[99] identified signs o prosperity (purchases of cars, comput and telephones) as proof that the standard of living has improved fairly dramatically in recent years for the vast majority (75%) of the Russian population. They classify 40 million people (27% of the population) as rich or middle class, 48% as tolerably well-off, and 25% as poor.

Ignoring Taxes As a Way of Life

Russians commonly justify tax evasion on the grounds that the rates are excessive. In reality, Russia's tax rates are comparable to those in the rest of Eastern Europe.

The real problem is that Russia imposes a dizzying variety of taxes, constantly changes the rules, and enforces them arbitrarily. In one recent survey, companies cited 3 main reasons for resorting to unreported cash or barter transactions:

- capricious tax collection,
- an unreliable banking system, and
- a desire to avoid paying bribes.

As a result, tax shortfalls are estimated at $100 billion a year. These shortfalls force the Kremlin to borrow money at sky-high rates. "Everybody pays a severe cost because of the reduced ability of the government to provide public goods," notes an economist at the European Bank for Reconstruction and Development. "By not providing public goods, it creates disincentives to investors, both foreign and domestic."

Russian Federation
MOSCOW

Formal Name: **Russian Federation**
Local Name: **Rossiya**
Local Formal Name: **Rossiyskaya Federatsiya**
Location: **Europe/Asia**
Status: **UN Country**
Capital City: **Moscow (Moskva)**
Main Cities: **St. Petersburg, Gorkiy, Yekaterinburg**
Population: **149,476,000**
Area [sq.km]: **17,075,000**
Currency: **1 ruble = 100 kopeks**
Main Languages: **Russian**
Main Religions: **Russian Orthodox, Muslim, Buddhist**

A Government Without Options

Crushing the tenevki is not a realistic option. In addition to being a hothouse for entrepreneurs, the shadow economy takes the place of a faulty social safety net by allowing a subsistence income to many people who would otherwise be unemployed. The trick will be for the government to simplify the tax code and gradually turn the tenevki into law-abiding taxpayers.

Polls now indicate that 80% of Russians see nothing wrong with evading taxes.

This has led the Tax Police to send SWAT-style teams on high-profile raids; softer methods include TV commercials that show that the sex lives of deadbeats suffer from worries over unpaid tax bills. The head of the State Tax Service recently summoned pop stars for a lecture on financial ethics. And the government has been floating tax amnesty plans, despite the general consensus among tax enforcement agencies that tax amnesty plans typically send the wrong message and backfire. Moral issues can be argued indefinitely, but that will not generate tax

10% of the Russian government's revenue comes from taxes on the sale of vodka – yet, most vodka consumed is distilled in the UgEcon.

ДЕНЬГИ НЕ ПАХНЕТ

Money doesn't smell.
– *An old Russian proverb*

Key Strategies for *Better* Taxes

The Dangers of Direct Taxation

Cicero, the great Roman lawyer, ran the senate when Caesar Augustus ruled the Empire, and many historians give Cicero credit for being the brains behind Augustus' modernization of taxes. Cicero was one of many seminal thinkers who condemned direct taxes as a danger to Roman liberty. His words ring as true today as they did 2,000 years ago:

Every effort must be made to prevent a repetition of direct taxation, and all possible precaution must be taken to ensure that such a step will never be needed. But if any government should find it necessary to levy a direct tax, the utmost care has to be devoted to making it clear to the entire population that this simply has to be done because no alternative exists short of complete national collapse.

Direct taxation, what we now call income tax, has always been an ineffective way to raise taxes. Prior to the last 70 years, relatively few people worked for large companies. Direct taxation has been an efficient method of tax collection only for the brief period from the end of The Great War – WWI, until the end of the 20th century.

The tidal wave of consumerism that matched the booming industrialization allowed governments in developed countries to continue direct taxation using the fiendish mechanism of withholding taxes. As long as most workers had regular jobs, taxes could be extracted before the workers ever saw the money. With the coming of the Information Revolution, traditional jobs have declined; a preponderance of the new jobs being created in the last decade of the century has been created in the self-employed and SME sectors.

These new sectors are not captive tax collectors like larger companies, and they are at the heart of the reason why *continued reliance on direct taxation is doomed to failure*. As the increasing tax burden is pressed on a decreasing captive tax base, the UgEcon options will flourish, and the burden on the shrinking cohort of taxed-at-the-source workers will no longer be able to pay for the social spending, the burden of the unfunded pension plans, and exorbitant costs of debt servicing. Like the fateful straw that broke the camel's back, we are precariously close to breaking the back of the captive taxpayer and what will soon be an historical artifact – the voluntarily compliant taxpayer.

The Tax Revolt is here, and it is growing. The government cannot continue to rely on direct (income) taxes or the system will implode, bringing with it great injustices for those who are dependent by nature or habit on the government.

Some changes can simplify tax collection and reduce the costs associated with the collection. The cost savings can be for both the governments who have to manage the collection and monitoring and for the average taxpayers who are forced to keep complicated records and to rely on expensive professional help to try to comply with very complex and ever-changing tax laws.

The French Revolution *(1789)*
One answer for arrogant politicians and nincompoop bureaucrats.

User Fees

Some of the fairest taxes are directly related to the service received: user fees. Early examples were tolls for the use of highways, bridges, ferries, and even for admission to fortified medieval towns.

In theory, these taxes should still be perceived as fair. But theory and practice often deviate; for example, gasoline taxes would be fair taxes today if they were used for developing and maintaining highways as they were initially intended. Instead, what has happened is that gasoline taxes have been easy to ratchet up because they are largely invisible (embedded in the cost of the product); in addition, the expense is relatively small and pales compared to the perceived value of using an automobile.

Thus, taxing gasoline has shifted from a user tax to a regressive form of general taxation. Although gasoline in Europe is about 5 times as expensive as in the US, shorter distances and an earlier move to more fuel-efficient cars have made the situation a little more palatable. Also, because of its bulk, gasoline is not a product that lends itself to smuggling on an enterprise level. However, few Canadians who travel to the US fail to return without full tanks of American gas, which, because of lack of tax parity, costs about 40% more in Canada.

Stricter Enforcement

The rules are very clear to the average, righteous, tax-captive wage-earner who sees tax deductions taken "at the source:"

If someone defrauds the system, the consequences should be very harsh.

However, any attempt to reduce the UgEcon by simply making enforcement stricter will result in more evasion activity because the enforcement

activity itself is rarely cost-effective to administer. It is enlightening to examine the details of Canada's 5-year-old enforcement initiative. (See page 96.)

Some Harsh Treatment for
the Tax Collector
in Revolutionary France

Changing the Tax Collection Points

California, a state generally sophisticated in tax collection, located in a country that is tax-compliant, identified and solved a tax evasion problem simply by changing its collection point. One revision of a tax law stopped the theft of hundreds of millions of dollars a year of tax money.

At the time, the state fuel vendor's tax was 17¢ a gallon, to be paid by the distributors. However, some distributors collected the tax and never remitted it to the state. A new law imposed the tax upstream at the manufacturing level, resulting in a dramatic reduction in the loss of tax revenue.

Tax Amnesties

The IMF has concluded that tax amnesties are not effective in economically developed countries with mature tax systems. Even if they show modest increases in revenue in the short run, compliance problems increase and revenues drop later on. The reason is simple: The average taxpayers believe that if tax amnesty happens once, it will happen again. Therefore, there is no motivation to change their behavior. (See Pakistan, page 88.)

Self-Assessment

In the US state of Massachusetts, if tax agents look at a tax return and judge that the taxpayer has taken an overly aggressive position, that taxpayer is sent a message: "This is a self-assessment program. You are being given an opportunity to correct your tax return." The taxpayer either makes a change or insists that it is correct, and his or her word is taken at face value.

If you had made a mistake or cut some corners in your last tax return, there would be no penalties if you corrected it yourself after the warning letter. On the other hand, if you did not take the opportunity to correct the return, and it were found to be deficient with the intent to defraud, you would quite likely go to jail. This potent deterrent to false filing has been proven successful, and other jurisdictions are considering similar approaches.

Tax Vigilantes

Many tax audits are based on leads provided by the public. Typical informants are competitors and sometimes compliant taxpayers who do not like watching someone else leave the tax bill to them. In reality, the vast majority of leads come from individuals infected with the "unhappy-camper syndrome" – ex-wives/husbands and girlfriends/boyfriends, soured business partners, or "losers" in business deals. The number of unsolicited leads has been increasing rapidly as the UgEcon grows.

One of the more sensational options being considered in several jurisdictions has been dubbed the "rat bounty" program. If someone turns in a tax evader, a percentage of the taxes collected (perhaps 20%) are paid – tax free and anonymously – to the informant.

Construction Subcontractors

The construction industry is particularly prone to participation in the UgEcon. Although home remodelling is clearly an area of substantial tax abuse, off-the-books payments are commonplace even on large projects. In times of construction booms, tradespeople are in demand; one of the leverages that they have with otherwise legitimate contractors is that they will only work for cash.

One way to correct this is to require contractors to report payments they make to subcontractors, including information about their business addresses and numbers. If undocumented payments to subcontractors were disallowed as deductions, the contractors' income tax liabilities would increase by the amount of the disallowed deductions. This system is already in force for construction contractors in countries such as Britain, Australia, and the US, where it has proved its worth in promoting compliance.

Help Wanted:

*Super Cop Needed –
Eliot Ness, Where Are You?*

Trans-National Solutions

In order to battle organized crime, law enforcement agencies must evolve beyond the state-centric paradigm. If national governments are going to succeed in their campaign against the UgEcon, countries must confer power to organizations that can act on a worldwide level.[100]

A successful effort will entail a more innovative use of multilateral mechanisms as well as more uniformity in national policies so that law enforcement officials can be as mobile and as efficient as the organized criminals they are chasing. Fully supported organizations with international jurisdictions focused on money laundering and illicit drug trafficking would permit national governments (as well as IGO's, INGO's, and NGO's) to make more effective use of limited resources.

While the opportunity still exists, all governments, especially members of the OECD, should design and establish mechanisms to combat the growing UgEcon fostered by organized crime on both the regional and worldwide levels.

Avoidance vs. Evasion: A Class Issue

Although the wealthy are able to use the loopholes created in the tax codes to legally avoid significant amounts of taxation, the same opportunities are not available to those less well-off. Without the expensive tax lawyers and accountants who are integral to the tax avoidance schemes, they resort to more basic actions – illegal tax evasion.

Business owners often use company-owned facilities, materials, and supplies for personal purposes. This is a course open to even the smallest business owner, starting with the restaurant owner who takes home food for personal use. One of the most common strategies, one that is used to some degree by virtually ALL restaurant owners, is simply to buy personal food from one or more vendors who sell to the business and charge the purchase to the company account. They believe they deserve a special break because they work nights, or long hours, or some other reason, and there is almost no possibility of detection.

Another gimmick that small businesses can use, and which is perfectly legal, is to pay income as salary to other members of the family. This option allows owners to move income from their high tax rate to the lower (or nonexistent) tax rate of younger or older family members.

Obviously if the work is done and the pay is reasonably close to market value, these are perfectly legitimate expenses. Tax advisers sometimes use the term "credible illusion of reality" as the guideline for employing family members. Employing a daughter (or son) who is a 16-year-old computer whiz to manage the website of a business has the illusion of reality even if the hourly rate is a little high and the hours are slightly padded. Stocking shelves in a corner store may be credible for a 10-year-old. Having a retired father and mother do custodial services for your business can pass muster, assuming that they at least live reasonably close by and are not bedridden. However, tax avoidance schemes that are perfectly legal can become evasion if they are only shams.

Our view is that governments see only the "tip of the iceberg," and that they really do not want to see the reality, i.e., the other 90% of the iceberg. *They cannot acknowledge the reality without having to acknowledge their own failures.*

Keeping New Business Out of the UgEcon

Compliance costs are relatively higher for SME's. Because they often lack the sophisticated accounting functions available to larger companies, administrative features of the tax system should be tailored to their situations. They also need to be consulted on pending changes in regulations so that they can be heard and participate in shaping outcomes, thus promoting compliance.

If incentives are offered, they must be very carefully designed. In many cases, the tax system may not be the best mechanism for assisting small firms, particularly start-ups. Therefore, other kinds of assistance – such as training, information, and guaranteed loans – need to be promoted.

Country-to-Country Tax Parity

Prior to the global economy, lack of parity in taxes between countries had triggered a dynamic aspect of the UgEcon: smuggling. If wine or spirits were cheaper in Spain than in France, enterprising smugglers simply moved the goods from the lower-priced market to the higher-priced market. Usually they were able to find other products that were taxed in reverse parity so that they could smuggle goods both ways to keep down their "production" costs.

At one point, cigarette taxes in some Canadian provinces were so far out of parity with the US that the black market mushroomed to a major industry. The sage resolution was not to increase enforcement but to reduce taxes. This dramatically reduced the risk/reward ratio: The penalty for getting caught remained the same, but the "profit" that could be gained dropped to the point that the risk outweighed the potential gain.

In today's global economy, tax harmonization is increasingly important. The growing integration of the world economy, aided by information technology and telecommunications, does not allow countries the luxury of maintaining radically different direct tax levels. Taxpayers, *especially corporations operating transnationally*, can simply transact business across separate tax jurisdictions to secure the lowest taxes and the best overall economic results. The result has been one or more of the following outcomes:

- Taxes have moved toward a harmonized status,
- Higher tax jurisdictions have lost taxes through a shift in locating manufacturing facilities and a loss of international investment, and/or,
- A brain drain has occurred, with costs so staggering that the phenomenon is denied by politicians responsible for setting the high taxes.

Tax Design and Social Marketing

Compliance problems can be anticipated, and to a large extent avoided, by the design of the tax policies themselves. A multifaceted approach is required, and the success of any policy to combat the UgEcon can only be measured over the long run by improved self-compliance – because enforced compliance can never be cost effective.

The expanded adoption of user fees and user taxes is a key element. These kinds of levies are generally perceived as fair taxes and open the way for reducing general tax rates; this in turn diminishes incentives for tax evasion, and therefore diminishes the size of the UgEcon.

Social marketing (getting people to believe that it is their obligation to pay all the taxes that they owe and that failing to do so is dishonest and constitutes a criminal action) is a long-term initiative. In the same way that product marketing is designed for a particular audience, social marketing must target different segments with different messages. In addition, it entails obtaining the support and active involvement of a number of partners, including all levels of government, labor unions, and private sector associations. Social marketing requires carrying out the necessary research and gathering broad-based support, because it is critical to ensure that the right message is established before implementation.

Ultimately the message must be some combination of carrot and stick:

1. *You have a moral obligation to pay* **just and fair** *taxes, and*
2. *If you are caught avoiding your tax obligations, you will be* **severely punished.**

The obvious issues are that taxes must become just and fair, and taxpayers must absolutely believe that risks outweigh rewards.

Money Laundering in a Washbasin

Folklore about money laundering describes suitcases full of $100 bills from illicit drugs or big-time bribes. In fact, money laundering is done with checks as well as cash, and much of it is done on a small scale, like most of the UgEcon.

Money laundering just means making sure that the funds cannot easily be traced back. Although depositing checks into an account leaves an audit trail, it is possible for an UgEcon worker to minimize the "tracks" left:

1. Take the check to the bank on which it is drawn and cash it there. The bank teller will ask for identification, but not many tracks are left because it never touches the UgEcon worker's account.

2. Endorse the check over to a regular supplier, someone with whom the UgEcon worker has done business for many years and who is quite willing to help out a good customer.

3. Deposit the check in a personal bank account. The odds of getting a detailed audit, especially as a low-profile taxpayer, are so low in most jurisdictions that detection is remote. An UgEcon worker using this strategy often changes banks periodically just to muddy the waters.

4. Deposit the check in a 2nd business account. This is the account in which the UgEcon worker keeps skimmed receipts. Money comes out of this account typically with a debit card for "walking-around cash" or it goes to a hidden investment account.

If the business is incorporated, the business owner simply makes sure that the tax preparer does not know about the existence of this account. Using a "dba" account ("doing business as" the name of an unincorporated business), the process is even easier. The address on the bank statements is a minor issue; many small- to medium-sized sole proprietorship businesses use a post box for bank statements, for legitimate privacy and control issues. Again, the odds of getting a detailed audit that would dig this deep are very remote, especially if the tax returns are prepared by a low-profile person.

Basic World Tax Code: Achieving Tax Parity

To keep multi-national companies and cyber workers from shopping for the lowest tax rates, industrialized countries will eventually have to reach a tax parity.

The Basic World Tax Code (BWTC) is a project of the International Tax Program at Harvard University. Since the mid-1980's, there has been growing consensus among economists and tax policy experts about the design of effective and stable tax systems. The BWTC idea came out of a need for a legislative framework for tax policies in developing and transitional countries.

The BWTC was initiated to provide an example of the laws that are needed for an efficient and effective tax system. The objective was to provide a framework or checklist of what is needed and not needed. Over the past few years, the BWTC has become a standard reference for tax reform.

The code, written by Professors Ward M. Hussey and Donald C. Lubick, assumes that the bulk of an emerging economy's revenue will come from customs revenues, the value-added tax, selected excise taxes, and a low, flat income tax. It contains a combined individual and entity income tax, but confines the individual income tax to a small portion of the population.

Income Tax

The BWTC imposes one income tax to which all persons and all business activities are subject. Progressivity is built in by a zero bracket amount that excludes the bulk of the working population, and the income tax is collected mainly by withholding at the source. It proposes a top rate for individuals and entities of 30%.

Value-Added Tax

The net tax rate is measured by the difference between the tax on the seller's output and the tax on the goods and services used in the seller's business, as evidenced by invoices. The value-added tax applies not only to production and wholesale activity, but also to retail activity. For revenue reasons and to ease compliance and administration, the tax is broad based in its application to goods and services, with exceptions kept to a minimum.

There is only one rate of tax, aside from a zero rate for exports, and it applies equally to imports and domestic production.

Excise Taxes

To ease tax collection, the taxes are levied on a relatively few taxpayers, on relatively few articles, and at relatively few rates. The taxes also are based on the value of the article rather than on units, and imports and domestic production are treated evenhandedly.

Property Taxes

Three property taxes are included in the BWTC: one on land and buildings, a 2nd on motor vehicles, and a 3rd on the gross assets of large resident entities. This 3rd tax serves as a minimum tax, which applies to the extent that it is less than the income tax.

Administrative Provisions

Power and responsibility are centralized in a single official, the Tax Administrator. Information with respect to trade (imports and exports) and domestic taxes is centralized in one database, making it easier to spot income and articles escaping tax, thus increasing audit proficiency.

In just a few years, the BWTC has become a standard reference for those embarking on tax reform in various parts of the world.

For more info visit the website at

Basic World Tax Code

http://www.tax.org/International/bwtc/english.htm

Flat Tax

> If there is any such thing as a "good" tax, it will have these attributes:
> **Certainty** (the amount, time, and place of payment are certain);
> **Collection** that is convenient and cheap;
> And that the burden of providing funds for support of government is distributed in roug[h] proportion to the benefits taxpayers receive from government.
>
> **Adam Smith,** the father of modern economic[s].

On each of these points, Adam Smith would favor a flat income tax over the current codes that cannot qualify in any respect as "good" taxes.

Proposals for a flat tax, primarily American, each differ; some allow deductions and some not. The simplest flat tax would require that everyone pay the same proportion of take-home income to the government. A simple flat tax makes filing a tax return as simple as filling out a postcard. (See samples on the next page.)

The flat tax would not be a perfect tax; there are no perfect taxes. But we do not live in a perfect world. Opponents of the flat tax will concede most points, but they argue that the flat tax fails the fairness test: The tax dollars that a family with $20,000 in income must pay represent a greater sacrifice than the dollars a millionaire pays. However, this point is irrelevant; our present tax system does the same thing. The loopholes enjoyed by the wealthy mean that the burden is not distributed equitably.

But equity is a subjective concept; what is fair is what people perceive to be fair, given their knowledge and value systems. The current income tax systems are certainly not perceived to be fair. The simplicity of a single tax rate paid by all regardless of the level or source of income appeals to the basic sense of fairness of most ordinary taxpayers. It, at least, seems fairer than what we have now. A flat tax is neutral; it treats every dollar of income the same, whether it is from wages, capital gains, dividends, interest, or rental income.[101]

Revenue Neutral

Two designs are under consideration in the US that could make a flat tax system bring in exactly the same amount of revenue as the existing income tax. However, the specific tax *rate* would depend on the deductions permitted. Therefore, allowed deductions and the tax rate are direct tradeoffs: The higher the allowances are set, the higher the tax rate would need to be to bring in the same amount of tax revenue as the current system.

Plan 1: All federal income tax revenues could be fully replaced by a system with a flat tax rate of 13.1% and no deductions. Allowing total deductions for a family of 4 to reach $36,800 would require a 19.9 % rate.

Plan 2: A less palatable alternative, embedded in the Armey-Shelby flat tax before the US Congress, would offset personal deductions by increased revenue from business. Taxes from individuals would fall by $51 billion while taxes from corporations would rise by $52 billion. This sleight-of-hand activity only hides taxes by passing them to businesses, who will, in turn, pass them onto consumers in the form of higher prices on goods and services. Although potentially more acceptable to taxpayers, this plan will make US exports less competitive and is, in general, inflationary.

Polling Data

A flat tax would levy a single tax rate on all income subject to tax. Income would be taxed only once. The complexity and unfairness resulting from hundreds of exemptions, credits, loopholes, and deductions now prevalent in the tax system would be eliminated to make the single tax rate as low as possible. Some alternatives allow personal and dependent deductions and other alternatives allow no deductions.

Public opinion polls indicate that fairness is clearly an issue of great concern with American taxpayers:
• There is strong desire to change the current tax code, as well as powerful support for replacing it with a flat tax: 2/3 of the taxpayers think federal income taxes are too high.
• Taxpayers want a flat tax by a 2-to-1 margin.
• 56% approve of a 17% flat tax with no deductions, and 41% support a 20% flat tax with mortgage and charitable deductions.
• 42% of respondents support the flat tax because it treats everyone more fairly than the current system.
• Out of 6 different potential reforms of the tax code, the flat tax was the clear winner.[102]

Individual Flat Tax Return

Imagine filing your tax return on a postcard. Write down your total wage and pension income. Subtract a generous family allowance ($33,800 for a family of 4) and take 17% of the balance.

That's your tax bill!

No death taxes, no capital gains taxes, no marriage penalty, and no Social Security benefit tax. You make out a check, drop it in the mail, and you're done with the IRS for the next 12 months. Instead of taking 11 hours to calculate your taxes, a flat tax takes you 11 minutes.

Form 1 ARMEY-SHELBY FLAT TAX FORM 2001

Your first name and initial	Last name	Your Social Security number
Present home address		Spouse's Social Security number
City, Town or Post Office Box, State and ZIP Code	Your occupation	
	Spouse's occupation	

1. Wages, Salary, and Pensions 1
2. Personal Allowance ....
   a. $24,400 for married filing jointly .... 2(a)
   b. $12,200 for single .... 2(b)
   c. $15,650 for single head of household ..... 2(c)
3. Number of dependents, not including spouse 3
4. Personal allowances for dependents (line 3 multipled by $5,500) 4
5. Total personal allowances (line 2 plus line 4) 5
6. Taxable wages (line 1 less line 5, if positive, otherwise zero) 6
7. Tax (17 percent of line 6) 7
8. Tax already paid 8
9. Tax due (line 7 less line 8, if positive) 9
10. Refund due (line 8 less line 7, if positive) 10

Corporate Flat Tax Return

Imagine completing your company's tax return on a postcard. Imagine the savings that you would enjoy by not having to maintain all the fastidious records that are now required for a business income tax return. No complex mess of schedules. Compute 10 items and send in your check.

Businesses, from the mom-and-pop grocery store to Fortune 500 companies, would subtract expenses from revenues and pay 17% on the remainder. All business income – including corporate, partnership, professional, farm, sole proprietorship, rents, royalties, and interest – would be taxed.[86]

Form 2 ARMEY-SHELBY FLAT TAX FORM 1999

Business Name	Employer ID Number
Street address	County
City, State and ZIP Code	Principal Product

1. Gross revenue from sales 1
2. Allowable costs
   a. Purchases of goods, services, and materials ..... 2(a)
   b. Wages, salaries, and pensions ..... 2(b)
   c. Purchases of capital equipment, structures, and land ..... 2(c)
3. Total of allowable costs (sum of lines 2(a), 2(b), 2(c)) 3
4. Taxable income (line 1 less line 3) 4
5. Tax (17% of line 4) 5
6. Carry forward from 1998 6
7. Interest on carry-forward (6% of line 6) 7
8. Carry-forward into 1999 (line 6 plus line 7) 8
9. Tax due (line 5 less line 8, if positive) 9
10. Carry-forward to 2000 (line 8 less line 5, if positive) 10

Consumption Taxes:

A Bold Step the World Needs to Move Forward in the 21st Century [103]

The only way to stop the growth of the UgEcon is to destroy income tax so completely that it can never grow back again. Income tax evasion costs compliant and captive taxpayers billions of dollars a year in lost revenues. It should be eliminated and replaced with user fees and a comprehensive tax on the consumption of goods and some services.

A consumption tax broadens the tax base by taxing the burgeoning underground economy. Everyone would have to pay a fair share of federal taxes on all purchases, regardless of income level. In addition, states/provinces have proven that they can more effectively administer a sales tax than an income tax.

The ideal tax code must include 5 basic principles to remove the incentives of the UgEcon: It must be fair, simple, encourage savings and investment, improve the balance of trade, and stimulate economic growth. The consumption tax is the only tax code that embodies all these elements.

1. Fair. The perception of fairness is essential to any tax code. Under a consumption tax, those who spend more would be taxed more. A Ford would have a smaller tax on it than a Rolls Royce. The loopholes disappear, and a fair tax code results.

2. Simple. A consumption tax would eliminate federal taxing authorities. The days of keeping tax receipts for at least 3 years would be over. No more sweating every year trying to figure out what you owe the government. (*Americans alone spend more than $300 billion annually just to comply with their income taxes.*) Because most companies today already keep records of revenues to pay state/province sales taxes, the basic, simple structure necessary to comply with a federal consumption tax already exists. The state/provincial taxing authority could collect the federal tax and pass it on to the national government.

3. Encourage Savings and Investment. Like a flat tax, no savings, investments, or capital gains would ever be taxed. By ending the double taxation on savings and encouraging investment, a consumption tax would energize the economy, lift stagnating wages, and create jobs.

4. Improve the Balance of Trade. Just imagine how many companies around the world would want to build their world headquarters in a tax jurisdiction that had no corporate income tax. Exports would not be subject to a consumption tax, and prices of products would be reduced in the international market because they would no longer need to cover the cost of corporate income tax. If all taxes were removed from production costs, export prices could drop at least 15%. This would undoubtedly lead to a surge in exports and strengthen the balance of trade. All imports would be subject to the consumption tax just like any other products. This approach would be completely legal under General Agreement on Tariffs and Trade (GATT), while giving participating countries an enormous, but fair, trade advantage in the global marketplace.

5. Stimulate Economic Growth. The Chairman of the Economics Department at Harvard University testified before the US House Ways and Means Committee that smooth, immediate transition to the consumption tax would lead to a tremendous growth in the economy. In fact, he also testified that a consumption tax would immediately increase the overall size of the US economy by 13% and then continue to run at 9% above current economic forecasts. The tremendous surge provided by a shift to consumption taxes would mean more work for all businesses and more jobs for all workers.

In other testimony, knowledgeable witnesses indicated that a consumption tax rate of roughly 15% to 20% would be adequate to cover federal government expenditures. This is significantly less than the average taxpayer pays today.

*Cheaters ultimately drive up the costs for everyone.
Enforcement is the most expensive method of collecting taxes.*

Effective Taxes Can Curb the UgEcon

In virtually all developed countries, media discussions abound regarding alternatives to the present income taxes. No one truly believes the present complex codes are worth keeping, but the problem is deciding on a replacement. Several alternatives have been suggested, such as a flat tax and a national sales tax; neither idea has caught on for various reasons.

The Problem with Flat-Tax Proposals

The flat-tax proposals are all derivatives of the plan developed in the late 1980's by professors Hall and Rabushka, of the Hoover Institution in California. The Hall/Rabushka plan maintains an income tax system, but the plan would be far simpler to manage and tax returns far simpler to prepare. (See pages 110-111.) Rabushka often states that it takes only 2 hours to explain his plan. That is probably 115 minutes too much time to spend on the explanation. However, the ways in which the flat-tax rate would evolve and how citizens could control its growth is difficult to see. It is also difficult to see how the flat tax could get at the UgEcon, which is not taxed directly or indirectly under any tax plan that is based on income taxes.

Although the flat tax is a dramatic improvement over existing models of income tax, it is flawed. It addresses the UgEcon only indirectly. Research has confirmed an intuitive relationship between higher marginal tax rates and higher rates of evasion. Lower rates, all other things being equal, lead to lower evasion because the benefits decline while the costs and risks remain comparable.

The flat tax does have an advantage in the point of collection – employers are motivated to capture the deduction because it directly reduces their corporate income taxes. In developed countries, the withholding system is in place and is fairly easy to monitor effectively. However, the drawback is in monitoring the increasing number of workers who are self-employed. A flat tax also does not retard the problems of blatantly excessive business expenses. (See page 22.)

The Problems with National Sales Tax Proposals

Sales taxes become problematic in that the point of collection is typically thought of as the responsibility of retailers, a sector of the economy in which small businesses are more densely represented. The inescapable reality is that small businesses are more likely to evade taxes because the owner (the beneficiary of tax evasion) is more likely to also be responsible for keeping the books and filing the tax returns.

This problem, however real, is exaggerated in that those small businesspersons who are likely to cheat on sales tax are probably already cheating on their income tax and would be inclined to do so under any tax system. Also, the economic importance of small firms in the retail sector in developed countries is usually grossly overstated. Small firms (exclusive of sole proprietorships) account for only 15% of gross receipts by all retailers, wholesalers, and service providers. Because the gross receipts of wholesalers would not typically be subject to a straight consumption tax, the true scope of the small, "problem" companies is negligible.[104]

How Progressive Are These Taxes?

"Progressive" here means to "take from the rich to pay the poor." But many economists believe that the poor pay for this largesse in the form of lower wages and fewer job opportunities because of slower business growth. Others argue that this is not clearly evident and very difficult to prove. Regardless, the flat tax with deductions is only moderately progressive. Consumption tax is truly progressive because the more you spend, the more you pay.

Big, Bigger, Biggest

The US federal tax code is more than 9,000 pages long and includes another nearly 100,000 pages of court case transcripts. Americans waste 5.5 billion person-hours of non-productive time each year just complying with this onerous tax system.

The New Tax System: Changing Who Is Taxed

Consumption taxes are really just sales or excise taxes – GST/PST in Canada or the VAT in most European countries. The US uses an excise tax (FET) on some products – alcohol, tobacco, and gasoline – as a form of consumption tax. Excise taxes are collected with great efficiency and effectiveness because the tax becomes part of the purchase price and cannot be avoided. Sales taxes also cannot be avoided without an exemption certificate. Consumption taxes are collected at a far lower cost than income taxes because there are many fewer collection points. They are more effectively collected because the collection method takes the individual out of the process, thereby reducing the opportunities for individual tax evasion.

Contrary to popular belief, Robin Hood is the taxpayers' bogeyman. He corrupted **the whole purpose of taxation, which is protection** – (mutual defence and internal security) and managed to get it tangled up with the awesomeness of the Magna Carta, democracy, motherhood, and probably even apple pie.

Robin Hood's noble theme of (theoretically) taking from the rich and giving to the poor, somehow backfired on the middle-class workers.

The consumption tax option taxes equally everyone's spending – captive and compliant taxpayers and UgEcon tax evaders, doing both legal and illegal activities. It increases tax compliance at the same time it reduces compliance costs.

The increased fairness, transparency, and legitimacy of the system will induce more compliance. A 90% reduction in the number of filers will enable tax administrators to more narrowly and effectively address non-compliance and will increase the likelihood that tax evasion will be uncovered.

The New Tax System

The New Tax System (NTS) is a combination of 2 types of consumption taxes:
- A Federal Excise Tax on "finished goods," collected at the point of manufacture or importation.
- A Federal Sales Tax on all other goods, collected at the point of sale.

Both of these taxes could have varying rates, by product class within industry, to minimize taxes on those items that are of the greatest economic importance to those with the least money.

Under the NTS, only businesses would pay taxes, either as excise taxes on finished goods or sales taxes on other goods. When a sale is made, tax is paid. Neither profits nor capital gains would be taxed. This will give the stockholders what they want: their profits protected and their businesses growing. And, business growth means more jobs.

The collection method presented here eliminates myriad opportunities for tax evasion and tax avoidance. However, this new system means a complete retreat from taxation of individuals, which is a dramatic switch of focus. The new focus needs to be on businesses, which now pay only about 4-10% of the total tax burden.

An Additional Refinement

Rightly or wrongly so, it appears to some observers of the UgEcon that the visibility of a tax may be as important as the rate of taxation in stimulating the UgEcon. We propose that the collection point for consumption taxes on goods could be pushed upstream from the retailer to manufacturers and importers. This has a double advantage in that it "imbeds" the tax into the price of the goods, creating reduced visibility and further reducing the number of collection points to 1-2% of the number in the current systems. This would not create any violations of free trade agreements, because domestic and foreign goods would be treated in precisely the same manner.

Taxing Services: A Tradeoff

One of the more complex issues addressed by the material in this chapter is understanding the tradeoff associated with applying a consumption tax, in whatever form, to *services*. Both the Basic World Tax Code (page 109) and National Sales Tax (page 112) include provisions for applying the sales tax to services as well as goods. The New Tax System model covered on this page and the preceding page excludes taxing services and limits the scope of commerce to which taxes apply.

The author, although fully appreciative of the improvements inherent in the BWTC and National Sales Tax systems, favors applying sales taxes only to goods. This is consistent with the NTS model and recognizes the reality that enforcing a sales tax on services is impossible: It is clearly one of the most flourishing areas of the UgEcon under our existing tax systems. Services are often rendered on an individual-to-individual or individual-to-small company basis; therefore, the collection point cannot be pushed "upstream," as is the case of taxing goods where the tax collection point can be designated as the manufacturer or importer.

Promoting Compliance

The relative simplicity of such a tax will promote compliance. Businesses will need to answer only a single question to determine the tax due: How much was sold to consumers?

In addition, the dramatic reduction in marginal tax rates will reduce individual gains from tax

> *We must manage an economy where every product and service has all taxes imbedded in the price, and, most importantly, the individual is no longer a part of the tax collection process.*[105]

evasion. If non-compliance costs remain comparable (or even increase, based on the increased likelihood of getting caught among the much smaller number of filers), then the expected profit from tax evasion will decline and the magnitude of tax evasion similarly will decline.

The most important factor favoring the NTS approach is that because it applies only to goods and not services, revenue agents can concentrate their enforcement efforts at dramatically fewer points. The collection points would be only about 10% of those under the current income tax system or other alternative tax systems.

With fewer collection points, equal funding for enforcement would increase considerably the audit rate for potential evaders, along with the probability of apprehending them. In other words, the risk of detection would increase and risk-adjusted cost of evasion would increase. Increased evasion due to the large concentration of small businesses in the retail sector would be outweighed by higher compliance because of greater simplicity and perceived legitimacy of the tax system. Lower marginal tax rates would reduce temptation, and the smaller taxpayer population would increase the risk of detection.

Lastly, monitoring could be computerized and would facilitate cross-checking by government auditors. Sales reports from manufacturers and wholesalers would reflect the quantity of product sold to retailers. An auditor could then ensure that the retailer's books either reflected a sale of these products or that the products were in inventory. An effective NTS plan would require that all businesses (including non-retailers) keep records in the ordinary course of business that would aid such cross-checking by government auditors. *Overall, this particular tax system is more likely to reduce rather than exacerbate the problem of tax evasion.*

Conclusion

Moving Forward

Economists, legislators, and taxpayers agree that the income tax systems in most developed countries are enormous obstacles to sustained economic growth. After decades of misuse by lawmakers, lobbyists, special interests, and socialistic income re-distributors, our systems of taxation are unfair, overly complex, and costly; they penalize work, saving, and investing. Simply stated, our onerous income tax systems are unfit to carry us into the 21st century. They stimulate rather than retard the UgEcon; unchanged they will lead to needless individual hardships and an overt rather than a passive tax revolt.

The Costs of Democracy

Clearly democracy and capitalism have conquered communism, but what the world has not seen conclusively is that we know how to pay for a democracy and how to control its costs. In many countries, especially Northern Europe and Canada, general taxes have been used to redistribute wealth. Even in the more self-reliant tradition of the US, Congress has increased the "handouts" that are paid from the Treasury to more than 50% of the total budget.

The only legitimate purpose of any tax is to provide protection and services that cannot be provided by the private sector. Unfortunately, since its enactment, the income tax system has fallen prey to a multitude of other purposes, including income redistribution, social engineering, and government micro-management of saving, investing, and spending decisions.

We have the right to demand that our tax system be equitable, efficient, and supportive of our greatest economic growth potential. Sadly, our current tax system treats individuals unfairly, exacts tremendous administrative and compliance costs, and hinders our economy from realizing its full productive capacity. As a result, the world's opportunities for an improved standard of living are jeopardized.

> *Nations should have a tax system which looks like someone designed it on purpose.*
> *– William E. Simon,*
> *former Secretary of the US Treasury*

The Urgency of Reform

We must fundamentally rethink the manner in which taxes are raised in order to construct a system that is equitable, efficient, and pro-growth. To achieve genuine tax reform, blinders must be taken off, special interests must give way to over-riding national concerns, politically motivated class warfare must stop, and the defenders of the status quo must get out of the way of positive change.

Remember the stealth of the forces that caused the collapse of the Soviet Union. Remember too that the earliest media speculation about the fall of the Berlin Wall came only a few weeks before it actually happened.

As the gap between the Haves and Have-Nots continues to bulge, we will be fortunate if we can get by with just a quiet tax revolt that will propel us gently into the post-nation state world. We just need to hope that the unprecedented cooperation of the EU, NAFTA, and WTO is a better indicator of what that post-nation state world will be than the rampant ethnic and religious rivalries and xenophobia that dominate our evening news.

Dutch Treat

The Dutch have cut their unemployment rate in half since it peaked in 1984. They did it by allowing the minimum wage to fall relative to the average wage. The government has tightened eligibility for unemployment and for sickness and disability benefits. Taxes were cut and rigid labor rules were relaxed – absolutely anti-trade union moves.

Taxes are clearly the key in the opinion of most economists. In 1996, a senior economist at The Hudson Institute conducted a survey of dozens of nations. The results were compelling:

Those countries that cut their income taxes in the 1980's enjoyed a 4 times greater rate of growth than those that did not.[106]

Same Song, 2000ᵗʰ Verse

It is not surprising that the global tax revolt is gaining momentum. Politicians of all ilks continue to ensure that they pull as much money as possible out of the pockets of the tax-paying public.

Bleak Data from Canada

In Canada, a fall 1999 poll by a major bank found that 65% of the people are just barely scraping by and that their expectations are bleak. For farmers in the prairies, 1999 was the worst year since the Depression. In separationist-oriented Quebec, 57% said they were treading water, and 24% said they were drowning. Despite expected growth of 3%- 4% in the year 2000 – one of the highest in the OECD – the life blood of the taxpayer is being sucked dry by insidious taxes. The only bright spots in the country were in Alberta and Ontario, where 40% of those surveyed believed that they were getting ahead. What both of these provinces have in common is a recent history of privatization, lowering of taxes, and reducing regulations.

In perhaps the most revealing data in the survey, only 35% of those surveyed thought their financial situation would improve in the next year. This is down sharply from 47% in a similar survey a year earlier.[107] These discouraging data are not coming from the context of a recession, but are happening in the heart of the biggest economic boom in 50 years, with the lowest unemployment rate in 3 decades.

Again, it is important to look at Canada as a key indicator for the world's economic climate. If the UN has distinguished Canada for 6 successive years as the "most livable" country in the world, and the situation is as bleak as the bank survey says, the rest of the world is in an even more dismal state.

Soak the Rich

Politicians and bureaucrats are the major recipients of their own largesse – a less noble variation of the Robin Hood image – they rob from the middle class to pay themselves.

After digesting this book, readers will appreciate that the rich have alternatives to paying taxes, as they always have, and corporations simply pass their tax burdens along to the consumers. In times before direct (income) taxes, merchants were always taxed when they imported goods and frequently taxed when they exported goods; these indirect (excise) taxes were simply added to the cost of the goods and paid by the consumer. Income taxes on corporations are defacto excise taxes in that they too are passed along to the consumer.

Taxpayers were deceived when they were "sold" on income taxes as a way of "soaking the rich." Occasionally a Leona Helmsley allows the taxing authorities to make a public example, but what the Helmsleys did was no different than what *every other business owner does* – bury a little personal expense in the company accounts. First-class air travel, luxurious hotels and "business meals," health and golf clubs, and choice seats at concerts and sporting events are often tax evasions (perks) that tax lobbyists for those industries have "bought" from our politicians. The perks are magically changed from evasion into avoidance with winks from lobbyists, politicians, and bureaucrats.

A Lesson from Dickens

This situation brings to mind a piercing passage in literature. In the Charles Dickens classic, *A Tale of Two Cities,* the old Marquis St. Evrémonde, when confronted by his nephew, Charles Darnay, about the reality of the pending French Revolution, defies that reality and says,

> *"My friend, I will die, perpetuating the system under which I have lived."*

The lackluster politicians and self-serving bureaucrats who waste our tax money think like Dickens' Marquis. Perhaps they have forgotten that the old Marquis was murdered within hours of his declaration?

The global tax revolt is ready to explode at the end of the 20ᵗʰ century. But instead of storming the Bastilles of the world, taxpayers need quietly and unobtrusively to *withdraw the right to govern* by consciously withholding taxes.

Conclusion Now is the Time to Actively

Greed is good!
— *Gordon Gekko,* in the film *Wall Street*

A Time for Moral Considerations

Avoidance and evasion are complementary and are as old as taxation itself: one of the earliest records goes back 4000 years to a Middle Eastern potentate who instituted a system of fines for those who avoided using the royal ferry by swimming across the river that ran through his domains.

It is time for avoidance and evasion to be fueled by moral considerations and not just motivated by the more cynical criterion of greed.

Greed From a Loss of Faith

Moralists argue that the UgEcon in developed countries is spurred by greed and has created a "me-first culture." It also has accelerated a break-down in social cohesion, which, in turn, has fostered the attitude that there is nothing wrong with tax evasion. Without a sense of collective responsibility for society, no moral impediment exists to the crime of hiding revenues from taxation or, more bluntly, defrauding government.

In reality, even when revenue collectors uncover tax evasion, a criminal penalty is very rare in most developed countries, only a fine that invariably amounts to considerably less than the accrued tax savings. Very little can be accomplished by more diligent enforcement of existing laws and sanctions. If governments increase the risk-to-reward ratio, they will find that they will create a backlash – honesty cannot be compelled. The most that can happen is an increase in the *illusion* of compliance.

> History teaches us that the great revolutions weren't started by people who are utterly down and out, without hope and vision. They take place when people begin to live a little better – and when they see how much remains to be achieved.
> — *Benjamin Franklin*

Need in Transitional and Developing Economies

The UgEcon is especially important in countries in transition and those with developing economies. These countries suffer from all kinds of acute (and often chronic) economic illnesses: lost export markets, backward technology, skyrocketing unemployment, dilapidated machinery and plants, decrepit infrastructure, immorality (obligations not honored and flourishing crime), lack of liquidity, and ballooning trade and budget deficits. They are conditioned to be dependent on handouts and dictates from various international financial institutions and donor countries.

The UgEcon is a perfect solution until the dust of transition and development settles. It enhances exports (and competitiveness through imports), encourages technology transfers, employs people, invests in businesses, and adds to the wealth of the nation, adding liquidity into a dehydrated market.

Unfortunately, the UgEcon is not out of the reach of zealous tax-compliant missionaries such as the World Bank and IMF. Funds needed for developing these countries are contingent on the largesse of already developed countries, often with short memories and pious and patronizing attitudes.

For example, when moral activists get outraged about child labor in Asia, they need to remember that child labor was rampant in OECD countries in the 19th century and relatively common well into the 20th century.

The UgEcon in developing countries cannot be judged by the standards of developed countries because it is integral to those countries whose workers toil at the edge of survival. The governments of have-not nations must keep a blind eye to it, for it is truly an economic blessing in a very thin disguise.

This important message is largely unheard and unappreciated in OECD countries as transnational monetary authorities make assistance contingent on governments cracking down on the only sector of their economies that is still alive and kicking.

Support the Global Tax Revolt

It Is Time to Stop *Getting the Shaft*

We hope that this book has made you more knowledgeable about the size, causes, and costs of the UgEcon. The consistent message has been that government waste, corruption, cronyism, and the social experiment of using direct taxation to redistribute wealth have universally destroyed the faith of the taxpayers in their governments.

The consolidation of large companies, coupled with self-employment and the cyber dimensions of our global economy, have created 3 distinct classes of taxpayers:

1. those who are captive (taxed-at-the-source),

2. those who *accept* voluntary compliance and

3. The Tax Revolters – those who *adamantly reject* voluntary compliance to governments that have lost credibility.

Goodwill could have stopped the revolution, but it is too late. *The worldwide tax revolt is here!*

The 1st casualties will be the captive taxpayers who will be forced to shoulder a burden so onerous that it will ultimately become an open revolt. As this book goes to press, farmers in the Canadian Prairies are refusing, en masse, to pay their property taxes.

I end the journey of writing this book having had an epiphany. My original belief was that if we could rekindle an interest in the common good, everyone would be able to see that the victims of tax evasion of the UgEcon are our hard-working neighbors, and we would find a way to overcome the loss of faith that most of us have experienced in politicians and bureaucrats.

A Conscious Revolt Is What We Need

After spending the last year researching the salient issues that fuel the UgEcon on a global scale and after studying the reasons for cultural patterns of tax evasion, I find myself fused to the concept that governments have – through ignorance, apathy, and self-interest – destroyed the trust that is necessary for a voluntarily compliant system to work. The problem is not something that can be corrected even by a radical change in the spending habits of governments (something not even remotely likely to occur).

Not unlike an imminent avalanche, conditions are ripe for an increasingly more overt tax revolt. Those with moderate incomes can increase the damage by passively hiding income and escalating questionable and fraudulent business expenses. The more well-off will find ways to move their assets offshore to a jurisdiction with stringent bank secrecy laws that allows assets to accumulate tax free, resulting in tax-free estate planning and another generation of tax evaders.

Since governments refuse to be responsible and redesign and reduce taxes and stop wasteful spending – let's all join the revolt and bring profligate governments to their knees.

Starve the Beast!

1 MacKinnon, Mark. "Underground Economy Takes a Big Bite," in *The Globe and Mail*, June 21, 1999.

2 Smith, James D. "Measuring the Informal Economy," in *The Annals of the American Academy of Political and Social Science*, 493 (1987): 83-99.

3 Zeisler, Karl F. Managing Editor of the *Monroe Evening News*, Monroe, Michigan, 1945.

4 Paglin, Morton. "The Underground Economy: New Estimates from Household Income and Expenditure Surveys," in *Yale Law Journal*, 103 (1994): 2239-2257.

5 Finance Canada. Budget 1997, Tax Fairness: 3.

6 Smith, Adam. *The Wealth of Nations*. Harvard Classics, 1909.

7 Dilnot and Morris, *The Reform of Social Security*, Oxford University Press, 1984.

8 Camdessus, Michel. (Managing Director of the International Monetary Fund) Address at the Plenary Meeting of the Financial Action Task Force on Money Laundering. Paris. February 10, 1998.

9 Davies, Glyn. *A History of Money from Ancient Times to the Present Day*. (rev. ed.) Cardiff: University of Wales Press, 1996.

10 *The Random House Dictionary of the English Language*. Second edition, unabridged.

11 Feige, Edgar L. "Revised Estimates of the UgEcon: Implications of US Currency Held Abroad," in *The UgEcon: Global Evidence of its Size and Impact*. Owen Lippert and Michael Walker eds. Vancouver, Canada: Fraser Institute, 1997. pp.151-208

12 Rogoff, Kenneth. "Blessing or Curse? Foreign and Underground Demand for Euro Notes," in *Economic Policy*, April 1998, pp. 263-303.

13 According to the IRS.

14 MacKinnon, Mark. "Many Formulas Used to Measure the Invisible," in *The Globe and Mail*, June 21, 1999.

15 Laurent, 1974.

16 Guttman, I. *Statistical Tolerance Regions: Classical & Bayesian* (Griffin's Statistical Monographs, No. 26)

17 Pozo, Susan, ed. *Exploring the Underground Economy*. Kalamazoo: Upjohn, 1996.

18 McCohan, Kevin F. and James D. Smith. "A Consumer Expenditure Approach to Estimating the Size of the Underground Economy," in *Journal of Marketing*. 50.2 (1986): 48-60.

19 de Leeuw, Frank. "An Indirect Way for Measuring the Underground Economy," in *Survey of Current Business*. 65 (1985): 64-72.

20 Speer, Tibbett L. "Digging into the Underground Economy" in *American Demographics*, February, 1995.

21 Kacapyr, Elia. "Current Conditions: Notes from Underground" in *American Demographics*, January, 1998. This section relies heavily on Dr. Kacapyr's observations, but has been expanded from a US to a global focus.

22 Glover, Paul (founder of Ithaca HOURS). The Hometown Money Starter Kit and video are available for US$40 from Ithaca Hours, Box 6578, Ithaca, NY 14851, 607-272-4330, or www.lightlink.com/ithacahours

23 http://www.transaction.net/moeny/community/index.html

24 Revenue Canada Interpretation Bulletin, Subject: Income Tax Act: Barter Transactions. NO: IT-490. Reference: Section 3 (also sections 9 and 69). July 5, 1982.

25 Eisner, Robert. *The Total Incomes System of Accounts*. University of Chicago Press, 1989.

26 Nasa, Sylvia. "Hardcopy," in *The New York Times*, April 26, 1998.

27 Jorge Mendoza, professor at Mexico City's Instituto Technologico y de Estudios Superiores de Monterrey (ITESM) who did his doctoral studies on Mexico City's underground economy.

28 Centre for Economic Studies of the Private Sector.

29 National Institute of Statistics, Geography and Information (INEGI)

30 Campos, Norma. (Research economist, UNAM)

31 Taylor, Marisa. Mexico Publishing Group. All Rights Reserved, September 1995. http://www.nafta.net/mexbiz/articles/blackblu.htm (last updated 11/7/95).

32 by an economist named Reuter (1983).

33 Gambetta, Diego. *The Sicilian Mafia: The Business of Private Protection*. Harvard University Press, 1983.

34 Cooper, Donald A. US Drug Enforcement Administration. McLean, Virginia.

35 *Glamour* magazine, June 1999, p.224.

36 Thornton, Mark. Alcohol Prohibition Was a Failure, Policy Executive Summary, Analysis No.157, July 17, 1991.

37 According to surveys by the US National Institute on Drug Abuse.

38 According to the US Drug Abuse Warning Network.

39 Perl, Raphael F. Foreign Affairs and National Defense Division [CRS Issue Brief for Congress] 88093: *Drug Control: International Policy and Options*, Updated January 7, 1997.

40 Magistad, Mary Kay. "Jaded in Myanmar" in *Washington Post*, March 15, 1993, p. A14.

41 Clotfelter, Charles T. "Tax Evasion and Tax Rates: An Analysis of Individual Returns," in *Review of Economics and Statistics*. 65 (1983): 363-373.

42 Watson, Harry. "Tax Evasion and Labor Markets," in *Journal of Public Economics*. 27 (1985): 231-246.

43 Jung, Young H., Arthur Snow and Gregory A. Trandel. "Tax Evasion and the Size of the Underground Economy," in *Journal of Public Economics*. 54 (1994): 391-402. North Holland.

44 "The Rise and Rise of Tax Compliance Costs," in *Tax Compliance Costs: Measurement and Policy*, Cedric Sandford, ed., Fiscal Publications, 1995.

45 Wehrell, Roger and Gordon Fullerton. *Competitive Advantage and Disadvantage in Home-Based Business*. Mount Allison University, Sackville, New Brunswick, Canada.

46 Orser, B. and M. Foster. *Home Enterprise: Canadians and Home-Based Work*. The National Home-Based Business Project Committee, 1992.

47 Arroyo, Dennis M. "Why is the Philippines so Poor?" December 21, 1998.

48 Alforque, Rudy. Contact: rudy@bnl.gov

49 Doulis, Alex. *My Blue Haven*. Uphill Publishing, Ltd., 1997. p.6

50 Armstrong, Jane and Rod Mickleburgh. "Climbing Golden Mountain Tough on Illegal Immigrants," in *The National Post*, Saturday, July 24, 1999. page A4.

51 The Underground Economy in the US: Some Criminal Justice and Legal Perspectives

52 Duffy, Andrew. "Tough penalties for smuggling illegal aliens," in *The Ottawa Citizen*, Friday, July 23, 1999. page A4.

53 Echaveste, Maria, Administrator of the US Labor Department's Wage and Hour Division, in Branigin, William, "Reaping Abuse for what they Sew, Sweatshops Once Again Commonplace in US Garment Industry," in *The Washington Post*, February 16, 1997. p.A01

54 Branigin, William. "Reaping Abuse for what they Sew, Sweatshops Once Again Commonplace in US Garment Industry," in *The Washington Post*, February 16, 1997. p.A01

55 According to Union Bank of Switzerland.

56 Perspective, "Europe's Medicine," in *Investor's Business Daily*, November 4, 1997.

57 Copyright (c) 1999 *East Cape News*. Distributed via Africa News Online. www.africanews.org

58 DeWitt, Larry. (SSA historian) http://www.ssa.gov/history/histwelc.html

59 A report to the President: [Excerpts] Submitted to the executive committee for consideration at its meeting on January 15, 1984.

60 Foreign Reporting Rules. Canadian Tax Foundation Submission to the Auditor General of Canada.

61 Cash, Adam. *How to Do Business Off the Books*. Port Townsend, Washington: Loompanics Unlimited, 1986.

62 The International Labour Organisation (ILO) and the Regional Employment Program for Latin America and the Carribean (REPLAC)

63 Liberally adapted from: Ghersi, Enrique. "The Growing Importance of Informality and Possibilities for Integration," in *The Underground Economy: Global Evidence of its Size and Impact*. Owen Lippert and Michael Walker eds. Vancouver, Canada: The Fraser Institute, 1997.

64 Mailman, Stanley. "Expatriation and Senator Moynihan's Tax Proposal," in *New York Law Journal*, April 24, 1995, p.3

65 According to the statistics released by the Directorate General of Budget, Accounting and Statistics (DGBAS).

66 "Changing Sovereignty Games and International Migration," Aristide R. Zolberg, University-in-Exile Professor, New School for Social Research, New York.

67 Kubat, Daniel. *The Politics of Migration Policies*. (2nd ed.) Center for Migration Studies, 1993.

68 Harris, Marc M. *The Expatriation Trend*. Cyberhaven.com Home of Business and Financial Resources.

69 Expatriation to Avoid Tax, Sec. 877. Title 26, Subtitle A, Chapter 1, Subchapter N, Part II, Subpart A, Sec. 877. This section is referred to in sections 2, 865, 894, 3405, 7701 of this title.

70 Krejcarek, Michele, E.A. "Defining Expatriation Rules for Aliens," in *Tax Practitioners Journal*, Fall 1996.

71 Bartlett, Bruce. (Senior Fellow at the National Center for Policy Analysis) Brief Analysis No. 278. September 4, 1998.

72 Schneider, Friedrich. (Johannes Kepler University, Linz), quoted by Bartlett, Bruce. (Senior Fellow at the National Center for Policy Analysis) Brief Analysis No. 278. September 4, 1998.

73 By 1987, economist Mario Deaglio of the University of Turin put Italy's UgEcon at a minimum of 15% of GNP and a maximum of 25%.

74 Franke, Heinrich, head of West Germany's Labour Office, 1986, quoted by Bartlett, Bruce. (Senior Fellow at the National Center for Policy Analysis) Brief Analysis No. 278. September 4, 1998.

75 Engelschalk, Michael. (Director for Financial, Fiscal and Enterprise Affairs, OECD) Tel.:(33-1)45.24.96.60, daf.contact@oecd.org

76 Johnston, Derek. (Spokesman for the RCMP)

77 Czerlau & Associates, (905) 333-6439, www.czerlau.com

78 lazarus.long@claslib.rational.ca

79 Keith, Hastings. June 1, 1994.

80 IRS Report Submitted to US Congress.

81 Skousen, W. Cleon. This copy is liberally based on a version of Skousen's work edited by Dick Bachert, Citizens for an Alternative Tax System. Manassas, Virginia.

82 Adapted from an article in the Australian Financial Review, August 19, 1999, and appearing in The Financial Post, August 21, 1999. Sydney and Toronto.

83 Copyright (c) 1995 American Heritage, Inc. All rights reserved. Reprinted by permission from American Heritage, November, 1995.

84 Compiled by the Committee on Ways and Means, Rep. Bill Archer, Chairman. Sources: Commerce Clearing House, Standard Federal Tax Reporter, 1996. Commerce Clearing House, Standard Federal Tax Reporter, 1997. The Library of Congress, Congressional Research Service.

85 Sovereign, Don. #TL16G: The Reliance Defense, Copyright 1994, Terra Libra Holdings.

86 Armey, Dick. (House Majority Leader) "Flat Tax - Not Just a Distant Dream." Internet: http://flattax.house.gov

87 McArdle, Thomas. "Cheating Uncle Sam at Tax Time," in Investor's Business Daily, Washington, DC. April 26, 1996.

88 Revenue Canada. "Ensuring Fair Customs and Revenue Administration in Canada." A Discussion Paper on Progress and an Invitation to Comment. March, 1998. Cat. No. 97-262(E)

89 Mills, Dennis, MP, Broadview - Greenwood, quoted in "How Fair Are Our Taxes," Reader's Digest, 1999.

90 Reporting of Payments to Federal Government Service Contractors.

91 Walton, Dawn. "Entrepreneurs going it alone, study finds," in The Globe and Mail, Wednesday, June 2, 1999. page B13

92 Extrapolated from data developed by The Canadian Tax Foundation.

93 Grant, Don. Quoted by: MacKinnon, Mark. "Underground Economy Takes a Big Bite," in The Globe and Mail, June 21, 1999.

94 Revenue Canada's Underground Economy Initiative, Fact Sheet. Minister of National Revenue. February 25, 1998. webmaster@rc.gc.ca

95 Revenue Canada. Compliance: From Vision to Strategy. 1997. p. 58.

96 The Diamond Registry, 580 Fifth Avenue, Suite 806, New York, NY, 10036 (Contact: Martin Stone).

97 US Economist John Tedstrom of Rand, World Report, 3/30/98.

98 Swedish economist Anders Aslund, World Report, 3/30/98.

99 Larisa Piyasheva and Igor Birman, World Report, 3/30/98.

100 An Integrated Approach to the Underground Economy.

101 Hite, James. (Senior Fellow, Strom Thurmond Institute).

102 Polls by: CNN-USA Today-Gallup in December 1994, Newsweek, The Luntz Research Companies, and Mitchell Research and Communications, Inc.

103 Archer, Bill. Modified to a global perspective and used with permission of US Congressman Bill Archer, Chairman of the Tax Writing Ways and Means Committee, from his insightful article, "The Bold Step America Needs to Move Forward on the Eve of the 21st Century."

104 According to the Joint Committee on Taxation (JCT).

105 Boskin, Michael J., ed. Frontiers of Tax Reform. Hoover Institution Press, publication #435.

106 Reynolds, Alan, (The Hudson Institute), as quoted by NCPA, 1997.

107 CIBC (Canadian Imperial Bank of Commerce) survey conducted by Compass in September, 1999.

108 Ford, Worthington C, Treasury official to the US Senate, 1894.

109 Abel, Allen, based on an internet posting by this Toronto author and broadcaster. http://www.thekidsnetwork.com/instructors.html

IMAGE CREDITS

Page	Source
iii	Lady Godiva by Hon John Collier. © Herbert Art Gallery and Museum, Coventry, England
viii	Saturn Devouring His Children, Francis Goya, Prado Museum, Madrid
1	The Honeymooners
3	Leona Helmsley. Canadian Press.
3	Marie Antoinette, Elizabeth Louise Vigee Le Brun, 1783 - http://www.batguano.com/VigeeMAgallery.html
6	"So I hear..." cartoon, Bentley Boyd, 7/98
11	Pig and Man, Yoshi Keller and Karo Ernst - http://members.tripod.de/yoshikeller/china/yangshou.htm
14	"The Sheriff of Nottingham" from Rhead, Louis. (1912) Bold Robin Hood and His Outlaw Band: Their Famous Exploits in Sherwood Forest. New York: Blue Ribbon Books.
17	"Drive to Drink" cartoon, Punch magazine, 1877
18	Mussolini, http://pomperaug.com/socstud/stumuseum/web/mrcidea2moussolini.htm
20	Dr. Milton Friedman, © The Nobel Foundation-http://www.nobel.se/laureates/economy-1976-1-bio.html
21	Einstein, Courtesy of the Archives, California Institute of Technology
26	Ithaca Hours, Paul Glover - http://www.lightlink.com/hours/ithacahours/
28	The Tower of Babel, 1563, by Pieter Brugel the Elder (1525-1569), Kunsthistorisches Museum Wien, Vienna.
31	Villa and Zapata, http://www.geocities.com/BourbonStreet/Quarter/3050/panchovilla.html
32	Don Corleone, "The Godfather," Paramount Pictures - http://www.paramount.com/motionpictures/index.html
33	Franklin D. Roosevelt, http://www.nps.gov/hofr/becoming.html
34	Amy Pofahl, http://www.chrisconrad.com/free_amy.htm
35	Einstein, Courtesy of the Archives, California Institute of Technology
36	Drug Peace Campaign http://www.drugpeace.org
40	Imelda Marcos. Canadian Press.
40	"Marcos as vampire" cartoon, John S. Pritchett
40	Ferdinand Marcos. Canadian Press.
41	Gen. Douglas MacArthur, Phillipines, Oct/44 National Archives
43	"People smuggling" cartoon, Ottawa Citizen, Friday, July 23, 1999, p. A15
43	Boat of Immigrants. Canadian Press.
44	Child Labour, Lewis W. Hine (1874-1940), National Archives.
47	"Blood pressure" cartoon, "Back Bench" by Harrop/Nissen, The Globe and Mail, 9/16/99
51	Ottawa at night - www.madamejava.com/ottawa/post.html
52	Peru (Llama) Andrys Basten - http://www.andrys.com/index.html
56	"Indians on Shore" cartoon, Saturday, September 11, 1999, reprinted with permission from The Globe and Mail.
58	"Brain Drain" cartoon, Syndicam Productions - http://www.syndicam.com/cartoons/cartoons.html
61	Street Vendor, Miekhail Metzel, "Surviving on Smoke," Associated Press/CP
65	"T-Rex Offshore" cartoon, Brown, The Financial Post, September 24, 1999
67	Rational Anarchists, Jerome Delay, Associated Press
72	"Crossroads" cartoon,
73	Franklin D. Roosevelt - http://www.nps.gov/hofr/becoming.html
74	"Look Who's Here" cartoon,
75	Pres. Jimmy Carter. Canadian Press.
75	Allen Keyes. Canadian Press.
75	Newt Gringrich. Canadian Press.
75	Pres. Ronald Reagan. Canadian Press.
78	"Beardsley Ruml" cartoon, public domain
86	"Rights of Man", Thomas Paine sculpture, Thetford, England.
87	Boston Tea Party
89	General Pervaiz Mushrraf. Canadian Press.
100	Tweedle Dee & Tweedle Dum sculpture Aurora's Attic - http://store.yahoo.com/aurora/com6344.html
101	"Drs... w/o Borders" cartoon, Gary Clement - The National Post, October 16, 1999.
102	"Volga Boatmen", painting by Ilya Repin, 1844-1930 (1873, Russian State Museum, Saint Petersburg) - http://www.duc.auburn.edu/academic/liberal_arts/foreign/russian/art/repin-boatmen.html
104	guillotine, Joern Fabricius - http://www.logp.dk/guillotine/Pages Gallery.html
105	Revolutionary France, anon. internet source
106	Eliot Ness, anon. internet source
109	BWTC - http://www.tax.org/International/bwtc/english.htm
114	Robin Hood, w/Errol Flynn - 1938 movie poster, MGM/UA
119	"Giant Shaft" cartoon, "Wizard of ID" by Brent Parker & Johnny Hart
Obc	"One Question" cartoon, Brown, The Financial Post, February 3, 2000